One Monk,
Many Masters

One Monk,
Many Masters

The Wanderings of a
Simple Buddhist Traveller

Paul Breiter

Parami Press
Vancouver, Washington

Published by
Parami Press, LLC
PO Box 65372
Vancouver, Washington 98665

ISBN: 978-0-9779774-3-7
LCCN: 2011943196

Printed in the United States of America

To patrons of Buddhism everywhere, especially the humble farmers of Northeast Thailand, who literally keep the Forest Tradition alive. And to Pansak, who embodied so well all that is admirable, and likable, in the Thai character.

Contents

Acknowledgments

This book began in retreat, in a splendid cabin on sacred land provided by the hidden yogi of the Forest of Awareness Holders. In such a place, positive thoughts arise naturally; what is meaningful in life becomes easily evident; and inspiration, gratitude, and recollection of great beings and spiritual companions overflow. I bow my stubborn bald head at the feet of that yogi's guru, Chakdud Tulku.

Thanks that are hard to express are owed to those who have guided me so slightly out of coarseness and immaturity over the decades, especially Ajahn Chah, Ajahn Sumedho, Roshi Kobun Chino, and the teacher of teachers, the lord and protector Lama Gonpo Tseten.

Thanks to the many friends who offered encouragement and suggestions after reading chapters as I produced them through a few years of plodding and pecking away, especially the venerable gang at Abhayagiri Monastery, Andrew Mittelman, and Bonnie Halpern-Cunningham.

When after several rejections I was ready to leave my stories for future generations to publish, the indomitable Paul Gerhards, who is publisher, editor, and staff of Parami Press, took on the challenge and spent countless hours over a whole year helping shape the manuscript into form. Telling a would-be author that his work needs revision is a thankless task, but he put his heart, perspiration, and funds into it, along with our copy editor, Jessica Swanson. I can only hope that they learned as much about the creative process as I did from our collaboration.

We are grateful to Shambhala Publications for permission to quote their excellent book *Zen Letters: Teachings of Yuanwu,* and to Bob Shamis and Jim Roy for providing photographs.

My wife, Lili, always encourages virtuous activity and is happy to pay the bills while I write things that may never be published and pretend to practice the Buddha's way. Never asking anything in return but only rejoicing in the good others try to do, she is a true inspiration and role model.

Introduction

My supremely kind and excellent teachers of the Buddha's Way have passed on. Many Dharma friends and old companions have died; one remarked that we only see each other at funerals now. Many of the places I lived in and traveled to in the 1970s, '80s, and even early '90s are no longer the same. So much of Asia has vanished under the onslaught of the logger's saw, the wrecking ball, and the building crane, been paved over with concrete and asphalt, crowded, choked, and smogged with rapidly expanding populations, smokestacks, and vehicle exhaust. "You'd better go see it while it's still there," I used to tell people who were thinking about visiting Thailand. So I thought I'd better record some memories while my mind and I are still here.

***

It is said that even the pleasant sensation of a cool breeze on a hot day is the blessing of a spiritual teacher. Such pronouncements sound fanciful indeed. Some of us can take them as inspiration for our practice, but for those in need of logic, it is there, too. The basic principle of Buddhism is that everything arises from causes. Like produces like. Pleasant experience results from positive actions, and the discernment to understand what is truly wholesome is learned from a spiritual guide. The positive results we reap in this life are the result of the wholesome actions we learned to perform in the past, whether it be the past of this life or lives before.

What can be more skillful than praising virtuous qualities and telling others of deeds of wisdom, love, and compassion, and appreciating the rarity of the opportunity to meet embodiments of these qualities? We accumulate merit by hearing of the lives of great beings. Wholesome traits blossom and the mind is uplifted. The Tibetan term for spiritual biography, *namthar*, means "complete liberation." That refers to the holy beings we read about in such accounts and the freedom they found in enlightenment, but the stories can also bring freedom and buoyancy to the mind of the reader. Lama Tsedrup Tharchin—a great, humble, lovable man—suggested such reading as an antidote to depression, one of the plagues of modern life.

***

Geshe Michael Roach, an American teacher of Tibetan Buddhism in the Gelugpa school, tells his audiences that for all he knows, they are all enlightened and just pretending otherwise to make him teach for his own benefit. Maybe no one will find anything of interest here; but for me, the process is inspirational and reconnects me with what has been most meaningful in this life.

There are many others who knew these teachers more intimately, in a personal sense, in appreciating their qualities, and in understanding and realizing their teachings. I have only skimmed along the surfaces of great oceans and vast deep lakes, but one does what one can. At the least, I can give some idea of the legions of transcendent masters and practitioners in the world in the hope that their tireless efforts to transmit their wisdom can result in ordinary people rising out of the mire of suffering and meaninglessness.

The enlightened masters and the institutions of their lineages are truly great, but their purpose is not self-glorification; it is to help people who are struggling to be free of suffering. Thus in close proximity to the teachers are often found confused seekers and just plain silly people (like me). This was the case in the time of the Buddha—the scriptures are full of the most outrageous goings-on of his disciples—and it is certainly true now.

The worldly way of critiquing people and ideas often involves either blind faith or cynical skepticism. The Buddha urged his listeners to take nothing on faith and to put his words to the test, "just as gold is burned, beaten, and polished." But there comes a point at which, having seen that everything so far has turned out to be reliable, one experiences a deep trust in the teacher and the teachings and is willing to take things on faith. Ajahn Sumedho, a Western monk of the Theravada Thai Forest Tradition, said, "Any fool can say how things *should* be. It doesn't take any energy to criticize." In ordinary life, we do more than enough fault-finding, and it doesn't bring us a whole lot of benefit. It is also a basic tenet that what we see in others is a projection of our own habit patterns. So let us now praise great beings, and instill habits of respect, reverence, and love for what is truly precious in this world. By contemplating the lives and deeds of people whose experience is beyond our own, we can elevate our minds and infuse them with positive qualities.

***

My first spiritual teacher was Ajahn Chah of northeast Thailand. I met him after I had been ordained for two months. I had never seen someone with such a presence or even imagined the existence of such a person. His living example of what the Buddha's teaching could accomplish was worth more than reading hundreds of books. He was radiant. He was happy. He was alive. He didn't spout philosophy—he didn't have to say anything at all to win me over—but he did encourage me and so many others to come meditate in the forest with him, with the warning that it might not be an easy life.

Ajahn Chah readily admitted that he was the most ordinary young man. He was full of doubts, he got angry, he was lustful and restless. But growing up in a Buddhist culture where taking robes and renouncing the world was not only common but was considered the highest calling, it was quite natural for him to follow the Buddha's way. He may have worked harder at it than most of us are willing or able to, but through all his trials and travails, he came out the other side. He didn't talk a lot about compassion, and never about having a mission, but without much planning he dedicated his life to serving others.

When I hear about spiritual masters, I usually imagine someone austere and aloof; yet Ajahn Chah, like many other great teachers, was full of juice, someone it was easy to love in a very pure and selfless way. At his funeral ceremonies in 1993, about a million people, including the king and queen of Thailand, passed through the gates of his monastery. The effect he had on people's lives throughout northeast Thailand is oceanic. Forest monasteries in the Ajahn Chah lineage have been established around the world, while his books have been translated into many languages and strike a chord among a great diversity of people. But for all that, he wasn't usually called by any particular title; he was *Luang Por,* "Venerable Father," to most people, and that simple appellation conveyed the love people felt for him more than any honorific could have.

***

I dwell here on Ajahn Chah because he was for me the gateway to the vital reality of Buddhism, the first person I ever met who illustrated the possibility of a better life, the kind of life so many people were yearning for in those days without knowing if such a thing really existed. He steered me through what I think of as my formative years, which became the foundation for what followed. He was the teacher I was closest to on a day-to-day personal level; I literally sat at his feet for years, though I often received abuse and ridicule there rather than divine transmission (and a good case can be made that his spiritual transmission often came in the form of habit-destroying abuse). I left the robes and Ajahn Chah's guidance, though not his influence, in 1977, after seven years as a monk.

My intention at that time was to continue Buddhist practice, to learn more of the vast ocean of the Buddha's teachings and to see if there was an alternative to monastic life that allowed one to authentically travel the path to liberation. I did so in fits and starts, often falling and bruising myself, much as I had as a monk. In the spiritual supermarket that California had become I was exposed to many different teachers and traditions in a few years, and the story lines often intersect and overlap. It wasn't unusual, for me and for many others, to dabble in three different traditions in one week. After a year as a lay person I briefly came to roost in the Soto Zen tradition, but still was open to meeting other teachers and attending events, eventually getting snared by Tibetan Buddhism, all the while keeping contact with Ajahn Chah's lineage. Looking back now, I can appreciate how my involvement with each tradition affected my involvement with the others. So the narrative is not exactly linear, of necessity hopscotching back and forth in time, since exposure to the different paths often occurred parallel to each other.

***

In the Buddhist world, and especially in traditional Buddhist societies in Asia, there is a culture of generosity and respect—respect for the quest and those who undertake it, respect for transcendence and those who realize it—that is the environment in which the teachings and the living tradition of enlightenment have flourished. Traveling through Thailand and other Asian countries as a layperson, I was accustomed to friendliness, hospitality, and warm welcomes at the budget hotels and eateries I frequented. Yet I came to realize a vast difference between that, as pleasant as it usually was, and staying in monasteries. When you check out of a hotel the staff will smile, thank you, and bid you to return, but that's in large part because you are spending money there. In a monastery, no money changes hands. One is welcome because one has an interest in practicing the Dharma, and one is invited to come again, not out of a wish for remuneration, but simply out of human goodness and mutual devotion to the Buddha's way. And the whole operation is kept going by the continual emergence of enlightened beings. Being a wealthy or powerful person or a celebrity doesn't make much of a difference. Within the monastery confines pretensions are shed, and ordinary people rub elbows with celebrities, generals, and captains of industry.

And great generosity very often is shown by those living in what most of us would consider poverty. Thailand is now a popular tourist destination, and visitors usually come away having witnessed the opulence of the well-known venues. The northeast of Thailand, where the practice of Dharma is most alive, is materially the least developed region of the country, and especially three or four decades ago it was difficult living there. But the openhandedness of the people bespeaks a wealth that is hard to find otherwise, and the same mindset, albeit with different cultural trappings, exists in other Buddhist societies.

Ajahn Chah said, "There are no rich people nowadays; at least I've never seen any. I only see people who don't have enough." In Buddhism, real wealth consists of inner qualities like generosity, lovingkindness toward other beings, wisdom, and, especially, contentment. These qualities still thrive and are revered in certain quarters, and in our disturbed world such places increasingly feel like islands of sanity.

We also now witness the transplanting of such ideals in the West. I hope that the stories contained herein will at least hint at the richness of the Buddhist realm, and that by the blessings of the Three Jewels—the Buddha, his teachings, and the community of his enlightened followers—virtuous aspirations will be fulfilled, and weary, troubled beings will soon enjoy peace and respite.

***

As I prepared this manuscript for publication, His Holiness Chetsang Rinpoche, head of the Drikung Kagyu lineage of Tibetan Buddhism, came to Florida, where I now live. I was instantly smitten, certain that I was seeing a Buddha. He is about the same age as I, and I thought, "Look at him, and look at me." But after the brief drama of dejection over my pitiable comparison, I thought that this is what the historical Buddha Shakyamuni must have felt eons ago, when at the feet of Dipankara Buddha he took the vow to become a fully enlightened Buddha himself, saying "I want to be just like him!" Such is the experience of meeting enlightened beings. When they aren't present in the flesh, reading about them may be the next best thing.

Part One

Following the Way of the Elders

1

Journeying East— the Search for God

Why leave the seat that exists in your own home to travel afar in dusty lands?

—Eihei Dogen

Punjab, India, 1969

You must come to meet our friend. He is an enlightened man!"

It was December of 1969. I was standing on the road into Jullundur, a dusty town in India's Punjab region, trying to hitch a ride. A pair of college-aged fellows had stopped to talk to me. With the insatiable Indian curiosity, they peppered me with questions, eager to learn why I was there.

"I've come to India to find God," I proclaimed. "India is the Holy Land." So they offered to take me at once to meet their friend. The town wasn't very big, and we were soon at the home of Professor Guruchan Singh Mongia.

Whether or not the professor was an "enlightened man" I cannot say, though as far as I could tell he appeared to be an ordinary person—but a very nice person, and a great host. Of course, we drank tea and talked, and, of course, he insisted I stay at his home. I soon got used to such hospitality in India and even started to expect it.

In the days that followed, we had many discussions, mostly of my background, my ideas, my aspirations. I had left home in May of that year to find peace of mind, beginning with an indulgent lifestyle on the Spanish island of Fomintera, a hippie paradise of sorts. In the World According to My Opinions, one only had to indulge one's desires to the point of true satisfaction, then one would relax in the most fundamental part of one's being, and the hindrances that blocked union with the Divine, being merely one's own tensions and frustrations, would dissolve of their own.

Having high aspirations is certainly a good thing, and it gave me some sense of purpose—and hope—to think in terms of the Divine, but in actuality I was a wreck, dysfunctional and miserable.

Since passing the days of childhood, when joy could be found in hitting a softball over the head of an outfielder, nothing had seemed right. Generally, everything bewildered me, and most things scared me. Nothing ever worked out as I hoped or as I thought it should. And nothing interested me very much. When I tried to think about "What I want to be" or "What I want to do," if I didn't come up blank I came up with apathy, despair, and nagging doubts.

Doing well in school was easy enough—but what was the point? I didn't dislike my parents or people of their generation and socio-economic standing, but I didn't see any meaning in living like they did.

In the society we were growing up in, we didn't see meaningful culture or traditions, and so had nothing to turn to that would buck us up, give us guidance or hope. But lucky me, lucky us, it was the 1960s. American life was undergoing upheavals, and if meaningful alternatives weren't yet out in the open, at least dissatisfaction was becoming fashionable.

When I left home, I felt in my bones that things weren't right, including my own mind. I had cobbled together a "philosophy" of how things work and how I could find everlasting happiness. I thought I was on to something profound; I'm sure many other 21-year-olds who had been through the psychedelic wars also thought that way. But basically, as I often repeated at the time to anyone who would listen, I felt like I was running for my life: "When the house is burning down, you don't think too much about where you're going or what you want to do, you just get out."

I had little idea of grand spiritual traditions that had been tested by time and had brought countless beings out of misery. My lifelong apathy made me undisciplined, made it difficult to see anything through, so even had I known of a way to deliverance, I wouldn't have been ready to follow it.

Still, I think it is human nature to expect that the next good thing can break the logjam and bring happiness. Even for those choosing alternative lifestyles, that attitude was still ingrained. Again, lucky me: I got to experience and indulge in most of the things I hoped and believed could bring me permanent happiness, and none of them worked, in fact they only increased the sense of frustration, despair, and bewilderment. And thus my presence in the plains of India after an overland voyage on the cheap through Europe, Turkey, Iran, Afghanistan, and Pakistan.

***

Professor G invited me to speak to one of his classes at the university, which I did one chilly morning, wrapped in a red blanket I had pilfered from a hotel in Kandahar, Afghanistan. The students looked at me with intense concentration and what I perceived as great interest as I began by saying, "I am here to tell you that the American dream is a nightmare." Later I found out they couldn't understand me, being accustomed as they were to British English. But I think the prof was pleased; when we got back to his house, he asked me to write an article for the local newspaper. Years later I discovered a copy of the article in my parents' house, under the headline "Confessions of a Dropout."

***

After several days of the professor's largesse, I moved on, getting back on the trunk road that runs from the Pakistani border to Delhi, my current destination before setting out for spiritual territory such as Varanasi, or perhaps the hill stations north of Delhi like Rishikesh or Hardwar. I was under the impression that in all those places holy men roamed the streets in large numbers.

I eventually came to roost on a houseboat in the holy city of Varanasi (Benares to Westerners) with several other travelers—you paid one rupee per night to the owner, and he would take as many people as could fit in the place. My housemates and I loafed around, wandered in the town, and did a lot of talking—usually hashish-inspired, though I was abstaining as it gave me tension headaches—mostly about travel and what we considered things of the spirit, but alas, no holy men appeared, though the occasional comical *sadhu* (a catch-all term for homeless spiritual seekers, wanderers, and mendicants) would attach himself to us, usually as a source of alms.

***

While in Varanasi, the closest I came to any sort of spiritual influence was going to the burning *ghats* (pyres) to observe cremations, and sitting by the banks of the Ganges River late at night and getting an intimation of what had made it a center of Indian religion for millennia.

Among our group of vagabonds was an Italian hippie couple who had befriended an Indian Buddhist man. He was a very kind, sincere, and gentle fellow, who invited us to his home in Saranath one evening. His family served us dinner, and then the Italian woman played the flute and her husband started dancing around like a lunatic, leaving me embarrassed for our host, who nonetheless took it in stride. His name was Guruprasad, "gift of the guru." Before he was born, his parents, who were unable to conceive, went to beseech a holy man for his blessing to enable them to conceive; when a son was born, they gave him this name in gratitude.

Guruprasad took us to the Deer Park, the site of the Buddha's first sermon. We gazed at the *stupa* (shrine) there and then sat in a teashop to talk with a Western Buddhist monk. The hippie couple didn't much approve of the monk's way of life and got into a contentious dispute with him. For me, seeing a shaven-head Westerner in robes was simply strange, so I sat on the sidelines while they duked it out. And I put this first meeting with Buddhism out of my mind soon after that.

***

After two months, when I was ready to get back on the road I met up with Peter, one of my traveling companions from Afghanistan and Pakistan. One night I decided to go to my favorite yogurt stand in the bazaar before heading back to the houseboat, and Peter arrived in a rickshaw. This was the kind of coincidence or fateful fork in the road that appeared several times in that period. Peter and I decided to hitchhike to Nepal. We got to the border without much trouble, usually being put in the comfortable sleeping spaces above the cabs of large trucks, and then took a bus to Kathmandu.

Before going there I had several dreams of Kathmandu Valley as an enchanted place, and so it was. But even being so close to major Buddhist shrines, monasteries, and teachers there I felt nothing and made no connections, mostly just hanging out for five months, dealing with constant dysentery and thinking about where to go next. Peter left for Darjeeling, and in August I decided to go to points south, with Calcutta my first stop.

***

The headache had begun the night before, but I hadn't paid it much notice. Now it was early morning, I was supposed to be flying to Calcutta in a few hours, and my head was splitting in a way I never imagined possible. There wasn't anything to do but see a doctor. I didn't think to check out of the hotel or call the airline (how many working telephones were there in Kathmandu Valley in those days?), but went out to the street and got a taxi to the International Hospital.

A young Dr. Srivastav, who assured me that he'd studied abroad, said he suspected meningitis. A tremor went through me. In recent years there were cases of meningitis in New York City, spread by pigeons, and it was usually fatal, but the good doctor assured me that the strain in Nepal wasn't so virulent. He wanted to test for it with a spinal tap, so they dressed me in hospital garb and had me wait in one of the wards.

The test came back positive, and Dr. Srivastav kept me for a week. While I was convalescing in Kathmandu after release from the hospital, I went to a bookstore and bought the *Life of St. Francis*, of all things. After finally getting to check in for that flight to Calcutta, while waiting in the airport I saw my pack in a pile of luggage under a sign that said New Delhi, but I didn't think too much of it.

Not surprisingly, my bag wasn't in Calcutta when I arrived. So I stayed for another week in the tropical heat of Calcutta—which had felt like walking into a wall as soon as I deplaned at the airport—while Royal Nepal Airlines tracked down my humble sack of possessions. Staying at the Salvation Army Hostel, I had my first look at the New Testament, which to my surprise inspired me.

To pass the time, I enjoyed a lot of good restaurants—a change from Nepal, where the only time I didn't have diarrhea was when I was in the hospital. I found a library with a decent selection of books in English and settled in for a while. I read some T.S. Eliot, the only poet I ever really liked, having studied *The Love Song of J. Alfred Prufrock* and *The Wasteland* in college. In his *Four Quartets*, considered the most mystical of his writings, he alluded to an experience "better than even a very good dinner."

I can't recall now if I sat up in my chair, but that quiet phrase spoke to me, loud and clear, of authentic, transformative spiritual experience. The past several months had been a time of illness, brooding introspection, and aimless desperation. My high aspirations had mostly vanished as I tried to get through the days wondering what I could eat that wouldn't cause my guts to rumble or explode, where I should travel to next, and when I would run out of money. But Eliot's words reminded me of my original intention in going East.

Then there was a book about a British colonial officer who, while on duty in the Orient, had gone on the Great Quest. He encountered a friend from his youth and described the two of them sitting quietly, smiling knowingly and communing in the experience of having found something beyond words. And after that, I was reading a book on Buddhism.

I, along with many of my generation, had read Herman Hesse's *Siddhartha,* and seen temples and monks in India and Nepal. But my curiosity had never been piqued: we were all quite sure that there was no "Way," and that, according to the *Tao Te Ching,* "those who speak do not know and those who know do not speak." This book on Buddhism was talking about something else I had never imagined, namely that desire and attachment are the cause of suffering. I'd been certain that fulfilling one's desires, in the right way of course, was the broad avenue to enlightenment. But those words on the page filled me with a strange foreboding.

Back in the hostel someone asked me if I had any interesting books to swap. I bartered my *St. Francis* for the *Life of Milarepa*—I'd never heard of the Tibetan ascetic saint, but I needed something to read, and Francis's tales of self-mortification didn't bring me much cheer.

Milarepa certainly wasn't showing me a good time either, but the vague sense of foreboding that I felt when reading about Buddhism in the library returned. Milarepa didn't exactly torture himself, but he underwent more than his share of privations under the tutelage of his master, Marpa the

Paul Breiter, Katmandu, Nepal, Summer 1970, prior to getting shave and haircut as required to enter Thailand.

Translator. Why anyone would want to live like that was beyond me, yet it cast a shadow that I couldn't get away from.

Meanwhile I kept on eating meals, walking around the bazaar being harassed by aggressive beggars and peddlers, and sightseeing with a group of Westerners staying in the hostel. They had an Indian friend who showed us the sights and one night took us to an opium den. It felt more like a working man's bar than a place of vice and mystery (though there was none of the rowdiness of a bar scene) and didn't produce any special experience save a nasty hangover.

I also daily took a human-powered rickshaw to the airline office, trying to find out about my bag. A fellow named Anthony, who proudly announced himself to be Anglo-Indian, helped me fill out a claim in case my bag never showed up and urged me to use my imagination in listing the contents. After a week it finally arrived, and I was on my way to Rangoon, in then-Burma.

***

Rangoon was a drag, reminding me of Schenectady, New York (home of General Electric and my alma mater, Union College), albeit with Buddhist temples, and I left there after three days.

The plane departed at six in the morning and arrived in Bangkok about two hours later. After checking into the Atlanta Hotel and getting a bed in the dorm for a dollar a night, I did what travelers do upon arriving in a new city and went to the Central Post Office to check for mail at Post Restante. There was a letter from my father, urging me to look up a friend and former dental patient of his who worked in the Bangkok Bank.

I showed the address to someone, who summoned a *tuk-tuk* (a horrible, noisy, pollution-spewing three-wheel taxi), and after a ride through streets of concrete block buildings that all looked the same, I was at the bank. I showed the name, Prasit M_____, to the first person I came across, and was soon sitting in his cubicle on the sixth floor.

When Khun Prasit (*Khun* and *Tahn* are polite forms of address, much like *Mr.* or *Ms.*, prefacing the given name, which is what Thai people go by) was a student at New York University in the early 1960s, a Thai man living in New York referred him to my father to fix his teeth. They kept in touch, and now here I was talking to him. My parents were rightly concerned about my wellbeing and survival; he showed me the telegram from his friend Bill in New York: "traveling in Asia, sick in Nepal, not a hippie."

Prasit had an easygoing manner and hospitable charm that immediately made me feel comfortable and at home. I'd been scouring the Exotic East for nearly a year. While my day-to-day existence was pretty aimless, the aspiration to find a better life and inner peace was always with me. Somehow I expected that around the next corner I was going to find Shangri-la, a place of effortless grace where the spiritual and secular meshed happily. Sitting with Prasit I felt that here, finally, was some of the Asian old-world graciousness I'd been looking for all that time. To be sure, I had experienced plenty of hospitality, kindness, and friendly interest in India, but there was something different here—a sense of spaciousness, a more easygoing, yet quite sober, approach to life, a depth in contemplating the big issues that was backed up by the tried and tested way of the Buddha, which has been a vital part of Thai life for centuries.

I tried to explain to him that I'd never been satisfied at home and so had taken to the road on my quest. I had faith that ultimate happiness existed, but I'd been unable to find it through my own efforts.

He heard me out and then said, "I think I know what you are looking for. There's something that might be right for you," and told me there was a lecture on Buddhism in a local temple that very night. "A lot of foreigners come here to learn about Buddhism, but they don't find the right places so they go home disappointed," he said.

The lecture was part of a series sponsored by a group led by his friend Sulak. He also said something about the "Bertrand Russell of Asia" being there, but I didn't make much sense of it. He then wrote a letter in Thai for me to give to his friend.

Prasit told me a little about himself. His parents had sent him to New York University, where he studied the principles of economic and social development.

"When I left, Bangkok was like heaven," he said. "When I came back seven years later, it was like hell. Life in Thailand used to be easy. In the countryside you picked fruit off the trees and got fish from the streams and the rice fields. You could have one cloth that you wear as a skirt, use as a towel, or wrap your baby in. Very simple." It certainly sounded idyllic and enticing; and having spent the past fifteen months living simply and now experiencing the waking nightmare of traffic, noise, and concrete that was Bangkok, I could certainly sympathize with Prasit's sense of loss. But I was soon to discover that a much different experience of Thai culture was in store for me.

He finished his work for the day and took me to his mother's house nearby, one of the newly constructed rowhouses that were starting to fill large swaths of Bangkok. Prasit was Sino-Thai. He told me that it was Moon Festival, a culinary event for ethnic Chinese, who lived in Bangkok in large numbers and, as in most Southeast Asian cities, were responsible for much of its commerce. His mother started feeding us, bringing dish after dish to the table.

Dinner over, we got up and walked out to the street, and he gave me directions to the temple. Walk to the monument, turn right, go a few blocks, turn left, you'll see the temple on your left after a while... or something like that. He and his mother were saying goodbye, nodding their heads and smiling, and off I went into the sunset.

But I was starting to fade, having had only a few hours sleep the previous night, which now seemed so long ago. I thought maybe I should just go back to the hotel, although I wasn't sure how I would get there. So I started hiking in the direction of Wat Boworn, the site of the lecture.

The monastery compound, with its trees, canals, stately old buildings, and ornate temples and shrines, was a sanctuary from the frenetic noisy streets. Stone lions and other decidedly Chinese figures stood guard around many of the buildings. An amazingly serene-looking standing Buddha caught my attention. I gazed at it for a few moments.

There was still time to wait before the talk. So I sat on a low wall and took an aerogram out of my shoulder bag to write a letter to a friend back home. "Howie, this is incredible, I'm sitting here in a Buddhist temple in Bangkok..."

But it was dusk, and I was jerked out of my reverie by swarms of mosquitoes chewing on my feet. Annoyed, I got up and walked around. Monks were starting to gather for the event. It was quite a sight to see all the yellow robes and shaven heads, men no doubt on a high spiritual plane inconceivable to me; but I noticed a lot of them pointing at me and smirking and giggling as they went by, more like schoolboys than holy men.

***

The speaker was an Indian monk named Sivalibodhi. He had the charm, facility of speech, and big luminous eyes I'd become familiar with in India. I wasn't familiar with the things he was saying, however—but they made perfect sense.

The Four Noble Truths, the Eightfold Path: there are causes for our confusion and suffering, which is not merely some personal aberration or the result of bad luck; and there is a way to remove those causes and experience peace, freedom, enlightenment. It sounded so precise and so reasonable—and so unlike the philosophy, psychology, and literature I had studied, which amounted to little more than guesswork.

"When I find what I'm looking for, I'll tell you what it is," I had pronounced before leaving home on the Great Quest. Yet I never imagined that the answer would lie in the direction of austere living or any sort of discipline. I followed my own patchwork philosophy of self-indulgence and met only with frustration. In the United States, in Europe, in the Holy Land of India and her little sister Nepal, my explorations yielded nothing during fifteen months of drilling dry holes. Hoping to somehow pull off a last-minute victory in Indonesia, I had come to Bangkok, where I planned to invest in an Indonesian visa (sixty dollars, a lot of money for most of us in those days) and figure out how to get there cheaply.

And now, contrary to my plans, here I was in this Buddhist temple. The Four Noble Truths, the Eightfold Path. Desire as the source of suffering, discipline as the way out. Strangely, it resonated with me, and though I didn't quite realize it at the moment, I was hooked.

When the talk was over and the monks filed out of the hall, I stood up, not sure what to do next. A small group of Westerners and Thais stood talking to one side. I approached but stayed on the edge of the group, until a Thai man noticed me and said hello. I muttered my name and stood there tongue-tied for a moment. Then I remembered Khun Prasit's letter. I pulled it out of my pocket and handed it to the gentleman, hoping he could point out the addressee.

He looked at the name written on the envelope and said, "That's me." Khun Sulak read the letter thoughtfully and introduced me to the group. The whirlwind began. People said hello and asked me about myself. An elderly American woman told me, "We have a group that meets with the abbot of the temple on Monday night for meditation and study. You're welcome to come."

After a few more pleasantries, Sulak asked me where I was staying and told me he would take me back to the hotel once he was finished talking with people.

A light rain was falling. The traffic, for which Bangkok was becoming justly infamous, was thin. Sulak said, "You ought to come to my store and talk to my manager. I don't really know much about Buddhism, but he does." So when he dropped me off he wrote down the information in Thai and English.

For a long time afterward I was under the impression that "the Bertrand Russell of Asia" was a reference to the Indian lecturer, Sivalibodhi. But I got to know him and found out that he was actually a lawyer who had recently ordained. When on one later occasion Sivalibodhi and Prasit were both at Wat Boworn at the same time, I was puzzled to notice that they didn't know each other.

Years later I learned that Sulak Sivaraksa was a renowned intellectual and a seminal thinker in applying Buddhist principles to the society. So one day the light went on: I recalled that first day in Bangkok and finally realized that Prasit was referring to Khun Sulak with his august comparison to the great English philosopher. Khun Sulak had written a number of books, and in 1978, fleeing persecution by the new military government, he was a guest lecturer at University of California, Berkeley. But for now I only had his humble disclaimer that he knew little about Buddhism and a piece of paper with the name and address of his bookstore, Suksit Siam.

***

Sulak had told his manager, Sutchai, that I would be coming. I was shown to his office on the second floor. He was a thin, somewhat intense man, but very friendly. A girl brought two bottles of Pepsi Cola, the social beverage of choice. It was ice cold and froze my empty stomach, which made it a little hard to focus attention on what Sutchai was saying.

He got right down to business. "Buddhism says that we suffer because of our desires. So we have to train to control ourselves." That was a novel idea. "Maybe we see a pretty girl, but we don't follow her," he said. "Maybe we give up these," he added sheepishly, indicating his cigarette.

"We meditate on the parts of the body. Hair, nails, teeth, and skin. They don't really belong to us. They grow by themselves and fall out by themselves. If we don't take care of them, they become dirty and unpleasant."

That knocked me for a loop. The most obvious thing, if you think about it—but I'd never thought about it.

***

Sutchai told me about the forest monasteries, the places where meditation was practiced seriously. "Whenever I get time off I go to stay with my teacher in the forest, where I can meditate all day. I love to do walking meditation—I can do it for hours. Someday I want to become a monk and live there." He explained that he lived with his father and took care of him, so as long as his father was alive he was stuck in the city—"like being in prison." Years later, when I was a forest monk myself, I thought back to Sutchai and wondered if he was still waiting for his father to die so he could fulfill his dream.

Then he started planning my internment.

"Once you become a monk," Sutchai said, "you can get a visa for one year at a time. Go to see the American monk at Wat Boworn, Tahn Dhammaramo. He will help you. And he can teach you meditation."

I didn't recall having signed anything, but he seemed certain I was making a commitment. I did want to learn meditation, it was true, but I thought of it as a skill to learn in order to calm myself down so that I could go about my life (miserable as it was), not turn my life upside down. What was happening to me?

I upgraded from the dorm to a single room for a whole 80 *baht*—$4—and did my version of meditation in the morning. In the afternoon I got directions for the bus to Wat Boworn.

The crowded bus lumbered along the hot and smoggy streets. After endless turns and stops, thirty or forty minutes later we reached the end of the line, across from the side entrance to Wat Boworn. I entered the gate and saw laypeople and monks strolling around. I asked for Kana Soong, the building where foreign monks were housed. Once there, I asked for Dhammaramo. Nobody spoke much English, but they seemed to have a great time dealing with me anyhow. I didn't particularly like being the center of attention and saw something sinister in the smiles and smirks, but there was certainly a more relaxed feeling, and a lot more breathing room, than in India, where everyone was so intensely curious about Westerners, and whereupon stopping to ask directions one quickly found oneself surrounded by an astonished, staring crowd. That was my first introduction to the renowned concept of *sanuk*, fun. For Thais, especially the working classes and rural people who populated the monasteries, almost everything is an occasion for having a good time. Seeing a Westerner added a little novelty, and trying to help him figure out his destination was entertainment. There was no hostility, only an abundance of smiles, but being generally uptight and self-conscious I tended to perceive the smiles as smirks somehow directed at my person.

***

Someone pointed to the stairs. I climbed to the top floor of the two-story building and stuck my head in the open door of the first room I came to and asked for Dhammaramo. A young man in ochre robes, with a shaven head and a quiet air about him, invited me in. He was Dhammaramo—my alter ego.

I recounted the events of the past two days that had brought me there and told him I was interested in learning meditation.

I couldn't imagine why this fellow was in that place in those robes, but he did seem very sensible and grounded—certainly he looked a lot calmer than I felt.

An American from Michigan, same age as I (twenty-two), he told me he'd been ordained for two years, and that ever since he was sixteen it had been his dream to become a monk. He was in the city temple to study and prepare for the life of an ascetic forest *bhikkhu* (the Pali term for monk, meaning "one who begs" as well as "one who sees danger," i.e., danger in the round of rebirths). His teacher lived in such a forest monastery in Udon Province in the northeast of Thailand.

I told him about my sojourns in this vale of tears, especially the frustration of the last fifteen months on the road, when I discovered that my ideas about how to achieve enlightenment didn't work. He assured me that there was hope, that there was a real path that could free one from suffering. I quoted the *Tao Te Ching*, a superficial reading of which was popular with hippie seekers, and reminded him that there is no path and no way, that "he who knows does not speak, and he who speaks does not know."

"Actually, that's not true," he calmly replied.

2

A New Name, a New Life

A heap of snares is the household life, crowded and dusty; life gone forth is open and free. It is not easy, while living in a home, to lead the holy life.

—The Buddha

Wat Boworn, Bangkok, Thailand, September 1970

Tahn Dhammaramo agreed to give me meditation instruction and suggested I do some study as well. He felt that the proper way to go about this would be for me to move into the temple. Before I knew it, we were on our way to the abbot's residence to ask his permission.

Walking further into the monastery compound, there was more foliage and more quietude. We walked along a small *klong* (canal), and soon came upon the abbot's *kuti*. Kuti usually refers to a hut or cabin, but the abbot's dwelling and many others in the monastery were more like houses, some with two floors.

The abbot invited us inside. He had a small study and a larger meditation room on the ground floor. We sat in the latter. The abbot's English was more than adequate, though deliberate and accented. He appeared to be quite a serious person. When Dhammaramo explained my situation he immediately said, "I permit," and then gave him some instructions in Thai. And that was it.

We walked back towards Kana Soong and went to the older building facing it. The sign outside grandly proclaimed it to be headquarters for the Dhammadhuta Foundation for Sending Monks Abroad to Teach Buddhism. But it was actually a mostly empty building where an eccentric old caretaker lived. It had a classroom on the ground floor, and upstairs were a small library and an empty room facing Kana Soong.

"This is your room," Dhammaramo told me.

"When should I move in?" I asked, expecting I would still have a bit more time "free" on the outside.

"Tomorrow," was his answer. The walls were closing in fast.

He introduced me to the caretaker and told me, "He acts a little strange sometimes. Don't pay any attention to him."

We went back to Dhammaramo's room. People started dropping by. There was Robert, a tall, calm, healthy-looking young American from Minnesota. He'd been in the Peace Corps in Thailand. Having already been meditating for several years, he decided to take ordination for a few months before returning home. He'd recently disrobed and was leaving soon. He had that air I thought of as being at journey's end, such as I imagined I'd seen in two Americans I'd met in London after they'd done three months of Transcendental Meditation with the Maharishi in India. Soon enough, I thought, I'll be in his shoes.

Then a small shaven-headed woman in white robes appeared. She had something for Dhammaramo and asked me if I would hand it to him. Seeing my puzzled expression, Dhammaramo explained that monks cannot take anything directly from the hand of a woman. It was my first lesson in the very strict monastic code of conduct, the *Vinaya*, laid down by the Buddha.

The three of them all seemed quite happy, and all they talked about was meditation. When Dhammaramo told them I was moving into the temple compound to become a meditator, they were delighted and assured me I was doing a great thing. But my heart was sinking fast. A monk's cell hadn't at all been part of my grand plan. I suppose that I too was expecting life to be full of sanuk.

Robert and Sudhamma, the nun, soon departed, and Dhammaramo asked a temple boy to hail me a taxi back to the hotel.

***

The next morning at breakfast, the Westerners in the hotel were talking about the usual things. One young man was with an attractive Thai girl, laughing and giggling. Probably stoned, I thought. But I had just been wrenched out of their world, which already seemed so far away. After breakfast I packed up, checked out, and walked up the *soi* (side street) to Sukumvit Road, where I got a taxi back to the monastery.

As the taxi made its way across town, I felt like I was about to dump myself on the steps of the orphanage. It was a lonely feeling.

I found Dhammaramo, who took me to the caretaker and got me the key to my room. "Come see me at three o'clock," he said, smiling gently.

That afternoon my life as a Buddhist began. Dhammaramo told me to meditate for a half-hour each morning and evening by sitting cross-legged and counting my breaths. Focusing attention on the air going in and out at the tip of the nostrils, I was to count to nine, and then start over again. He said that the usual count was to ten, but for me it was nine. He also mentioned his own schedule: he slept from 10 at night until two in the morning and then got up to meditate until dawn. He may have told me this in order to make my new meditation schedule seem easy by comparison, but it was intimidating to hear about.

"Set an alarm clock or burn a stick of incense," he said, "and make up your mind not to move until the time is up. You'll get hot, you'll start itching, and your legs will fall asleep, but don't get up," he advised. He patiently fielded my questions and gave me a couple of books to read: Nyananponika's *Heart of Buddhist Meditation*, which was at the time the classic explanation of the Buddha's teaching on the

Four Foundations of Mindfulness, and *Introduction to Buddhism* by Khantipalo Bhikkhu.

"Khantipalo normally lives here, but he's spending the rains retreat somewhere else. You'll get to meet him when he comes back in October." He smiled mischievously and added, "He's more of a scholar than a meditator. His name means 'Protector of Patience,' but he's very impatient. Anyhow, you can come here at three every afternoon and we can discuss your meditation and reading."

In the early evening I went out to the bustling street and ate stir-fried rice noodles (for three baht, equal to fifteen cents) and also bought an alarm clock. At eight o'clock I sat down to meditate in an awkward cross-legged posture—I wasn't terribly flexible. It was awful. Just like the man said, I was hot and itching. My legs fell asleep and I didn't see how I could bear the pain for the entire half hour. But I got through it.

The next morning, to my surprise I woke up earlier than usual. I loved to sleep. It was my last refuge from misery and confusion, and when I heard how little Dhammaramo slept I couldn't imagine leading such a life. But I woke feeling more refreshed than I usually did after much more sleep. And I did the meditation torture once again. As time went by, especially once I was preparing for ordination, I would get up before dawn, take the sitting position and say to myself, "The abbot will be proud of me!" I certainly needed something to spur myself on.

In the afternoon, I would go to see Dhammaramo. He encouraged me and answered my questions, some of them practical, dealing with the nuts and bolts of meditation, some of them loopy, coming from the eclectic mishmash that most of us self-styled seekers and philosophers subscribed to.

As days went by, the meditation got a little easier, but still a desperate, lonely feeling came over me every afternoon as meditation time approached. I extended the sittings by five minutes every so often, and added walking meditation. Sitting got less excruciating, and occasionally there were patches of calm unlike anything I'd experienced before.

The books, though a little dry, were giving me a solid sense of a real path. I'd been a voracious reader for the past few years, and I kept borrowing more books. I also found some in my building. I started reading the *suttas* themselves, the Buddhist scriptures of the Pali Canon.

The writing was on the wall. There was simply no way to argue with the things I was reading, no faults in the logic, no cracks in the edifice. There was beauty in it, for sure, but it was clear that I would have to give up my way of life (whatever that was) and set out on something completely new and unplanned for, with no crutches, with nothing familiar to fall back on. Not only was desire the source of suffering, not only was there suffering in life, but the whole of life as we lived it was nothing but suffering, according to the scriptures. That wonderful Pali word *dukkha* with its many translations, from "suffering" to "stress" to "the pervasive unsatisfactoriness of existence," had entered my vocabulary.

The suttas often present the matter in a positive light. Seekers who went to see the Buddha and had their perplexities undone would exclaim things like, "It is wonderful, Lord, it is marvelous! It is like someone bringing a light into the darkness or setting upright what had been overturned." So they were telling me there was hope, lots of it in fact, that countless humans had found their way out of suffering and desperation, and that there was no reason I could not do that as well.

In the library in Calcutta, I had come across a simple description of Buddhist teaching: desire was the cause of suffering. And soon after, on my very first day in Bangkok, I heard about the Four Noble Truths and the Eightfold Path: suffering and the way out of suffering.

As with medical treatment, first comes the diagnosis. What seems mysterious and hopeless is often quickly recognizable to the physician. The Four Noble Truths start by diagnosing unhappiness and explaining its causes. Unhappiness isn't an aberration or the result of bad luck, but as understandable as what happens when you mix the wrong chemicals in a laboratory.

Texts like the *Dhammapada,* short verses grouped according to subject believed to be one of the oldest records of the Buddha's words, and the *Theragatha,* inspired verses of the Buddha's enlightened disciples, clearly marked the divide between the worldly way and the way to liberation. I could see that I needed to follow this path, but it was calling for levels of discipline and austerity that I didn't see myself capable of fulfilling. I summed up my conundrum with the thought,

"The Buddha's teachings are perfect; the only problem is, you have to do it yourself."

Like Prufrock's insect, I was pinned down and writhing.

One afternoon when I went to see Dhammaramo, Robert was there, along with two teenage Americans, recent high school graduates. The teenagers were inspecting the Wheel of Life, the classic illustration of the twelve links of dependent origination that charts the cycle of suffering from birth to old age and death. Dhammaramo explained what each illustration stood for: needles piercing the eyes represented sense contact, for example, while a man drinking represented craving, or *tanha,* which literally means "thirst."

They pondered thoughtfully, and finally one of them asked, "So how do you get out?"

"He got it!" Robert said, delightedly.

Back in my room, I read the *Dhammapada.* "Just as a fish thrown up on dry land writhes and gasps, just so struggles a mind newly withdrawn from sense-pleasures." Writhing, gasping, flopping around—that was me.

But I began to understand: rather than simply a technique, the teachings in conjunction with the monastic environment offered a complete overhaul of one's way of life. Of course it's unlikely one would stay in a monastic environment to learn meditation without beginning to suspect that there is some point to monastic life, that it might well be conducive to practicing what the Buddha taught. Without anyone pushing it on me, I felt pressure building to do something, to make a commitment. It was becoming clear that my untamed mind was the reason I was so unhappy and that my previous ideas about how to find unshakable happiness were useless. But ordaining? It was a drastic step to take and certainly didn't fit any of my preconceived notions about what to do with my life.

When I was younger, I was enthralled with Henry Miller—maybe I was just clinging desperately to someone's offer of hope—and had the idea that life should be art. I, however, wasn't going to be a mere painter, writer, or musician (never mind that I had no talent in those fields). I wanted to be a "life artist." Experience had been teaching me that I didn't have a clue what I was talking about or what I was trying to achieve. But now here was something that put it all together. I went back and forth, mulling it over, trying to tell myself I could merely stay for a few months, learn what I had to learn, and be on my merry (miserable, actually) way. But the voices kept nagging.

Sunday rolled around—not that it mattered which day it was. Robert came and asked if I would like to go to the zoo with him.

Zoo-going had become something of a pastime. I'd gone in Calcutta and Rangoon, mostly out of boredom. I was glad for the chance to get out of the compound and go look at animals.

Since moving into the monastery, I'd had no contact with the outside world except for Pra Sumeru Road, the street that ran in front of Wat Boworn, where I went to eat fried rice and buy tins of cocoa, milk powder, and instant coffee. At the zoo, it was a little overwhelming to be among the crowds. The animals no longer looked so idyllic. They were simply trapped, ignorant beasts, restless in their cages. The image that still remains, decades later, is of the polar bear. It looked just as uncomfortable as I was in our new tropical home.

We stopped in the shade a few times to drink coconut juice and eat ice cream. I started noticing that the people weren't really much different from the animals. They were driven by restlessness, not knowing what they were doing or why, only that they had to try to do something, had to keep moving.

This Buddhism was taking everything away from me. Nothing was safe. Even a trip to the zoo turned into a contemplation of dukkha. I was good and worked up that night.

The next afternoon, sitting in my room on the second floor, I read about the wanderer Subhadda, the last person to receive ordination during the Buddha's lifetime. One of the wandering ascetics in search of liberation who populated north India during that period, he'd heard of Siddhattha Gotama and decided to go see him to resolve his doubts. After a brief verbal tussle with Ananda, the Buddha's attendant, who didn't want his boss to be disturbed when his life was coming to an end, Subhadda was given an audience. His doubts were cleared away and he was inspired to join up. When told that wanderers of other sects were usually placed on a sort of probation for four months, he said, fine, it can be four years, just count me in. So the Buddha, seeing that he had a keeper, told Ananda to shave his head and ordain him on the spot.

It was like being struck by lightning. I raised my head and looked out the window. It was a sunny day; back then, you could still see blue sky in Bangkok.

Here I was, torturing myself over whether or not to try ordination, and this guy just walked right up and did it. Well, if he can do it, so can I, I told myself. That became my battle cry.

When time came for the afternoon session with Dhammaramo, I told him I wanted to ordain. At least, I still thought, it won't happen too soon, there must be hoops to jump through, approvals to get, things to arrange.

"Fine," he said. "Let's go ask the abbot."

Whoops. He put on his upper robe, and we walked over to the abbot's kuti. The abbot greeted us with his usual stern look, spoke in his usual gentle voice, and assented with his usual chuckle, telling Dhammaramo to make the arrangements.

That was September 1, 1970. When we got back to Dhammaramo's room I said, "Don't let me off the hook if I come back and tell you I changed my mind." The next day I learned my ordination was set for September 14. Someone was coming from Los Angeles also to ordain, and he and I would study together.

Michael arrived after a couple of days. I went to introduce myself. We got to talking, and he said he planned to stay a year. "If he can do it, I can do it." So I upped the ante from the six months I had started to think would be a reasonable commitment. And within a few days I realized that two years was probably more realistic. I hadn't yet wholly subscribed to the standard Buddhist idea that we carry into this lifetime a huge mountain of bad habits that can take decades of hard work to undo, but wrestling with my mind in meditation every day and quietly reflecting on all the dukkha I had experienced throughout my twenty-two years was showing me that meaningful change might not be easy to accomplish in a short time.

We were assigned to a demanding tutor who trained us in the ordination chanting. He was a senior monk with the ecclesiastical title of *Pra Kru,* "Venerable Teacher" (the Thai *Kru* being derived from the Sanskrit *Guru*). He turned out to be a nice old fellow, but we couldn't get all the nuances of the precise vowel and consonant sounds he wanted as he drilled us over and over. He had his own building right across from Kana Soong. Many senior monks were similarly ensconced, often in much more luxurious quarters than the abbot.

One of the prerequisites for ordination, stipulated by the Buddha at the request of his father, was to obtain my parents' permission. I wrote to them and explained my plans. They weren't thrilled about it, feeling I was deluding myself as usual—and how utterly alien it must have seemed to middle-class American suburbanites in 1970—but said that if it was what I wanted to do they wouldn't hinder me.

When Ajahn Chah was in London in 1979, a young man who was training with Ajahn Sumedho at Hampstead *Vihara* asked for ordination. Ajahn Chah informed him of the necessity of parental consent. His father, a well-to-do executive, came to visit one day.

"I know your type," he told Ajahn Chah. "You're evil. I am not allowing my son to ordain in your cult!"

Unruffled, Ajahn Chah asked the man, "If your son were to take up with a gang of toughs and be living on the margins of society, what would you do about that?"

The father thought for a moment and said, "Well, he's an adult, isn't he? I can't stop him from doing what he wants to do."

"If that's the case," Ajahn Chah replied, "then he is certainly free to make his own decision about ordaining!"

The fellow is still in robes.

***

So far my self-directed search for happiness had been an abysmal failure. Now it seemed all that would change. Yet I was seized with terror over this venture—especially so because it took away the future. I began to realize I couldn't put a time limit on this; it wasn't at all like going to college, knowing that at some point in time you could get your degree and move on. There was nowhere to move on to that would allow me to escape my own habit patterns if I didn't do something about them myself, now. The monastic discipline, as I contemplated it, didn't cut you any slack. There was very little opportunity for distraction. If I were on the outside, I saw, it would be all too easy to pass the days, months, and years in frivolity and never get down to business.

One afternoon I blurted out to Dhammaramo, "I sometimes feel afraid I'll be annihilated."

He calmly replied, "I certainly don't feel annihilated." Then he added, "I hope I don't look that way."

This is one of the oldest canards about Buddhism—that it is nihilistic and teaches a path to nothingness. I wasn't yet aware of such philosophical contretemps, but I can understand how it could be understood that way. I was experiencing it at gut level.

***

Michael's ordination came on September 13, and mine was the following day. We were ordaining as *samanera*, novices. In Thailand, novice ordination is normally given only for those under age twenty, which is the age required for full ordination as a bhikkhu. And in those days almost any adult male, Thai or foreigner, could walk into a temple in Bangkok and soon find himself a bhikkhu, with little knowledge of what that really entailed and little guidance on how to live. But some places took the approach that novicehood was a stage of training on the way to full ordination, and such it was at Wat Boworn.

Dhammaramo shaved my head and escorted me to the main chapel, where a bustling little man named *Nai* (Mr.) Sai was waiting for me. He was one of the laymen who lived in the temple compound and was a gopher for the abbot and senior monks. He gave me commands in Thai, none of which I understood, and steered me by taking hold of my shoulders with his hands and giving an occasional push in the back. Dhammaramo seemed to enjoy the show; he had warned me that Nai Sai would make the most of his temporary authority and that I should just do as ordered, though my not being able to understand a word of Thai made it something of a slapstick comedy.

First I had to change my clothes and put on white robes, the initial step in what is called "going forth from home to homelessness." Then, carrying my brand-new set of yellow robes, I approached the abbot seated in front of the ornate shrine, both of us witnessed by many imposing Buddha statues. The abbot was flanked by monks on each side, sitting in rows perpendicular to him.

The few photographs taken on that day make the place look cavernous and gloomy, and they certainly matched my mood.

I presented the abbot with a tray of the traditional offerings of incense, candles, and flowers and awaited my cue to start the recitations I'd been training in over the past weeks. I first requested ordination. Holding the set of robes as I knelt before the abbot, I recited the ancient formula, saying that I was taking refuge in the Lord Buddha; the Dharma, his teaching; and the Sangha, his community of followers, and asking to be accepted into the fold as one gone forth into the homeless life of a novice monk.

The abbot, Venerable Chao Khun Sasanasobhana, later to become the Supreme Patriarch of the order in Thailand, accepted the set of robes, and I sat down in front of him. He gave a brief explanation of refuge and the significance of ordination in English. In his slow, measured speech and with a look of serious dignity, he began each piece of advice with "You should know…" He also gave brief instruction on the "root meditation" of nails, hair, teeth, and skin—that very topic Khun Sutchai had stunned me with on my second day in Thailand.

"To people of the world," he said of the components of our external appearance, "these things are important. People try to make them look beautiful. But now you are a follower of the Lord Buddha. You shave your head. You cut your nails. You take care of these things because you know they can become dirty and unpleasant. But you are not seeking happiness from the world anymore."

With that, he put the *angsa,* a sort of open-sleeved shirt, over my shoulder, and handed me the rest of the robes, my cue to exit left.

The next step was to return to the dressing area, where I turned in the whites and was wrapped in yellow robes. There was clearly no turning back at this point. Years later I discovered a set of photos I had sent to my parents. In particular, when I had the yellow robes on and was heading back to see the abbot, a smiling Dhammaramo by my side, I looked like someone coming from his best friend's funeral; on the back of the photo I wrote, "Don't look very happy, do I?"

I returned to the hall for the granting of refuge and taking of the precepts, which is what constitutes the ordination. Taking refuge, I submitted myself to the Buddha, Dharma, and Sangha and asked for their guidance and protection. The abbot recited the verses of taking refuge three times, with me repeating after him. Then he recited and I repeated after him the ten precepts of a samanera.

Five precepts form the basic moral code for anyone aspiring to be a follower of the Buddhist way, and they are considered the basic ethical guidelines for human life: abstaining from taking life, stealing, sexual misconduct, lying, and use of intoxicants. For the samanera, the prohibition on sexual misconduct becomes celibacy. The next five precepts are acts of renunciation: abstaining from taking food between noon and sunrise, entertainments, personal adornment, high and luxurious sleeping places, and handling money.

The abbot then informed me that I was now a samanera. I received a new name, *Varapanyo*, which in Pali means "Excellence of Wisdom." Normally I might have said something like, "If I'm so wise, how did I get myself into this?" At that moment I was truly at a loss for words.

In a daze, Samanera Varapanyo left the chapel to begin his new life.

The newly ordained Samanera Varapanyo with Nai Sai, September 14, 1970. Photograph taken by a GI who came to study with Dhammaramo at Wat Boworn and offered to sponsor the author's ordination.

3

Body of Complete Enjoyment

These days everyone worships knowledge, but not many people worship goodness.

—*Ajahn Chah*

Wat Boworn, 1970

I'd been in robes for two months, meditating, studying, and floundering. The traditional three-month rains retreat (*vassa* in Pali, *pansa* in Thai) ended in October, and several Western monks showed up in Bangkok, most of them staying at Wat Boworn. I got to meet many of the veterans Dhammaramo had told me about. They were obviously in much better shape than I was, they all seemed to be very fine men, and their understanding of the Dharma and their explanations of forest life were clear enough, but somehow nothing was kindled in me. It usually felt as if I was being told, "This is what you will need to do. Take your medicine."

Then two monks showed up from Ajahn Chah's monastery. One was Santidhammo Bhikkhu, known today as Jack Kornfield, who ordained after a stint in the Peace Corps. The other was Suvijjano, or

Douglas Burns, an American psychiatrist who had been stationed in Thailand with the U.S. Army.

Ajahn Chah was barely mentioned in Wat Boworn, since he belonged to the Mahanikaya monastic tradition. Wat Boworn was part of the much smaller Dhammayuttika Nikaya (or simply Dhammayut) lineage, which was something of a reform movement and generally maintained higher disciplinary standards. Most of the renowned masters in the northeast of Thailand, where the forest lineage was strongest, belonged to Dhammayut. But these two monks were practically bursting with enthusiasm about Ajahn Chah. It felt like they were speaking from the realm of day-to-day experience rather than theory and ideals, talking about how they live rather than what should be attained. Their praise of Ajahn Chah was effusive, and even in my depressed state I felt uplift at hearing their stories.

***

They also praised the American monk Sumedho, who had been with Ajahn Chah for a few years. They described him as someone who was obviously reaping the fruits of meditation and ordained life. In addition to that, he spoke Thai and was very willing to help newcomers, whereas from what we'd been told about the Dhammayut forest monasteries, new guys were pretty much on their own and so should first have a good foundation in study, meditation, and Thai language too.

Ajahn Chah himself came to Bangkok and Wat Boworn soon after. I was swept up by his presence. I had never met anyone like him, or even suspected that people like him existed. He didn't seem to think that we needed a lot of study or that not being able to speak Thai would be a hindrance. "You're welcome to come, if you think you can bear it," he said with a smile. A few weeks later I took him up on his invitation.

***

Ajahn Chah often said that it was after he became a teacher and abbot and had to deal with all sorts of people that his wisdom really increased, though in the eyes of some disciples he was merely caught up in talking and socializing. Those who met him later in his life were invariably struck by his radiant happiness and naturally drawn to him. I think most people felt they'd never seen anyone who seemed so comfortable with himself and who enjoyed life so thoroughly. Though he lived an extremely simple existence guided by a detailed code of vows that included poverty and celibacy and avoidance of almost all forms of entertainment and gratification, there was no sense of privation or tedium about him.

The teachings of Mahayana Buddhism (the "Northern School," which appeared several centuries after the Buddha's lifetime) speak of the Three Kayas, the aspects of enlightened mind. One of the translations of *Sambhogakaya,* usually represented by deities with any number of arms and faces, often in unearthly forms, is the "body of complete enjoyment." It can be interpreted in many ways and on many levels—sometimes not relating at all to ordinary experience—but the term often comes to mind when thinking about Luang Por Chah and his complete enjoyment of life.

My initial impression of him during his visit to Wat Boworn was that he looked like a big, happy frog sitting on his lily pad. Newly ordained, I was struggling merely to hold on to my robes in those days, but upon meeting Ajahn Chah I immediately thought, "If all you have to do to be like that is sit in the forest for thirty years, it's worth it."

I made my first visit to his monastery, Wat Pah Pong, shortly after that. When I got there, he was in southern Thailand, unable to return because of heavy rains. Based on my earlier impression of him, I had a vivid image of Ajahn Chah sitting in an open jeep, stuck in the mud with rain falling heavily, enjoying himself immensely.

After he returned, the small group of farang who were at Wat Pah Pong (Sumedho, Suvijjano, the Englishman Dhammagutto, and I) went to see Ajahn Chah one evening. As Dhammagutto and I were newly ordained and had come from city monasteries, he spoke of the benefits of practicing in a forest monastery.

"When you live in the forest, half the job is already done," he said. "Living in a city monastery is like trying to meditate in the marketplace." That brought to mind my frustrations at Wat Boworn. I recalled the ice-cream vendor walking through the monastery and shouting to advertise his goods, and I started laughing. The image stayed with me for a long time, in large part because of the lightness of spirit with which Luang Por said it. It wasn't said in a tone of condemnation or criticism, but of amusement: this is just the way things are, and it's actually quite funny—which might be a good summary of Ajahn Chah's view of life.

***

Day in and day out, at all hours, Ajahn Chah received visitors, monastic or lay, Thai or foreign, doctor or rice farmer, in a way that is almost unparalleled among spiritual teachers. He had no personal life, nor did he seek disciples or fame. He didn't turn people away or try to hide from difficulty. He wasn't straining to be enthusiastic about things or to find the bright side and think positively. Joy flowed naturally, as did his teaching.

Ajahn Chah didn't plan things out, though once he made his mind up to do something he would focus relentlessly on it. Yet he was always ready to abandon anything on the spot and change course. The world came to find him, and nothing seemed to throw him. His inner wealth and lack of anxiousness were palpable. I think he enjoyed having farang disciples and felt a freshness in talking with people who had different cultural habits. We also presented fresh challenges, but he took it all in stride.

He could also be stern, terrifying even, as well as imperious, overbearing, and cantankerous. And he was a terrible tease—everyone's weaknesses and foibles were fair game for a teaching moment or just a dose of humility.

Classic definitions define a *bodhisattva* (buddha-to-be) as manifesting in whatever forms are needed, including as a bridge, medicine, food and shelter, a companion and a guide. Luang Por in the course of a day, a month, or a year might show many different personae and act in many different roles (and as abbot and teacher he also did provide the material support necessary for life). He was always giving—he wasn't trying to gratify himself. Nor did he have *things* to enjoy. It was just his mode of being. Certainly he was able to enjoy things like good food, but he could drink horribly bitter *borapet*, a medicinal vine boiled or pickled to make an infusion often drunk in lieu of anything else being available, just like a cup of tea.

When we were in Seattle together years later, Ajahn Chah asked if I could find some cigars for him. I came across a tobacco shop and bought a package to offer. Then one afternoon I went for a walk in the neighborhood, and as I returned, from several houses away I smelled the distinctive aroma of a cigar. When I got to the home of our hosts, Luang Por was sitting in the back yard, puffing away and having a grand time.

He was endlessly amused, but not in the way that needs to belittle others. When he did tease us, we usually knew he was teaching something, attacking pride or other habits and not people. He pulled things out of thin air, puns no one else would ever conceive of. After the meal, very relaxed as he joked with the senior monks—while the juniors were anything but relaxed, weighed down with a day's food and wanting to leave—he often had the air of a raconteur in a bar. He loved to tell stories, and retell them endlessly, enjoying them more each time. In my first year at Wat Pah Pong, as I struggled to adjust and survive, I was involved in several incidents that became part of his canon of tales. Sometimes I told him myself of a troublesome episode, other times the grapevine would relay it.

As he had me remain in samanera status for a long time, I was down at the end of the hierarchical row in the eating hall. One hot season a local doctor sent his two young sons to stay at Wat Pah Pong. They took *anagarika* (renunciant) vows, wore white, and sat next to me. They were curious about this farang, a rare sight in Ubon in those years, and always wanted to talk with me. Their father brought them things to supplement the lean dry season fare, and they offered me a bag of peanuts. I kept them in my *yahm* (monastic shoulder bag) and added a handful to my food each morning.

Then the inevitable occurred. One morning I awoke to find my yahm had been chewed through and the peanuts scattered all over the kuti—a mouse had discovered them. I threw the peanuts into the forest and in consternation went to show the yahm to Luang Por. He asked if I'd put any food in it, so I told him about the peanuts. He thought that funny (of course) and had someone sew the yahm for me, since I hadn't yet learned to use a sewing machine.

The next morning there was another hole in my yahm. I went back to Luang Por. He thought this was really hilarious. "It still has the smell of the nuts," he explained. Once again, he had it sewn, and I washed it well. Over the years that followed, I can't count how many times Luang Por would say things like, "Varapanyo really suffered when he first came to Wat Pah Pong. A mouse chewed his yahm!" or "Poor Varapanyo, he was hungry when he was a novice so he stored some nuts in his yahm. Then one day he came to me and said, 'Luang Por, a mouse chewed my yahm!'"

During hot season, the kutis, with their tin roofs exposed to the sun, often became unbearable in daytime. Mine had a bathroom underneath with toilet, water barrel, and enough space to bathe. As it was made of concrete and was sheltered from the sun, the bathroom was more comfortable than the kuti in the daytime, so I did what seemed logical and brought a mat down there to take a rest at midday and sit in meditation. Of course someone noticed and reported it to Luang Por, which again was repeated over the years—such a thing just wasn't done by Thai or Isan (northeastern) people. "Oy! Varapanyo suffered so much when he first ordained: he used to sleep in the toilet!" And he would always get a great laugh out of it, no matter how many times he told the story.

***

These events occurred during my novitiate. I was a novice for about twenty months, longer than most of the other farang spent in that status. Taking the full ordination (*upasampada* in Pali) of a bhikkhu became an "ought to" with me, and every so often I would remind Luang Por that I was still a novice and wondering when he would give the go-ahead for upasampada. But he kept telling me there was no hurry.

He took ordination seriously, and he told us repeatedly that we should be committed to spending five *vassa* (rains retreats) as bhikkhus. He saw that as a reasonable period of time for a person to make a real change in habits, to establish a foundation of morality and mindfulness, and to start gaining insight in meditation practice (what he once described, in my own case, as being able to understand about five percent of the teachings).

According to the historical accounts in scripture, when the Buddha first began teaching after his enlightenment he would ordain worthy candidates simply by saying *"Ehi bhikkhu,"* literally "Come, bhikkhu," adding something like "Lead the holy life for the ending of suffering." As time went by the numbers of those wishing to follow the Buddha increased, with a whole range of characters showing up, some more suitable than others. The ordination procedure evolved to something more formalized and elaborate, and a probationary period was instituted to test the resolve and suitability of those seeking to become disciples of the Buddha.

It wouldn't have taken a feat of clairvoyance for Ajahn Chah to see that I wasn't very sure about what I was doing or where I was going. Sometimes he liked to bring things to a boil and push people to take the next step, but his methods were tailored to the individual. In most cases, he felt that the monastic routine would provide the immersion in living Dharma that could mature the individual. The Buddha taught that the mind is impermanent and uncertain, it is of the nature to accumulate suffering, it is not oneself or one's own—but it can be trained. And so as days and months passed, the way of life became more real and meaningful to me, and without forcing the matter I felt ready for the plunge.

***

Shortly before the beginning of vassa in 1972, Ajahn Chah sent about twenty of us—three farang and a group of locals—for ordination at Wat Wahrin, in the nearby town of the same name. Luang Por wasn't yet invested with the title of *upajjhaya,* preceptor. He could give novice ordination but not upasampada. As soon as the ceremony was over and I had one more robe, the *sanghati,* which is usually folded and placed over the shoulder, things felt different. When we met with Luang Por soon afterward, he told us that we were adults now and had to give one hundred percent, whereas for novices fifty was the norm. His tone was sober. I got the message that things were not going to be the same.

The bhikkhu has many more rules to guide his behavior. A long novitiate, as well as living in an environment where discipline and ethics are revered, prepares one to take the task seriously, even when nobody is looking. Two years before, if someone had told me that I would soon be living in a monastery in Bangkok and preparing to take robes, I would have been incredulous—they might as well have said I was soon going to the moon. But now I was all in, and there wasn't anything else I could conceive of doing.

***

A freelance journalist reviewing *Venerable Father*, my account of the years I spent with Ajahn Chah (which I first self-published in Bangkok in 1993), wrote about my "love-hate relationship" with Ajahn Chah. People reading or hearing about the way he operated often remarked that he seemed sadistic. And living in his monasteries was certainly not easy. One Amazon reviewer of *Venerable Father* entitled his piece "Forest Monastery Human Rights Abuses."

Buddhism talks of "skillful means," *upaya* in Pali and Sanskrit, the original languages of the scriptures. It can refer to the way the individual develops his own practice or the way one benefits others, including in the role of teacher. One of the things that distinguished Ajahn Chah from other teachers in Thailand was his hands-on relationship with large numbers of disciples, his readiness to accept almost anyone and take on all comers. Skillful means meant something different for each student. Buddhism is often compared to medical treatment: the Buddha is the physician, the Dharma is the medicine prescribed, and the Sangha are the medical staff that help one through the treatment. We are the patients; we are sick, we are in dire straits, we are in need of help. Like all metaphors, it only goes so far. It talks about helping us in the course of this life, whereas the suffering rooted in the mental continuum goes on and on endlessly throughout a succession of lives until the causes are eradicated. In other words, the situation is drastic and may require drastic action informed by wisdom and compassion.

In the flesh, most people were charmed by Ajahn Chah and felt him to be the warmest, liveliest person they'd ever met. But he was a superb actor and you never knew what you were going to get.

Ajahn Chah once said that we look at enlightened beings and conceive of them as being like ourselves, so it can be hard to figure them out. Specifically he said we think they have the same conceptions of "me" and "mine" that we do. But awakened ones are awakened precisely because they've freed themselves from the hunter's nets and steel traps of self-cherishing and self-conception. When they deal with others, they do so in response to the needs of others, not out of a need for self-fulfillment. It is said to be like the sun shining, without intention or deliberation: that's just what the sun does, and it shines on all without discriminating as to who is worthy and so on.

Like the sun, he could be warming or he could be fierce; without deliberation, he was able to respond to the needs of those who came to him. Especially with ordained disciples, who basically were standing up and saying "OK, give it to me with both barrels," the treatment could be harsh and painful. Within the boundaries of monastic discipline, one trusts that no harm will be done save to one's ego, and master and disciple (master especially) are ready to let the chips fall where they may. That may be one of the reasons Ajahn Chah started making the requirements for ordination more stringent in his later years—he wanted to weed out those who weren't ready for that kind of commitment.

The vocabulary used in the Thai language describing the relationship with a spiritual teacher speaks of having deference and even fear. When I mentioned to another Western monk that the Thai monks and nuns often seemed to be terrified of Ajahn Chah, he replied, "I'm not so sure that's a bad way to be." The example of the teacher is something the disciples try to live up to, but it's not easy. The teacher's presence is a constant reminder and standard, and there is usually some tension in play. With a complex code of discipline that applies to all aspects of daily existence, it's easy to fall off the straight and narrow path. The teacher not only watches for errant behavior but can read a lot from disciples' deportment, sizing up one's practice from the way one walks, speaks, eats. But no matter how the teacher puts the screws to you, there's never any doubt that he only has your welfare in mind.

Ajahn Chah was often a Santa Claus figure, right down to round and jolly and an almost-red suit of clothes. But as they say about Santa, "He knows when you are sleeping, he knows when you're awake, he knows if you've been bad or good...." At times we may have thought he wasn't really paying attention to everyone and everything going on in Wat Pah Pong and his other monasteries, but sooner or later we'd usually be brought up short and realize that not much escaped his view. Over the years, therefore, my relationship with Ajahn Chah was often rocky. It could be blissful just to sit in his presence. Sometimes he gave me tasks and responsibilities, such as translating for the other farang monks, which were a joy to perform and made me feel good about myself at a time when I had almost zero confidence or sense of worth. But it could also be frightening and painful to deal with him, and I never knew what to expect. He especially didn't allow people to stagnate, and whenever I got in a comfortable rut, a jolt was usually in store. He often said in later years how it hurt him to do what he needed to do for me and joked that he would be afraid to go to the West because "Varapanyo probably wants to get me back for torturing him."

***

Though my personal relationship with Ajahn Chah is what remains most vivid in my memory, it was the daily grind in the monastery that was the real training. I'm quite certain that is what Ajahn Chah intended. And a lot of it was just plain endurance, constantly forcing one to rouse energy and to do and put up with things one would rather not be involved in.

The gong was struck at three o'clock every morning. A military metaphor may have been unintended, but many of the gongs used in monasteries were fashioned from bombshells discarded by the U.S. Air Force base outside of Ubon city. Their peals resounded to all corners of the monastery and into the nearby villages.

Walking in the dark with an empty stomach to go meditate and chant praises in an ancient language to the founder of an Eastern religion was not anything I would ever have imagined myself doing, but there I was. A few hours later, I carried an alms bowl and followed a group of monks to a village a mile or two away, where mostly old, grizzled farmers put steaming lumps of glutinous rice in my bowl. And a couple of hours after that I finally got to eat something. Half an hour of supposedly mindful eating—in actuality stuffing down the food in fear of being hungry through the night and following morning—and that was it for the day's sensual pleasure and physical sustenance.

After that, it was back to the kuti in the forest, alone with my wild mind. Some cleaning, some meditation, some rest, and then the gong rang again at three in the afternoon.

We gathered at wells around the monastery. A couple of monks pulled up water in five-gallon cans and poured it into other cans, and those were hoisted onto long bamboo poles. A monk or novice took each end of the pole and carried the water to places around the monastery to fill big ceramic barrels. While we worked like that, a crew of older monks swept and cleaned the meditation hall.

After that there might be some sweeping of the grounds to do. Some of us would always head to Ajahn Chah's kuti, to clean up, to be available for anything he needed, or just to hang out. Sometimes laypeople came to visit him, sometimes there would be a visiting monk. There could be a lot of aimless chatter as the laypeople chewed Luang Por's ears off, but a profound Dharma talk was just as likely to happen. There was a soft drink on occasion, and newcomers were often given a cup of tea, Luang Por himself offering it from the thermos his attendant novice had prepared.

Ajahn Chah's kuti was an island of peace and levity in my early days there, but I learned later on, after I had made the commitment to become a disciple of Ajahn Chah and stay at Wat Pah Pong for as long as it took, that you approached at your own peril. Life with Luang Por was Dharma combat, and you never knew if his hand would be holding out a cup of tea or brandishing a sword.

There was usually an evening practice of meditation and chanting, followed by a senior bhikkhu reading and commenting on a text explaining the Vinaya, the scriptural code of discipline. Of course, when

I was new I didn't understand any of what was being said, so it was another "opportunity" to sit through pain in my legs and restlessness. Then it was back to the forest for more meditation and a little sleep.

It was a demanding daily round, and the life was spartan, but it was peaceful. Even for someone habitually in turmoil, the tranquility of the forest was striking and would unexpectedly pull me out of my dramas again and again. The simplicity and neatness of the daily existence, with little time or opportunity to think about what I wanted or how I preferred to do things, tangibly reduced the mental clutter. The teachings came more alive. The Dharma made more sense there in the forest, where the way of life was probably not much different from that of monks in the time of the Buddha.

***

When the Buddha was about to leave this world, he told his disciples, "Let this Dharma and Vinaya that I have taught be your guide." Ajahn Chah once explained to a visitor how he taught disciples from other cultures. "I just tell them, 'Pick up this glass and put it over there.' Then after some time, I tell them, 'Pick it up and put it back here.' If they ask why they should do that, I say, 'Your responsibility is not to ask about it, just to pick it up and move it!'" And he explained that after (figuratively) doing this for a long time, some change and sensitivity come about in the mind.

The day-to-day routines could seem just as non-spiritual and uninspiring as moving a glass back and forth. What made them different from what we might have done if left to our own devices were the supporting, or surrounding, factors. Everything was done according to the Vinaya, which emphasizes and fosters simplicity, honesty, non-harming, unselfishness, and non-attachment. We were always taught to establish mindfulness in whatever we did, whether formal meditation, working, eating, or coming and going. And there was the presence, example, guidance, and shadow of the teacher too.

***

Everyone was welcome to join Ajahn Chah's party at any time. Sometimes, with his monks at Wat Pah Pong, he wouldn't let you leave the party. On the *Uposatha* (observance) days, during evening

Dharma talks, or before or after the meal, for example, he would keep us sitting and sitting while he taught, joked, discussed very minor business, and so on. We would be achy, restless, hungry, angry, wanting to go meditate in our kutis or sleep, while he was demonstrating right before our eyes that suffering is not necessary. The problem was that we didn't recognize there was a party going on, and while it was unlikely he would be able to force us to see that, I think he felt that if he kept on pointing in the right direction sooner or later some of us would get it. But no matter how dense or resistant I could be, there were always occasions when I would be at his kuti or listening to his Dharma talk in the *sala* (meditation hall), and in the immediacy of his joy and radiant presence, or from the piercing clarity of his words, everything would drop away, all the great burdens and petty concerns, the mental aches and pains and sometimes the physical ones too. Or it could simply be the forced sitting still with no possibility of escape that made you let go after listening to your own mind going round and round on the same tiresome track.

The last time I saw Ajahn Som, the colorful abbot of Wat Tam Saeng Pet (Cave of Diamond Light Monastery, one of the early branches of Wat Pah Pong), he was standing outside one afternoon, chewing betel nut (*areca*), a mild stimulant popular in many Asian countries that turns the mouth and saliva red, and occasionally stepping aside to spit out the juice. We had one of those rambling conversations that people who are in a hurry might consider pointless, but which often yield up nuggets of gold. One of the things he said was, "Most of us humans have a lot of karma to work through. Luang Por Chah is someone with little karma." He meant negative karma, of course, the positive being *parami,* spiritual perfections.

While Luang Por's perfections of morality, endurance, diligence, wisdom, and so forth were obvious, I never thought much in terms of generosity (as it's usually considered "layperson's practice" in Thailand and somehow inferior to keeping monastic vows and practicing meditation), yet now it strikes me how totally generous he was and what richness, what wealth, he projected. "I realized that with my begging bowl and one set of robes I was the richest person in the universe

and all beings were my children" is one of the statements the Buddha
made about his enlightenment. That was more than 2,500 years ago,
but in more recent times many of us had the good fortune to meet a
living embodiment in Ajahn Chah.

Ajahn Chah, May 1979, Insight Meditation Society, Barre,
Mass., Photograph by Jim Roy.

4

Endure, Varapanyo, Endure a Lot

Being in [monasteries in] northeast Thailand is like being out on an oil rig somewhere. You know you're there because you have a job to do, but you wouldn't be there for any other reason.

—*Khemanando Bhikkhu*

Wat Boworn and Wat Pah Pong, 1971-72

My first, exploratory visit to Ajahn Chah's monastery was in December of 1970. It certainly felt like a suitable environment to be in if I wanted to pursue meditation practice and the path leading out of suffering. But spartan living in splendid isolation was intimidating too, so it took a couple of months to get up the courage to return there.

The first time I thought I was ready to spend the rest of my days in the forest it didn't go at all smoothly. A few other farang monks and novices had come to practice with Ajahn Chah, and he sent us all to stay with Ajahn Sumedho at Wat Tam Saeng Pet, a huge forest monastery complete with mountain and caves.

Before too long, I was about as desperate as I'd ever been.

A few months of meditation practice had broken open the ants' nest of my mind, and I was in a state of near-panic much of the time. Unable to digest the sticky rice, the staple of the northeastern diet, I kept losing weight and had little energy to get through the enervating hot season days. In addition to all the usual difficulties of monastic life and being alone with my mind most of the day, the *pindapat* (alms round) routes were all at least a two-hour walk. I started to think it might be better for me at Wat Pah Pong, with shorter pindapats and more group practice, and the reassuring presence of Luang Por Chah.

***

As if by magic, a vehicle always appears to take ordained people to their destinations, with a driver who seems to have nothing else in the world to do. On the way to Wat Pah Pong, my driver there stopped in Ubon city, whether at Ajahn Chah's orders or out of his own concern for this skinny stranger in robes I'm not sure, to take me to see a doctor. It was the clinic of Dr. Utai, a kindly Chinese man who spoke good English.

It was late Sunday afternoon. He examined me and prescribed some vitamins, and then as I got up from the examining table my glasses slipped off my skinny head and shattered on the floor. It felt like yet another big wave rolling in from the ocean of misery, further submerging my spirits, but barely three seconds passed before Dr. Utai jumped up and said, "I will offer a new pair!" The driver took me down the street to an optician's shop, and the next day I was brought back to pick up my new pair of glasses.

I was so amazed, and comforted, by the gentleness and kindness of Dr. Utai that I kept him in mind for a long time. When my sister came to visit and fell ill, my first thought was for her to see him. When I started having a problem with a knee, I went to see him in the hospital. Luang Por started calling me *"luksit Mor Utai,"* Dr. Utai's disciple. Ajahn Chah was probably taking aim at my hypochondria, but still I never forgot that first incident.

***

Before I ordained, at the age of twenty-two, I never had to support myself. Any jobs I'd had were to get extra spending money or to help pay for travel. I was used to others footing the bill without having to consider what it was costing them, so I guess it seemed logical to me that someone was now providing food and a place to stay. When I was in robes, it didn't take me long to get accustomed to having my entire existence subsidized by people who didn't know me.

Just trying to make it from one day to the next, I wasn't terribly sensitive to what was going on around me. So in spite of the extraordinary generosity of strangers, mostly I grumbled about the difficulty of my living situation, sometimes meager food, lack of the things I was accustomed to and desired. "What's the big deal about providing things that people like?" I would ask myself, certain that if it were me in pants and shirt, showing up at the wat in an automobile, I would outdo everyone with lavish offerings. Yet when I

Varapanyo Bhikkhu, Bangkok, 1972. Taken in a photographer's shop prior to renewing his visa.

later disrobed and was scraping out a subsistence-level, no-frills life (by American standards), there seemed little left over to support worthy causes and people. I managed to occasionally donate to Oxfam and send coffee or tea to the monks in Thailand, but it was far from being a way of life, and looking outside myself to see what I could do for others was more of a task than a habit.

***

Staying at Wat Pah Pong didn't turn out to be any easier than Tam Saeng Pet, and I soon convinced myself to go to Bangkok for the vassa.

Wat Boworn kept the monastic discipline strictly, even if more in letter than in spirit, and there was usually at least one experienced Western monk in residence who could help newcomers. The abbot was respected as a genuine practitioner too. The food would be better and the pindapats much easier. Such went my line of reasoning.

When I went to announce my decision to Luang Por Chah, he didn't try to dissuade me, only telling me and the American novice who was translating, "Sumedho says Varapanyo thinks too much."

At that point, nine months as a novice, I was little more than a casual visitor at Wat Pah Pong. I had noticed Ajahn Chah's sincere concern for me when he visited at Tam Saeng Pet and looked me over, but he probably saw me as a little fish that had to be thrown back into the pond for a while. I spent time with him some more before leaving, but even his august presence couldn't do much to alter my unrelenting desperation.

A train ticket and a ride to the station were procured, and soon I was back at Wat Boworn. The abbot accepted me back and assigned me a kuti, telling me to rely on one senior English bhikkhu from Ajahn Mahaboowa's monastery who was spending vassa there.

The small group of farang at Wat Boworn took meals together and studied Vinaya with Venerable Jutindharo, and we joined the abbot on Mondays for his teaching and meditation with Western laypeople. But I was fumbling my way through it all. One afternoon, after a session with Tahn Jutindharo, I was helping wash teacups. There was no sink to wash things in; we squatted on the concrete downstairs and made do with a hose and basin. With soapy hands, I picked up a teapot as I conversed with another novice. The pot slipped from my grasp and shattered on the cement.

"Uh oh," said samanera Bodhesako. "That's Jutindharo's favorite teapot."

In trepidation, I climbed the stairs to deliver the bad news.

"*Mai pen rai* (It doesn't matter)," Jutindharo said with a sweet smile. "Impermanence."

I breathed a sigh of relief and decided to leave the other novice to finish the cups. But a few mornings later, I was assigned to slice mangoes for the meal. They were ripe and juicy, and it wasn't easy to cut them into neat pieces. When I offered the tray to Jutindharo, his face darkened.

"What is this mess?" he demanded. "Not a single thing can you do right! You don't respond to training at all."

Speechless, I slunk back to my seat. After that I started taking my meals alone and stayed in my kuti rather than joining the tea and Vinaya sessions. But there was no haven there either. I was on the second floor, in a room above a Thai monk. One afternoon there was a knock on my door. An irate novice, an Indonesian named Teddy, was standing there.

"The monk downstairs is trying to prepare for exams! But he can't study because of all the noise you are making!"

I'd never had much contact with Teddy, but he'd always been pleasant when I did speak with him, so his sudden fit of anger gave me a shock. And I couldn't figure out how I was making noise. It was just that kind of time.

My despair became a yawning chasm. It got so bad that even when I sat down to take a simple cup of tea, my whole torso would feel squeezed unbearably. There was hardly a moment's respite throughout the day and night. My weight dropped to around 115 pounds. In college, I'd weighed more than 170, and when I first came to Thailand, one year before, I was 140 pounds, and that after months of dysentery in Nepal.

I was more exhausted and apathetic than I had been even at Tam Saeng Pet. The kuti was usually sweltering and it was an effort just to get up off the floor. When I did get up it was hard to sit still to meditate. But one day it felt literally like "do or die." I forced myself to get up and started doing slow walking meditation in circles in the room.

And I kept on walking. At night I went outside and walked around the monastery. Usually I worked my way over to one of the smaller buildings behind the main chapel and walked back and forth there for a couple of hours. In the morning, after the meal, I was terrified to get off my feet, knowing that drowsiness awaited me. Old rock lyrics would run through my head at that moment every day: *You can't sit down, you can't sit down.* So I would take off my upper robe, hang it up, and start cleaning the room in the same slow, mindful way as I did the walking. I dusted and scrubbed every square inch of that room many times in the following weeks.

In the daytime I went to a huge new building on the other end of the compound from the chapel and did walking meditation inside, walking back and forth, around in rectangles, up and down the stairs. The slow walking calmed me down a tiny bit, but mostly it brought things into focus. The physical sensations often intensified. I would stop to stand still and contemplate what was going on inside the body. Sometimes I felt I was on the field of battle, facing Mara, the Evil One, mounted on his war elephant and surrounded by his fearsome legions.

It became clear that I belonged in the forest, where the environment was so much more tranquil, so much more conducive to mindfulness and meditation practice. Being basically on my own and struggling against the noise and crowded conditions of the city wat, I could better appreciate and understand the value of group practice and communal living in the forest monastery, and especially of having the guidance and good example of people like Sumedho and Ajahn Chah. I started counting off the days until the end of vassa. But I couldn't just bide my time. I knew I had to make effort in the present, I had to face the experience of dukkha. If I just returned to the forest hoping that someone else would do everything for me, or that somehow I would all of a sudden be ready to shake off apathy, I would be back at the bottom of the deep hole.

***

Immediately after vassa ended I did return to Wat Pah Pong for the long haul. When Luang Por decided I wasn't running away this time, having observed and directly questioned me about my aims and plans over a period of a couple of months, he took hold of me and put me to work doing *acaryawat,* serving the teacher. I spent time with the novices who attended him and learned the ropes from them. There seemed no limits to their patience with my bumbling, freaked-out ways as well as my limited command of the Thai language (and hardly any understanding of the local Isan dialect). If there was a "what's in it for me?" attitude on the part of any of them, I sure didn't see it. I also got to know several of the monks, and they were all most encouraging.

One thing that became obvious was the earthiness of the Northeastern monks. There certainly wasn't any kind of immorality in their behavior, but they didn't fit the stereotype of being straight-laced and ethereal that probably comes to mind for many of us when seeing people in religious garb or thinking about those leading lives of renunciation. Part of it is cultural—earthiness could logically be expected from farmers, which is what most of the monks and novices had been before ordaining. In a broader sense, monks don't have anything to be embarrassed about. Ajahn Sumedho noted that even Ajahn Chah could be quite crude in his humor.

Young monks who have been in robes for just a few years tend to be very restrained, but when they've been ordained for a decade or so they often become more much more relaxed. Personalities resurface, though cleansed of grosser forms of defilement. There were lots of interesting characters at Wat Pah Pong. I sometimes would look at senior monks and wonder what they might be doing if they were laypeople. I could see some as schoolteachers, certainly. Others might have been the local tailor, or the stereotypical barber who talks nonstop. Some had a looseness that I could imagine becoming lechery in lay life.

Still, these amusements were sideshows, and there were hard realities to face on a daily basis. The conversation that stands out most in memory was with Ajahn Kam, one of the senior bhikkhus. We were sitting with Luang Por one cold windy night at his kuti, drinking tea and talking about a lot of things, but especially the trials of practice and monastic life. Before we adjourned, Ajahn Kam turned to me and said, "*Ot ton,* Varapanyo. *Ot ton,*" which translates roughly as "Hang in there and tough it out" or literally as "Endure, Varapanyo; endure a lot."

***

The northeast of Thailand is certainly not a wealthy area, and in the 1970s, the people had even less than they do now. But the habit of giving is strong among rich and poor. From one branch monastery to another over the years, the story was pretty much the same, people at all levels of society lending a hand to sustain the existence of those in robes, with Pra Farang usually getting extra attention.

It begins with pindapat, the daily alms round. Walking for alms creates a symbiotic relationship: those who have renounced the world become completely dependent on the generosity of the faithful for their very survival, and the patrons depend on the ordained ones for spiritual guidance. Throughout the Kingdom, people are up before dawn, preparing food for the bhikkhus and samaneras who will be coming to seek their daily sustenance. In Bangkok, there were a few regular donors I would stop at, along with some people who were out every morning and gave their offerings for the day to the first monks who came by. Then there were those offering food for special occasions such as a birthday—itself a revelation, the idea of giving rather than expecting gifts on one's birthday—who would get dressed in their finest, set up a table in a well-trafficked spot, and scoop rice out of their best tureen and offer colorful curries in little plastic bags and dainty treats wrapped in banana leaves. Yet none of this to me compares with the way it's done in the Isan, where most villagers are out every single morning. Often they give only sticky rice, but several will go the monastery afterwards and bring or prepare more food. These are some of the poorest people in Thailand. The northeast is periodically afflicted with drought and poor crop yields, yet somehow there is always enough to feed the Sangha.

A few of us were sitting with Luang Por Chah at his kuti one afternoon when seemingly out of the blue he said, addressing one of us at random as he often did, "Santacitto! There's not much to the practice here. The Buddha wanted us to go pindapat every day. He wanted us to walk through the villages, see the houses, see the people, see the chickens, and contemplate." He didn't elaborate on it any further, but over the years I considered that statement many times, and especially as a layperson later struggling to survive, I felt he meant that ordained people should be aware that lay life is not something easy or idyllic. Walking through villages in the Northeast in those days certainly showed me that life was rough in many ways and the people who fed me were not at all wealthy; in a normal person, this also ought to give rise to much appreciation and gratitude. And those poor, humble folk exhibited more happiness and graciousness than I was capable of, and more than I usually found among the middle and upper classes in the United States and also in more materially developed Asian societies like Japan and Taiwan.

***

There is a reason ordained people are supported unconditionally, something that separates them from the rest of humanity: renunciation. Monks, novices, and nuns are tasked with penetrating the causes of suffering, dedicating their lives to the goal of liberation without holding anything in reserve. In the Thai language, renunciants are even referred to as a "gender," so different are they held to be.

Still, in some ways it may take a foreigner's viewpoint to really appreciate the sharp edge of the way of life. For most Thais several decades ago, many of the privations of forest living were not so different from or more difficult than what they knew in lay life in a simple society in the tropics. For pampered souls like me, on the other hand, hardship seemed to be advancing from all sides.

The ants, for example.

A visiting American monk at Wat Pah Pong once remarked, "This place should be called Wat Pah Mot (Forest Monastery of Ants)."

Mot lin, black army ants that have a sting so painful it's hard to imagine, can bring down a centipede. And a centipede, in Thailand, can bring down a snake. Mot lin especially swarm out after rain, and Wat Pah Pong had more of them than any other place I saw. Fortunately, they don't climb, otherwise the forests would be uninhabitable. The first time I was at Wat Pah Pong at the height of rainy season I started having nightmares about the monastery being filled with mot lin and them coming up into the kutis, which were raised on pillars for just this kind of reason.

Usually they march in columns, crossing the forest paths—"It's frightening to see, like watching the Panzer Division," remarked a monk who once stepped off his kuti stairs into a mass of them and thought he might die, so painful was the experience. You can step over one column, but there may be more than one. When encountering this I would first survey the scene with my flashlight (they generally come out at night, adding to the challenge), plan a route, then back up to get a running start and jump over the columns one after the next. But if they've broken ranks to attack prey, such as a fat worm, sometimes there's no way through or around and you just have to retrace your steps and find another path to your destination.

Red tree ants, which fall on you while you sweep leaves and nip at your head, can bring down mot lin. Then there's a smaller ant that can carry away the red tree ants, presumably to eat them.

Some ants get in your kettle and mug. Some little ones sniff out anything sweet, seemingly from miles away; you might have a little sugar tied shut in a plastic bag and hanging from a clothesline, and one day you open it to find ants inside. Keeping sugar in a kuti was like beating a loud drum to summon the ants from the far reaches of the forest.

Mot kun come up through the floor in the night, even going through the weave of the mosquito net, and start chewing on you with an itchy *(kun)* bite. *Mot nahm* are similar, but smaller and with a sharper bite *(nahm* = thorn).

There are small black and white termites too. They make enormous mounds in the forest and come to munch on kutis. Large termites fly, shed their wings, then go to ground. Their bite can take out a chunk of skin.

There are nasty medium-sized, reddish stinging ants that march in columns similar to those of mot lin and are often encountered on pindapat. One type of large brown ant likes to make nests among books. Occasionally they get into a sweet drink. They have an unforgettable sour taste.

You can usually tell how bad an ant's bite or sting is by blowing on a column. The more frantically they scatter, the more powerful they are.

But the zoological challenges paled in comparison to the hand-to-hand combat of dealing with my own mind, day after day, minute by minute, with precious little distraction. Sometimes I would say to myself, "I'm such a lovely guy, why do I want to torment myself like this?" But at day's end, when I was lying down on the hard floor for a few hours' respite, I would often jut out my figurative chin and say, "I'll get you yet, you bastard." The life wasn't easy and I had plenty of dukkha, just as I had at Wat Boworn and in my lay life before ordaining. But I knew I had finally gained traction on the path by committing to staying in an environment where Dharma and Vinaya were lived and breathed; and whenever my feet started slipping, Ajahn Chah was usually there to grab hold and pull me along.

Varapanyo in Ajahn Chah's kuti, August 1974. Santacitto Bhikkhu is seen in the background. Photo by Barbara Breiter.

5

Ajahn Sumedho

Any fool can say how things should be.

—Ajahn Sumedho

Wat Pra Sri Mahadhatu, Wat Pah Pong, and Tam Saeng Pet, 1973

My first year in college I had one of those rare instructors who provoked students into investigating the world and themselves. In one lecture, he talked about myth. He said that myths are something relevant to their time and place and fill a need, allowing contact with dimensions of life from which we normally feel disconnected. In modern times (that was 1967), he said, a mythic figure might be someone like Bob Dylan.

Six years later, I found myself walking behind Ajahn Sumedho on pindapat. We were in the environs of Wat Pra Sri Mahadhatu, on the outskirts of Bangkok, where he was staying at the time. That area was almost rural in those days, and the pindapats were bright and peaceful occasions.

The tradition of spiritual seekers living on alms in Asian societies is older even than Buddhism. In the Buddhist monastic way, monks must go for almsfood every day, as they are not permitted to buy or store food. The monasteries thus have to be within walking distance of the laypeople, and they are always open for anyone to come. In Thailand, almsgiving has become a part of daily life, and except in the most remote regions, it is inconceivable that monks and novices would go hungry. But in fact the laity are under no obligation to donate food or anything else if they don't feel the mendicants are spiritually worthy—so there is, theoretically at least, incentive for the monks to live in the right way—and scriptural accounts show that in the Buddha's time monks were often not able to take food offerings for granted.

Monks and novices set out after the first light of day. They have usually been awake for a few hours already. Not having taken food since the previous morning, body and mind are light. In rural areas the landscape was still and quiet, with maybe an occasional passing vehicle and farmers leading water buffalo to the fields. I think Westerners soon get over whatever stigma they may have felt about "begging"—ordained people are treated with so much respect in Thailand that it can be hard to feel humbled—and for me, walking out into the new day with empty hands, in the wake of the morning's sitting meditation, was often a joyful experience. It was usually done in silence. Occasionally there would be inspired Dharma conversation, but Ajahn Chah, who was clearly from the "talk is cheap" school, saw more value in silence and urged that on us.

The prescribed method of seeking alms is to stand silently outside of a house sufficiently long to determine whether anyone might be coming out to make an offering. But in the villages in Thailand people are lined up waiting for the bhikkhus and samaneras. In the cities, all sorts of delicacies are put in the alms bowls, along with the ubiquitous rice, but in the villages sometimes there is little beside the rice.

Since there were just the two of us, Ajahn Sumedho and I, we took our food back to our large and comfortable kuti, chose what we wanted from the full alms bowls, and put the rest aside for the temple boys, usually students who got room and board in exchange for assisting the monks and doing chores. In the large city monasteries, the monks are on their own for many of their activities, like pindapat and eating, while in the forest everything is usually done communally, with the local laypeople interacting.

Some villagers go to the monastery daily, bringing more food or cooking there. Some items may be stockpiled in the kitchen under the stewardship of laypeople, nuns, or white-robed *anagarikas*. On occasion city people will come, and the sound of a vehicle approaching usually signals special food offerings.

After a brief period of bustle in getting everything prepared, the food is offered to the Sangha. A blessing is chanted, the meal is taken in silence, and after the cleanup that's it as far as involvement with food goes. It often seemed like a big production, involving several hours from the time we left on pindapat to the time we got back to our kutis after the meal. But after living as a layman and considering just how much time is spent on shopping for, preparing, and eating food and then cleaning up (not to mention the time consumed by going to a restaurant), as well as the hours of paid work that are needed to be able to buy food, the monastic approach seems most streamlined.

***

I hadn't seen Ajahn Sumedho for about a year. While he had always been an impressive figure, it was evident that he had matured further since our previous encounter. Over the years, whenever I saw him after a period of time, he always seemed to display new facets of spiritual development. He was physically impressive, too. At well over six feet tall he towered over the Thais and was bigger than most of the other farang monks. And his strong, deep voice underscored the authority with which he spoke.

He and I had inspired conversations on the walk to and from the houses during those two weeks I spent with him at Wat Pra Sri. His words conveyed clarity and profundity in that uniquely accessible way of communicating he has. It was a great honor to walk in his footsteps as we made our alms round. I began to think that here was someone who provided a truly meaningful mythic figure for our times. He was a model that young people would do well to aspire to, much more so than any frenetic musician or poet.

***

Ajahn Sumedho didn't go much for categories and standard Buddhist terminology, but he fit the bill for what the scriptures call *dukkhapatipadakhippabhinya,* one whose path involves suffering but who comes to realize the Dharma quickly.

Ordaining in his early 30s, the monk once known as Robert Jackman had more life experience than most of us who took robes in the 1960s and '70s. A native of Seattle, he served four years in the U.S. Navy as a medic, earned a Master of Arts degree, and was a social worker and a Peace Corps volunteer, all prior to his ordination in 1966. Always something of a seeker and thinker, he told me he'd been a voracious reader. "I used to sit in coffee shops and libraries reading books, and I finally started to wonder, what's the point of life if all you can do is read about it?" He also had a religious bent from an early age, eagerly taking part in church activities, but as he grew up and perceived suffering in himself and all around him he began to think that "God must be a terrible boor and have a really bad sense of humor" to create such a world. When he came across Buddhism, he said, "I had faith in it because it told me I didn't have to believe in anything."

After a year of practicing method meditation, he heard about Ajahn Chah. He went to stay at Wat Pah Pong but chafed at the discipline, still wishing to be a hermit meditator, and after one year there he went to live on a remote hill in Sakon Nakhon province. He became seriously ill, had a major breakthrough in his practice, then "realized what a silly person I was." He made up his mind to go back and surrender to Ajahn Chah.

Ajahn Chah didn't make life easy for his first farang disciple. Luang Por loved to tell stories about Sumedho and occasionally jab in the needle. As often happened, things reported to Luang Por got magnified, embellished, and recounted over and over.

One episode involved eating *som tum,* the raw papaya salad that's made fiery spicy in the Northeast. Sumedho was caught by surprise the first time he ate it, with comical results. Comical at least to Ajahn Chah, who, as the story grew, portrayed him picking up handfuls of it, stuffing it in his mouth, and catching on fire. Luang Por would imitate Sumedho smearing som tum on his face, like a baby trying to eat.

***

Ajahn Sumedho believed he was generally respected by the monks because he practiced hard, but to the laypeople he became something of a circus attraction, "like a monkey," as he put it. All they knew of America in those days was from Elvis Presley movies, and they wondered why an American would want to come live in an austere forest monastery when he could be home "riding a big motorcycle and singing and dancing in the street."

I first heard of Ajahn Sumedho in late 1970. I'd been ordained for about two months and was still at Wat Boworn in Bangkok when the two monks, Santidhammo and Suvijjano, came from Wat Pah Pong and raved about Ajahn Chah and Sumedho. I continued to dither for a while, but after meeting Ajahn Chah and getting increasingly frustrated by the noisy environment of the city temple, I finally summoned the courage to take the overnight train to Ubon province to see what life was like at Ajahn Chah's monastery.

When I arrived at Wat Pah Pong, the monks were just getting back from pindapat. I met Suvijjano and one other farang, Dhammagutto. And then Sumedho came. Suvijjano introduced me to Sumedho, who welcomed me with an ear-to-ear grin—sort of unmonklike, I thought, having been around so many dour types in Bangkok.

I stayed for about three weeks. He was generous with his time, taking us to see Ajahn Chah on a few occasions and inviting us to his kuti for tea and conversation. There was something natural and unforced about his bhikkhuhood. He would admit that food could be delicious, that things could be attractive, but he had the wider view that such things are bound up with their opposites. He would say, "It's natural to like sweet things. You give your girlfriend chocolates—you don't give her *samor* (a small sour fruit taken as a laxative and a frequent post-noon "refreshment" for monks in northeast Thailand) pickled in Ajahn Chah's urine." He had great trust in Ajahn Chah and confidence in monastic life. Being at Wat Pah Pong and experiencing Sumedho's presence and common sense—and of course Ajahn Chah's too—was very uplifting. I decided that after getting my visa renewed in Bangkok I would return for a longer stay.

***

A couple of months later I was back at Wat Pah Pong, just as hot season was beginning. Sumedho was at Wat Tam Saeng Pet, and Luang Por was sending farang there to stay with him. So after a few days at Wat Pah Pong, Dhammagutto and I, who had returned together, were on our way to Tam Saeng Pet.

Sumedho was sick with malaria, which was a recurring illness for him. A novice led us to his cave on the hillside. He was sitting cross legged, wrapped in his robe. He greeted us, and we asked how he was doing. Grinning broadly, he said, "Not very well." That was impressive. He didn't look like he was suffering just because he happened to be very ill.

I had accustomed myself to the idea of life at Wat Pah Pong, even after a very short stay—clutching at straws, as the mind is wont to do—and felt some security in the routine there. Now I was in a huge, mostly empty monastery, consigned to a cave and left to practice on my own. The first night's jolly meeting in the sala, with a full kettle of some steaming sweet liquid to drink, allayed some of the unease, but as the days went by I sometimes wondered what I was doing there.

Ajahn Sumedho obviously loved solitude, but he wasn't the kind of recluse who got spooked by having to talk to people. We would often converse after the meal, sometimes outside the sala, sometimes on the forest paths leading back to our caves. Some evenings we gathered in the sala or one of the caves. Most of us would have something to say about practice, recounting difficulties, insights, and opinions, but Sumedho was the one we looked to for the last word. He was just "Sumedho" to us then—"Ajahn" was a title reserved for inscrutable senior Thai monks, it seemed, and it wasn't until a few years later that we started referring to him as Ajahn Sumedho.

On one occasion, he talked about peaks of inspiration and valleys of despair in practice. I think most of us Westerners were obsessively concerned with success and achievement. We expected our minds to be always clear, brilliant, and inspired, and felt something was wrong if we weren't always happy and making measurable progress in meditation. Instead, we were racing right past the real point of practice: seeing the impermanence of absolutely everything. And Sumedho may well have pointed this out at that moment, but my thoughts were elsewhere after hearing about the peaks. I was starting to gain enthusiasm for meditation practice, having had a couple of months of markedly improved experience, and I began to think that I had climbed out of the valley for good and was sure-footedly heading to the summit.

Sumedho also said something I didn't grasp for a long time. He said wisdom is like space. "We notice objects, but we never notice the space around objects," he said, without further elaboration.

***

Sumedho started guiding my meditation, having me pay attention to the way the senses worked, to get a feel for what my body was. He told me to do things like grasping parts of my body with my hands when I woke up, which had a peculiar grounding effect. "Hands are for grasping," he said. "We're born because of grasping."

During his first year as a monk, the only reading matter he had was Nyanamoli's *Word of the Buddha,* which he read about a hundred times. He became convinced that the place to break the chain of *paticca samuppada* (dependent origination) was at the link of grasping. Dependent origination is depicted in that Wheel of Life painting that I had seen in Dhammaramo's room when I was first studying in Bangkok. It outlines twelve links in the cycle of existence, beginning with ignorance and ending with ageing, sickness, and death, finishing with the statement, "Thus comes about this whole mass of suffering."

He introduced me to one of his great loves of the time, the *hua tou* or *koan* method of meditation as explained in Charles Luk's *Chan and Zen Teachings,* using doubt to open up the mind. Sumedho certainly wasn't promoting a lifetime of *anapanasati.* Anapanasati means mindfulness of breathing, being aware of inhalations and exhalations, sometimes focusing on the air entering and exiting at the tip of the nose, sometimes focusing on the rising and falling of the abdomen with the breath. It is a staple of Theravada Buddhist practice, and in some systems, it can be practiced into the higher stages of the path, but that wasn't Sumedho's outlook. He compared it to learning to play scales on the piano, saying, "You have to learn scales in if you want to play piano, but that's not all you practice." He recommended doing ten or fifteen minutes of anapanasati in a session and then switching to something more insight-oriented. "Just watching your breath can make the mind dull," he said.

Samadhi (one-pointed concentration) came easily for Sumedho, much more so than for the rest of us, and that might be why he didn't place great emphasis on meditations that focused on a single point. He frequently pointed out the pitfalls of suppressing all mental activity and abiding in blank or blissful states. "Ajahn Chah says it's like covering grass with a rock. You don't see the grass and it grows more slowly, but when you take the rock away the grass is still there." Rather, he said, the aim of the practice was to uproot the causes of suffering through developing insight. Samadhi is a foundation of insight, but concentration practice in itself can be a dead end.

The koan practice—specifically, raising the question "Who is the one thinking (and walking, eating, and doing any other activity)?"—was effective, perhaps too much so. I started to feel like I was descending into the depths of myself way too fast; everything was hitting the fan, and it seemed more than I could handle or even force myself to try handling. I think what was happening was that by questioning what went on in the mind, and by searching for a self or person experiencing and doing things and not finding it, the supports for habitual deluded suppositions about my existence were getting knocked away. The usual reference points, even though they only brought me confusion and suffering, were being revealed as meaningless: in the long run, a good thing, but in the short run terribly unsettling. Or to put it in the common parlance of that era, when actually getting a close-up look at the characteristics of impermanence, unsatisfactoriness, and lack of a self as pointed out in the teachings, I was freaking out. One night after an evening meeting I asked Sumedho if I could speak with him.

We went to the dyeing shed and sat in meditation together for a while. Then I told him I was having a really hard time and didn't see how I could continue—not that I saw any alternative, which was the most frightening part.

He'd already related to many of us how he struggled in his early days, how he reached his own depths and finally let go. Now he was telling me that sometimes there was nothing to do but grit your teeth and bear it, and that when it changed, which it always did, you were left with a deep understanding of impermanence that could see you through anything. Finally he said, "You wouldn't *believe* what it's like" when you do let go.

Because he had met with great difficulty in his practice and come through it, he was someone we could relate to and someone to look to as an inspiring model of what could be. And I think it gave him real empathy—he always said that compassion comes from first seeing suffering in yourself and then realizing that others suffer just the same. Still, it seemed, there was no safe haven anywhere.

***

Early on, before my self-exile to Bangkok, part of the forest routine that depressed me most and made me feel all alone, a vast and endless task before me without an iota of pleasure to look forward to, was sweeping the monastery grounds. In forest monasteries, there are lots of trees. In the tropics, trees are shedding leaves all year round. So there is a lot of sweeping to do.

Working in silence is the norm, since the sweepers are too far apart to be able to converse. Working in concert, sweeping on and on into the afternoon and moving from one area to the next, can feel like an orchestrated performance. And as clouds of dust rise and mix with perspiration, the repetitive movement, a full sweeping stroke with brooms that are often taller than the sweeper, can put you in a meditative state. As the ground is cleared of leaves and debris, it feels like the mind is being cleared. Ajahn Chah sometimes spoke of just this experience. But at that time I hadn't heard such uplifting talk and found sweeping to be a particularly oppressive form of drudgery.

Ajahn Sumedho and I were probably not the only ones who initially disliked sweeping. Sometimes it was just the physical effort involved, sometimes it was the feeling that "I should be meditating instead of doing this!" For me at first, there was also a sense of desolation, another dreary chore in a joyless existence, standing alone and scratching the dry ground.

Talking about the daily life as practice, Ajahn Sumedho urged putting energy and mindfulness into everything we did. "When you sweep the leaves," he would say, "make it a meditation practice," or, "do it with mindfulness, not thinking you should be in your kuti sitting in meditation," or other party-line statements. During my stay in Bangkok, I used to recall the misery of sweeping and immediately Sumedho would pop into my head, saying, "When you sweep the leaves…" But later, when I returned to Wat Pah Pong after getting scared enough to start putting effort into monastic life ("when you're cornered things become very clear" as Trungpa Rinpoche used to say), the sweeping became something I even looked forward to. It was meditative, it was graceful, it made me feel like I was part of a harmonious group. We worked together until it was done. The monastery grounds and forest paths looked so wonderful, clean and renewed—yet even as you admired your work, the leaves were falling again.

Ajahn Chah compared the sweeping to clearing debris out of the mind. He compared an uncluttered mind to a cleanly swept path, and he said, "So you come to realize, 'Sweeping is not bad after all. We sweep the leaves to make the monastery neat and clean, and we sweep the defilements out of the mind to make it neat and clean."

***

Over the years I saw Ajahn Sumedho every few months. His words were always to the point and memorable. Tall and upright, full of vigor and without hesitancy, he was a tower of strength. And he never seemed to put his own needs or desires first; many years later I realized that I had never seen him do anything selfish. Yet he wasn't trying to project any certain image, and he often spiced up his advice with stories of his own foibles and difficulties.

He freely poked fun at the way he tended to get ahead of himself. When he first ordained he thought, "I would be happy if I could become just a little bit better—if I could quit smoking, that would be something." He did quit smoking, and later on Ajahn Chah too decided to quit. He pleaded, "Sumedho, you've got to help me!"

But as his practice progressed he started thinking big. Once on a train to Bangkok he was thinking he had realized truths that could help create a utopia, and he saw himself as Spiritual Adviser to the United Nations. His heart was full of love for all beings. But as soon as he arrived in the bustling city he immediately became angry and irritated.

Another time, he was living in a cave and enjoying blissful meditation. He decided his profound insights should be preserved, so he started writing poetry. "After a while, it began to feel like the whining of mice, and I wondered if it would ever stop," he said of his writing.

He was especially tuned in to doubt. He saw farang after farang come and air out all sorts of doubts: about themselves, about the teachings, about the practice, the teacher, the way of life. He had a take-no-prisoners attitude and was always urging us to burn our bridges. At the same time, he recognized that doubts did occur and couldn't simply be suppressed, so he recommended looking directly at them as just another mental occurrence, and even to use doubt, such as in the *hua tou* method of asking, "Who is the one that is thinking?" But he could apply force when needed. Once during another difficult hot season I told him how one visiting farang monk had told me that the body is the vehicle for practice, and if the living situation made it too weak, then one couldn't practice properly.

He replied, "Varapanyo, I've listened to all these farang, and they're all full of shit."

***

Visiting Wat Pah Pong from the branch monastery where I was spending the vassa in 1974, one night I had tea with Ajahn Sumedho at his kuti. He said he was becoming more and more dispassionate. "I'm not enamored of living anymore. I don't dislike life, but I'm not clinging to it." Being with him on such occasions usually put me in a meditative way, enabling me to see myself more clearly and feel a sense of detachment from what I saw. It was obvious that he spoke from experience, and he transmitted something tangible. Maybe that's what is called blessing, or grace.

On one occasion the following year, at a similar evening tea-klatch, just as I thought we were ready to adjourn Ajahn Sumedho insisted I listen to him recite a sutta. It was on the topic of *ditthi* (views or opinions), and it took the framework of the Four Noble Truths: views, the arising of views, the cessation of views, and the path leading to the cessation of views. After his recitation, he remarked that there must be some reason for it being presented that way, i.e., that views and opinions themselves, when clung to, are the cause of suffering. This soon became a main theme of his teaching.

That night he also talked about the practice in general and meditation as the vital point. "And what is meditation?" asked rhetorically. "Sometimes it's sitting there with a sick mind and listening to all the shit that's been accumulated over a lifetime." He talked about forbearance and going against the grain. "When your bladder is aching, you can just sit and watch your reaction instead of immediately getting up to go urinate." After a pause he added, "Your mother would never understand that."

6

In the Language of Ajahn Chah

The texts are right, but they're not right.

—Ajahn Chah

Wat Pah Pong, 1970s

Among other things, Ajahn Chah was a pragmatist. He made the Buddhadharma relevant and practical. He used and explained the traditional concepts and vocabulary of the Dharma in a way people could relate to and apply to their experience.

One illustration of this is the way he talked about the twelve links of dependent origination. He compared it to falling from a tree: as you're going down, you're not likely to be taking much note of what's passing in front of your eyes, counting branches and leaves as you go. You just have the experience of falling and the pain of hitting the ground. Yes, it's true that ignorance conditions mental formations, mental formations condition consciousness, and so on, leading through many steps to feeling, desire, attachment, and suffering, but it happens so fast that it's like the experience of falling from the tree. So, he said, "The texts are right, but they're not right."

He would also often say that experiencing something like anger is much different from reading the word "anger" in a book. So his advice was to "fight outside the model." "When you're studying, study the model," he said. "But when it comes time for combat, you have to fight outside the model."

According to scripture, there are four levels of enlightenment, beginning with the stream enterer (*sotapanna*) and progressing to *arahant*, one who has removed all the mental defilements and attained complete peace. Ajahn Chah wasn't overly impressed by people who proclaimed their attainment of stream entry. He said "Sotapanna is fish sauce," indicating that it's just a concept to give some flavor to the practice. But he sometimes said that if your mind is free of the defilements for a little while, you are temporarily an arahant. He answered someone's query as to whether he himself had attained that exalted stage by comparing himself to a tree. "Birds come to rest in the tree; they eat its fruit, and they may say the fruit is sweet or sour or whatever. But the tree itself has no such ideas; 'sweet' and 'sour' are just the chattering of the birds."

The scriptures also say that a layperson who becomes an arahant will die unless he or she ordains within seven days. To Luang Por, this simply meant that one who attains that level will naturally die to the mundane concerns of lay life (so we lay practitioners needn't fear what might befall us if we travel the path to the end).

***

Luang Por tried to make the Lord Buddha accessible, talking about him in terms we could relate to and explaining some of the mysteries of the Tathagata (the term the Buddha used to refer to himself) in down-to-earth ways. One of the linchpins of his training was the commitment to five years as a bhikkhu, after also having spent considerable time wearing the white of an eight-precept anagarika and then as a novice. While we were slugging it out in the early years, he would often say things like, "It was the same for the Buddha. His first five years he suffered tremendously. In his sixth, he found peace." And Luang Por would use the term *sabai*, the fits-all Thai word for every sort of happiness, well-being, and ease, rather than the usual *sangop*, "tranquil." I always thought that however farfetched it might sound, it was nice to know we were considered to be playing in the same league as the Buddha. And for those of us battling in the trenches of monastic life, barely able to lift our gaze above the weeds, it was helpful to be able to think about what the Buddha attained simply as well-being.

Once he was talking about the Buddha occasionally going on retreat, far from the community of monks. I asked why, even after having attained complete and perfect enlightenment, the Buddha still needed to go into solitary retreat.

To Luang Por, there was no mystery. "Sometimes the monks would be quarreling and couldn't resolve their differences," Ajahn Chah explained, "so the Buddha would leave them and go into the forest alone. When people learned that the Buddha wasn't around, they'd stop offering food to the monks. When they got hungry enough they became remorseful and mended their ways."

The three jewels of Buddhism are the Buddha, the Dharma, and the Sangha. To Ajahn Chah, *Buddha* meant the One Who Knows. In Thailand, the word "Buddho" is a standard object of meditation. Once knowledge and awareness arise within, we have Buddho, so it's not necessary to keep repeating the word, he would say. Putting it in those terms meant that we all can have a share in the Buddha refuge—it is something accessible.

Dharma means everything we experience, because, Ajahn Chah said, "That which is not Dharma does not exist." Ajahn Chaluey, a Dharma friend of Luang Por's who lived by the ocean in Hua Hin province, used to say that he had realized morality and Dharma thanks to mosquitoes.

The *Sangha*, like the other two, can be interpreted on different levels, such as ordinary companions on the path or the enlightened practitioners who are a true refuge. But Luang Por reminded us that whenever four followers of the Buddha gather, there is a Sangha.

Sometimes practitioners are divided into *sekha*, those in training, and *asekha*, those for whom no more training is needed. The asekha level, Luang Por said, is a place where there is nothing more to relinquish and nothing more to develop. Asekha might be considered synonymous with arahant, though not always. Luang Por said that in order to teach others one should be asekha, but it's doubtful he thought that everyone who teaches should be an arahant. I think he meant that no longer being mired in one's own concerns is a precondition for teaching others. And, as with so many other things, he was giving a pointer, maybe a word of caution not to be in too big a hurry to save the world, and leaving it up to the listeners to honestly gauge their own practice and ability.

Ajahn Chah frequently spoke of "the world" in the scripturally literal sense: the Pali word *loko* means "darkness." At a group interview at IMS in Barre, Massachusetts, a questioner asked what we should do to help the world, and Luang Por pointed her back to that meaning, saying that eliminating the darkness in our own minds and letting light (*aloko*) be born is the way to truly improve what we perceive as the world.

***

Many Thai people hold Buddhist words to have great, high meaning perhaps so lofty as to be beyond their reach. The term for wisdom, *panya* (*prajna* in Sanskrit), is generally used in an exalted way, but Luang Por would often needle us for being foolish by saying, *"Mai mee panya,"* "(You) don't have wisdom." He talked about his early days at Wat Pah Pong, when village dogs came to chase and often kill the squirrels. It saddened him, so he built a wall around the monastery—and quite a wall it was, topped with barbed wire and pieces of broken glass. Coming back from pindapat and viewing the wall, I often wondered if it was there to keep things out or keep us in. But whatever the case, Luang Por ran into criticism.

"You're supposed to be a meditation monk. Why are you busy with construction? Why are you so concerned about squirrels? Why are you trying to alter nature?" So he decided he had to let go, in spite of his good motivation, but over the years he noticed that the squirrel population thrived.

He later commented, "The presence of dogs made them more cautious. They developed their own sort of panya."

He was always trying to bring people out of the realm of theory.

Even the concept that all conditioned things are impermanent—embodied in the first line of the traditional funeral chant and known to almost everyone in Thailand—was to many something remote and likely meaningless. In a hard-hitting funeral oration he gave in his home village of Bahn Gaw, he said, "We always hear this recited. Well, what is this impermanence all about? It's just what is sitting here right now—it's us." And he was quick to remind people that we are all facing the executioner, and it's just a matter of who gets called first and who later.

Those who had studied some scripture and came to spout meaningful quotations got short shrift. When a disturbing letter came from the States about possible inappropriate behavior on the part of a monk who was visiting his parents there, Luang Por seemed concerned. A layman present at the time took it upon himself to counsel Ajahn Chah. "As you know," he said, "the scriptures compare disciples to four kinds of lotus flowers…" Luang Por cut him off with, "They don't know from lotus flowers, these guys."

***

Having Westerners at Wat Pah Pong and having taken two trips to the West, Luang Por naturally heard people speaking about God and was often questioned about how that concept fit with Buddhist theory. He explained it sometimes in terms of the law of karma, sometimes as ultimate reality beyond words and concepts. Flora and fauna were among his favorite sources of analogies, and he compared ultimate reality to an apple: you can see it and talk about it, but until you taste it, you don't really know what it is. And once you taste it, anything you might say about it is secondary and doesn't convey the actuality.

***

Luang Por loved word play, I think both for its humor and for the way varied usages could get a point across. In the early 1970s we were frequently visited by Americans from the U.S. airbase in Ubon. When Sumedho took off for central Thailand and India, I was often the only farang monk who could speak Thai, so visitors were sent to me, or I would be called to Luang Por's kuti to meet them. One of our visitors was Jerry, who talked about the worries and difficulties of family life.

"*Krawp krua krawp laew,*" Luang Por told him. *Krawp krua,* which translates as something like "controlling the kitchen," is the word for "family" (Luang Por elsewhere has cited an older translation, "roasting circle"). *Krawp* can mean to cover, occupy, possess, and also deceive; Luang Por was telling Jerry that he was being *krawp*-ed by his family concerns. Though we've all heard plenty of people speak of the struggle and burden of having a family, I never heard anyone put it the way Luang Por did, and those tricks with language seemed to be second nature to him.

***

An account of life in Thailand wouldn't be complete without some mention of the confusion that comes about because of misunderstanding the language, usually the tones. The same sound with a different tone can have a completely different meaning—but sometimes the wrong meaning fits well enough to carry one along for a good while. When responding to a question about how we can see ignorance when it is ignorance that obscures our vision in the first place, Luang Por said, "*Khun kee mah tahm wah mah yoo teenai*"—"You're riding a horse and asking, 'Where's the horse?'" I thought he had said "*Koot kee mah tahm wah mah yoo teenai*"—"You're shoveling dog waste and asking, 'Where's the dog?'" The latter seemed to work fine, but then I had second thoughts and asked Luang Por for clarification.

One of the most powerful talks I ever heard him give was at the nuns' quarter, spoken in Lao, on the subject of the five "aggregates"—the psycho-physical constituents of bodily form, sensation, perception, conception, and consciousness that are ordinarily taken to be oneself and one's own—being like thieves and murderers. He said that practice should be like clearing the forest (*tahng pah*) without cutting down the trees: We should clear away attachment to the aggregates without trying to alter or destroy the aggregates themselves. But I thought he was talking about making a path (*tahng* also, different tone) through the forest, which I duly translated for the other farang at Wat Pah Pong and entered into the notebook I called "Chah Speaks." It seemed functional, and there it stayed for quite some time until one day I realized what Luang Por had actually said.

***

One of the plagues of practice in a monastery is useless talk (to be fair, there aren't many other distractions or mindless pastimes). Most teachers sternly remind their monks over and over again to stop talking. Luang Por often did that, but sometimes he'd say, "Let it die in your mind. When you want to say something, hold off for a moment, look at it, and let it die there." He also often urged us to "converse in the mind," meaning to reflect on and analyze our experience, saying that this is the "factor of enlightenment" (Pali *bojjhanga*) known as "investigating the Dharma (*dhammavicaya*)." Seven such factors are listed in Buddhist scripture: mindfulness, investigation, effort, rapture, tranquility, concentration, and equanimity. Ajahn Chah didn't often teach on the various lists and classifications found in Sutta and Abhidhamma, and when he did use the terms he was flexible with them: on one occasion he spoke of dhammavicaya as specifically meaning the kind of discursive analysis that takes place in a state of concentration, not merely as ordinary reflection.

There were always questions about the existence of past and future lives, from both Westerners and Thais. Luang Por was not the kind of teacher who built a case step by step, using logic and scriptural quotations. In answer to this one, he would usually ask, "Was there yesterday? Is there tomorrow?" But he also remarked that no one has ever experienced tomorrow, because once it comes it's no longer tomorrow, it's today.

He didn't discount the existence of other lives, but expressed that becoming and rebirth were primarily to be understood in our experience here and now. "Anger is born in the mind, and we enter a different state. Desire is born, and we become something else yet again." And he told us to die before we die, meaning to contemplate our own death again and again and also to die to our impulses and habits, and age before we age, to contemplate aging and see that we are aging right in the present moment and are in fact no different from the elderly and infirm.

7

Into Exile

If your mind is not right, even a needle is heavy.

—*Ajahn Liem*

Nong Hy Monastery, 1974

During the time of the Buddha, as now, India's monsoon season was June through September, making it difficult for wandering monks to live outdoors and travel the countryside. Farmers complained to the Buddha that monks were tramping through their planted fields. So the Buddha stipulated that they stay in monasteries on "rains retreat" or, in Pali, *vassa*. Today, regardless of the local climate, Theravada monks and nuns throughout the world follow the tradition of going into retreat during the months of July, August, and September. Vassa is a time of intensive meditation practice and study. Travel and other activities are curtailed.

A Theravada monk's or nun's life is measured not in years but in vassa, how many rains retreats, or simply "rains," he or she has sat through. In my case, it was more a matter of how many I survived. I was ordained toward the end of the 1970 vassa. Then, I had little idea of what I was getting into and for how long. It was only after I had signed on with Ajahn Chah that I committed to spending at least five vassa as a bhikkhu.

My first two vassa—one as a novice in Bangkok and the other in one of Ajahn Chah's new branch monasteries—were extremely difficult, but I felt as I was going through them that there was much to be learned, and that just seeing it through was already beneficial of itself. But by the third vassa (which was actually considered my second, as the seniority clock begins with bhikkhu ordination), enduring for enduring's sake was getting old; or maybe the challenges weren't severe enough to keep me from falling into a rut. There was not much inspiration this time, and I had no warm and fuzzy thoughts of Ajahn Chah to sustain me. For a couple of months before vassa he had been greeting me with a scowl or a look of indifference, and then abruptly sent me away to his branch forest monastery in Ampher Muang Samsip, under the abbotship of the respected scholar Ajahn Maha Amorn, thinking it would help get me out of some sloppy habits I'd started building.

After the vassa, I returned to Wat Pah Pong. Ajahn Chah didn't seem very happy to see me. I suspect he hadn't received a glowing report from my abbot of the previous months.

Ajahn Chah was keeping an icy distance; I thought I might get some warmth from Ajahn Sumedho, but when I spoke with him, he was unsympathetic. One evening several of us met with him in his kuti. I took the opportunity to tell him of my difficulties during the rains retreat.

He listened patiently to my whining, complaining, and vacillating. Then he let me have it.

"These are monasteries," he thundered. "You can't go into these places and demand everything be to your comfort. You create disharmony. You've got a reputation as a troublemaker."

He stayed on the offensive. "If you're committed to this way of life, you have to make up your mind to endure, and stop complaining and putting conditions on things. It would be better to die than to continue like that. It would be the manly thing to do."

His words stung, but there wasn't much in them I could argue with.

In monastic life, one knows that such scolding is not a personal attack, and hard feelings are (generally) not held. I had plenty of respect for Ajahn Sumedho, and also didn't see any viable alternative, so I tried to step up my feeble efforts.

I slunk around for a while, trying not to attract attention. My sister, traveling the world after graduating college the year before, had written to say that she would soon be coming to visit, which threw me into even more turmoil—in my confused, downtrodden state, how would I be able to receive her? She came for an extended visit, which took some of the heat off me. Ajahn Chah became cordial, even downright fun and friendly on occasion, but I got the sense he was just biding his time with me. After my sister left, in January of 1974, I was back in the crosshairs.

In a state of great turmoil I went to Ajahn Chah early one morning. I sat underneath his kuti waiting for the sun to rise and for him to come downstairs.

It had become painfully clear that I was not very welcome in Ajahn Chah's neighborhood. Prostrating myself physically and emotionally, I asked what I should do.

"You want to teach your sister, you want to teach your parents, but you don't want to teach yourself," he berated me. Then, after a pause, he said, "Go to stay with Ajahn Sinuan."

In monastic life, it doesn't take long to move without leaving a trace. I cleaned out my kuti—when you depart from a monastery you leave nothing behind and have no claim on a kuti or anything else if you return—packed my few belongings into my alms bowl, washed the blanket and hung it out to dry, and headed for the gate. Three dusty, lonely roads—a walk, a ride on a truck, and another walk—and a few hours later I was in Ajahn Sinuan's monastery, usually known as Bahn Nong Hy for the nearest village.

All I knew about Ajahn Sinuan was that he was the third seniormost disciple of Ajahn Chah, though younger than the other senior disciples were. His monastery was only fifteen or twenty miles away, but he was rarely seen at Wat Pah Pong. Expecting another gruff disciplinarian, I was pleasantly surprised by his easygoing manner.

I was given a small kuti of bamboo and grass, with rough planks of uneven size and shape making up the floor. It didn't have much to offer on cold, windy nights. The night I arrived I was provided with nothing but a straw mat for the floor. It got cold and I used my robes for a blanket, but they weren't nearly enough. Around midnight, I went to the open-air *sala* (main hall) to see what I could find and ended up bringing back more mats to cover myself with. In the following weeks, I often thought of my colleague Venerable Viradhammo snug in his cave at Tam Saeng Pet and consoled myself by calling my new abode The Bamboo Cave.

The monastery schedule wasn't too intense, though the life was truly spartan, and there was a feeling that one needn't be perfect and on guard all the time. The food was simple, often coarse and smelly, but adequate.

It was a large monastery with few monks, so sweeping the grounds took three afternoons every week. Sometimes we were given the evening off and didn't meet in the sala for chanting and meditation, although having more free time in which to torment myself was often more difficult than any of the rigors of monastic training.

The daily routine was rarely broken. Having no one to hang out with, my practice became regular. Ajahn Sinuan engaged me in conversation occasionally, asking about life in the West or my ideas on practice and ordained life. He had a refreshing straightforwardness that seemed to be imbued with an attitude of respect for my thoughts on things, something that other ajahns didn't always display. And he emanated a strength that was reassuring.

Morning chanting began a little later than in other monasteries. We didn't have to sit and listen to long talks and readings, and we got some nights off from group practice. Overall, there was a more easygoing attitude at Wat Nong Hy than elsewhere. Sometimes, though, even I felt the routine was a little slack. Although I had plenty of time to slug it out with dukkha on my own, Ajahn Sinuan was always available for a pep talk when I needed a lift in spirit. And I appreciated that he felt Western monks were serious about practice and that he respected us for our commitment.

Ajahn Sinuan didn't give long Dharma talks, but when he did speak he showed real depth. He gave good reminders about the daily routine and pointers on the specifics of meditation that I found helpful. One of the distinctive practices at Ajahn Chah's monasteries is prostrating. Whenever you sit down or stand up, you prostrate three times. When I first went to Wat Tam Saeng Pet, one afternoon a novice came to visit me in my cave. He sat down and prostrated out into the distance, leaving me wondering where the unseen Buddha statue was. Finally, I did hear Luang Por Chah talk about the importance of doing this a couple of years later. Ajahn Sinuan advised us to prostrate slowly while recollecting the virtues of the Three Jewels rather than just mechanically going up and down.

His sense of humor was undeniable, in that Isan manner which is able to take most everything in stride. One morning after the meal, he asked me if I was aware that a nun had died. "She died two days ago. I went to the nuns' quarters yesterday and conducted the funeral," he said. I knew nothing about it—we had no contact at all with the nuns and only saw them from a distance in the morning as they worked in the kitchen. Sinuan laughed and said, "It's like a frog dying—nobody knows."

He knew Ajahn Sumedho pretty well. They had been together at Wat Pah Pong when Sumedho first arrived, Sinuan not yet an abbot. One evening on *Wun Pra* (the observance day held on each of the four lunar phases), talking to the small group who regularly came for meditation and chanting, Sinuan spoke about farang monks. He told the laypeople that we were in search of something meaningful and not just ordained out of tradition like many Thai monks. "Tahn Sumedho came to Wat Pah Pong many years ago to study with Luang Por Chah, and he's still there," he said. "Through practicing Dharma, he's discovered a radiant, bright light. It's not the kind of light that others can see—it's within himself."

***

As weeks and months went by, I began to feel less insecure and started to think that I just might be able to complete the five vassa of bhikkhuhood that Ajahn Chah said was our baseline commitment. I would rouse my spirits with such optimistic thoughts as "Only thirty-two months and seven days until the end of my fifth vassa." As bleak as that may sound, and sometimes felt, for the first time I at least had a sense that a finish line was in sight. What might come after that, I couldn't begin to consider.

***

One night I dreamed I was in Brooklyn, wandering around familiar neighborhoods of prewar red brick apartment buildings, but feeling lost and afraid. Then I found myself on the street where my father's dental office was, and standing outside his door was Ajahn Sinuan, long broom in hand, sweeping leaves. He was a reassuring sight in the dream, and indeed, I was starting to feel like I'd been adopted and had a safe haven for a while.

The life was extremely simple at Ajahn Sinuan's monastery. Except for the very rare occasion when someone arrived in a pickup truck—the road that came to the monastery from the trunk road about two kilometers away looked more like a Himalayan yak trail than a road—we might have been living in the nineteenth or seventeenth century. We had no electricity, no running water, no gas. That wasn't unusual for a forest monastery in northeast Thailand in the early 1970s, but everything at Wat Nong Hy and the surrounding villages was a little cruder and more basic even than at Wat Pah Pong and the other branch monasteries I'd been to.

I'd once heard Ajahn Chah joke about the area and its people, an ethnic group known as Soey, which Sinuan belonged to. When Luang Por was in America, one day we got to talking about Wat Nong Hy and Ajahn Sinuan, and in a throaty, serious voice, Luang Por said, "Sinuan is really a hick!"

He described a recent visit there for the christening of a water tank they had just built. Sinuan was renowned for his unique approach to construction, believing as he did that plans, blueprints, and methods were not necessary: one only needed to use common sense. Sinuan seated Luang Por and entourage around the tank, his new pride and joy, and then told the novices to start filling it. He was clearly nervous, said Luang Por, and growing more so by the minute. Luang Por did an imitation of Sinuan sitting there, bobbling his leg up and down. Then as the tank started to fill, it sprung a leak.

One of the monks who originally went to Nong Hy with Sinuan to establish the monastery told me, "Ajahn Sinuan is a person with the very least wisdom," and he described some of the tragicomedies that resulted from Sinuan's stubbornness and bad decisions. But whenever I heard such stories about Ajahn Sinuan, I never felt that anyone had the slightest ill will toward him.

***

Ajahn Sinuan often spoke about how tough it was in the early days at Wat Pah Pong, but, as abbot of his own monastery, he didn't push people to practice in that way. Most of us can only try to imagine how we would have endured life at Wat Pah Pong in the 1950s, when he trained there. The food was extremely lean, and just getting a bowlful of rice often entailed wading through waist-high water to reach the nearest village. Malaria was rampant, with no treatment available. Basic supplies like candles and oil for lamps were almost nonexistent. And Ajahn Chah was a demanding taskmaster. Sinuan said, for example, that in the hot season he would shut them in the eating hall after the meal and lead them in sitting meditation for a few hours. That meant sitting with a day's food just swallowed and the temperature rising under the low tin roof to over 100 degrees. Sometime around midday, Ajahn Chah would dismiss them and have the doors opened, and they would stagger out into the sunlight.

Sinuan liked to boast about how diligent he was, though his manner was so nearly childlike that it wasn't obnoxious to listen to. He said he would do things to "let the others see" that he wasn't afraid of pain or discomfort, such as picking up a large centipede and letting it bite him—it is supposed to be incredibly painful, causing even seasoned meditators known for their strong samadhi to cry out in pain— or eating food that disagreed with him. But Luang Por Chah wasn't overly impressed by these shenanigans. He often told of how the roof of Sinuan's kuti blew off in a storm and Sinuan didn't fix it. Instead, he said, he was "practicing equanimity." Luang Por held this up as an example of taking the words of the Dharma in exactly the wrong way:

Sinuan's kuti was probably ruined and Luang Por didn't notice him gaining great wisdom from it.

***

I got more or less settled in, but felt like I was grinding out the yardage in a tough ground game, and each day was long and filled with challenge. I recalled scriptural analogies of domesticating and training wild animals and would sometimes say to myself, "Hold the rope, Sinuan!"

After a few weeks, which had seemed like many months, it was time to go to Wat Pah Pong for *Magha Puja,* the Buddhist holiday most widely celebrated in Thailand, commemorating the Buddha's first teaching to the *bhikkhusangha* (order of monks). We went the usual way, walking the two kilometers to the main road, getting on a pickup truck with a lay attendant from a nearby village, then getting off at Bahn Gaw and walking to Wat Pah Pong.

We got to the monastery in late afternoon and found Luang Por out front directing a work project. I had it in mind that we would be welcomed inside the monastery, shown to kutis, and go to bathe at the wells. Because he was a senior ajahn, I assumed Sinuan would be attended by resident novices while I drank tea with the farang monks.

But as soon as Luang Por saw Sinuan approach, he pointed to a huge pit that the workers had dug and said, "Sinuan! Fill it!" Ajahn Sinuan without hesitation took off his upper robe, grabbed a shovel, and went to work. After a minute, I realized that my Ajahn was working and I wouldn't be going anywhere, so I took off my robe and joined him. We shoveled and shoveled and shoveled. Dusk approached and the mosquitoes were out, chewing at our ankles as we worked. "A little more and you can probably bury me in this hole," I remarked to Sinuan.

We finally did get the job done, and I finally got a kuti, a bath, and an invitation to coffee with the few resident farang, after which we met at Luang Por's kuti. It turned out to be a momentous weekend that left me in higher spirits and in better esteem with Luang Por than I had been in a long time. I think my finally being able to go to a branch monastery and not make waves was a big plus in Luang Por's eyes— not because he wanted the troublemaker out of sight and out of mind, but because it indicated to him that I might be maturing a little—and he was his old charming and funny self again. There were inspiring conversations with Ajahn Sumedho, as of old. And as often happened, the brief break from the daily routine gave me a new perspective on what I had been doing recently and provided momentum for going back and carrying on the battle. Being able to discuss practice in my own language with the small group of farang who gathered for the occasion was refreshing too.

I had been dreading the onset of hot season, and as I settled back in at Ajahn Sinuan's monastery, I worried that one more oppressive summer could be my Waterloo. But the hot weather came later than usual and wasn't as bad as in previous years. Still, the living wasn't easy, and when the temperature started rising it was harder to get through the days, harder to find some energy to do walking and sitting meditation at night. Often I felt I was merely putting in time, logging my hours and hoping for a break somewhere down the road. Then one night after a few hours of sweeping the grounds, instead of a novice coming around to the kutis with the usual two little menthol candies, the bell rang, meaning we should gather at Sinuan's kuti. Full of curiosity, I put on my upper robe and walked over there.

There was a big kettle of hot coffee. I drank three large mugs and went back to my kuti and did high-flying meditation for several hours, without a trace of dullness or fatigue creeping in until after midnight. All my faith in Buddhism was restored. And as I finally lay down to get a few hours sleep, I said to myself, *"Café saranang gacchami."* (The formula for taking refuge in the Buddha, the Dharma, and the Sangha begins "Buddhang saranang gacchami…")

***

May rolled around and Visakha Puja, the holiday commemorating the Buddha's birth, death, and enlightenment, was near. I distinctly remembered Luang Por saying he wanted all the farang to gather for the occasion, so I asked permission of Ajahn Sinuan and made the trip to Wat Pah Pong the day before Visakha. But when I got there, Luang Por was at Tam Saeng Pet and no one knew anything about a meeting.

Having arrived, I felt like staying for a while—compared to Nong Hy, Wat Pah Pong was almost a four-star hotel—so I got into the daily routine and planned to go to the dreaded dentist in town to justify a stay at Wat Pah Pong. I also thought I should wait for Luang Por to come back in case he had anything in mind for us (he didn't). I needed two visits to the dentist, so I got to stay a couple of weeks.

Then I figured I might as well stay another week, because Ajahn Sinuan was coming to Wat Pah Pong for Luang Por's birthday and the Sangha meeting that was scheduled to accompany it.

There wasn't a birthday party, but we did the ceremony of asking forgiveness of the teacher for misdeeds of body, speech, and mind. After the brief ceremony, Luang Por asked if anyone had any issues or concerns to talk about. Only Sinuan dared to speak. He was embarrassed and saddened to see senior ajahns falling asleep during all-night teachings and meditation, he said, because it set a poor example for the laypeople as well as the junior monks. I'd often heard him carry on about that, usually naming certain ajahns who were in Luang Por's favor—I suspected he was jealous—and he boasted to me that no one ever saw him falling asleep, though that was probably because he never stayed up past midnight, claiming health problems.

Luang Por received Sinuan's righteously offered comment with a stone face. After a pause, he said he wanted to talk about prostrating (bowing). It gets worse all the time, he said. Prostrations are important and should be done properly, going all the way down and coming back up all the way for each one of the three repetitions. Then he added offhandedly, "Sinuan has stopped prostrating altogether," and did an imitation, bending his head slightly and fluttering his hands, as the highbred city ladies do, eliciting muted chuckles and sly smiles from the Sangha.

We stayed for Wun Pra, with the usual all-night meditation in the sala with the laypeople, and I got just an hour's rest before morning chanting. After the meal, we took our leave.

I assumed there would be a pickup truck, if not to take us back to our monastery then at least to the main road where we could get a bus or pickup to Nong Hy village. Several trucks were waiting outside the gate, as there were many monks and laypeople leaving the monastery after the Wun Pra and other celebrations, and if we waited there, we certainly would have been invited to take a seat. But Sinuan wanted to leave (and, I suspected, wanted to show how humble and/or tough he was), so we walked on by. I was on wobbly legs after the night's exertions, which had been followed by the usual pindapat walk of several kilometers, and peeved at Sinuan's stubbornness. Sinuan, however, was fresh as a daisy, having gotten plenty of rest, as was his custom.

After about an hour, a passing truck stopped and invited us to board. At that point, I was prepared to hate my Ajahn if he refused, but he accepted. We got off at Nong Hy village, with another two kilometers to walk to the monastery. Sinuan paused to talk with some villagers. In no mood to wait or listen, I walked on alone, a pretty blatant breach of etiquette.

I staggered into the monastery and to my kuti, where I put my bowl down and collapsed, tears streaming. "Is this what I have to do?" I asked myself. "Is there no end to this sort of thing?" Luang Por once said that if you haven't broken down and cried at least three times, with the tears flowing down to your shoulders, then you haven't really begun practicing. That was cold comfort, and I was pretty glum for the rest of the day.

As it was the day after Wun Pra, there would be no evening chanting. Unexpectedly the bell rang early in the evening, so I headed to Sinuan's kuti, expecting some annoying nonsense and wondering how I would react. I was the last to arrive. On the floor in front of Sinuan was a large kettle. The aroma of Thai coffee was unmistakable.

I did three prostrations and sat down. Sinuan didn't waste any time—which, for Thailand, already made the occasion special—but had the coffee poured. "This is for you," he said, addressing me. "When I saw Varapanyo staggering down the road, my heart was filled with sadness and pity. You looked like a seventy-year-old man."

I was moved by that, and also deeply relieved and delighted to see my mug filled up with steaming coffee. Sinuan went on: "In future, if anyone criticizes Varapanyo, I will stand up for you. I will tell them you are obviously not in good physical condition but still you make your best effort. I will say this in a Sangha meeting if necessary."

It was an act of overt kindness, a gesture that other ajahns wouldn't have made, but the sweet memory of and gratitude for it soon faded. In the following weeks I had run-ins with Ajahn Sinuan and one day even said I would leave. He didn't offer a sympathetic ear this time. He upbraided me for my behavior, recounting my misdeeds over the last several months and saying I was like a poisonous viper, repaying all his efforts with ingratitude.

Fine, I thought, I'm really getting out of here. I went back to my kuti and packed my gear. But when I looked at the empty kuti, sadness overtook me and I thought better of it. I went back to my Ajahn and asked if he would allow a crazy person to stay in his monastery, offering many apologies for the way I'd carried on. He had done a lot to help me through the rough patches, and a bond was formed that not only enabled me to stay but made me want to stay, and made it all the harder to leave.

***

In a perfect world, bhikkhus might be able to meditate one-pointedly day and night. But I think Ajahn Chah and many other masters recognized that most aspirants needed some support, part of which meant other skillful activities to round out the days. Chanting with Thai translation had recently been instituted, and Sinuan was big on it. I memorized the chants walking to the village for alms round and enjoyed accompanying Sinuan and a couple of full-voiced novices in reciting them—the rest of the group was slow to learn them, probably being functionally illiterate. Then one night, while chanting in the sala, I thought, I've learned all the translated chants—what to do next? The answer popped out: learn the *Patimokkha*.

The Patimokkha is a compilation of the 227 major rules of monkhood that must be recited fortnightly in a meeting of the entire bhikkhusangha. The recitation, done from memory with a prompter sitting by with the text, takes forty minutes to an hour, and not many bhikkhus learn it. Ajahn Sumedho was the only farang to have ac-

complished that to date, earning praise and admiration all around—
though Sinuan liked to do an imitation of him, holding his nose and
reciting the first part in a nasal voice. It generally represents a big step
forward in a bhikkhu's career, and several farang monks used to spec-
ulate who would be the next after Ajahn Sumedho to recite the Patimokkha. It hadn't meant much to me, since I was mostly focused on
just getting by, and would have been glad to let someone else earn the
laurels, but now it seemed like the thing to do. I requested a copy of
the small booklet with the Patimokkha in Thai script and took it on
pindapat every morning. After a couple of months, I was ready and
told Sinuan I'd like to recite it at the next Uposatha ceremony. It went
well and Sinuan made me the designated reciter.

Varapanyo with his father, Irving Breiter, during his
parents' August 1974 visit to Wat Pah Pong. The two are
standing in front of the platorm where Ajahn Chah would
meet visitors and oversee construction projects. Photo by
Barbara Breiter.

My parents came to Ubon that summer to see for themselves what
their son had gotten himself into. We had arranged to meet at Wat
Pah Pong, and as it was once again vassa, when travel is limited to

emergencies, family matters, and urgent need to consult the teacher, I requested a seven-day leave from Nong Hy to visit with them.

On my way from Nong Hy to Wat Pah Pong, the bus broke down. We sat on the road for a good long while until repairs could be made, so I arrived hours later than I had planned.

"What are you doing, walking in here at night?" Luang Por Chah demanded when I went to his kuti to pay my respects.

"The bus broke down."

He laughed. "The guy with bad karma." Then he posed a little riddle: "Tired?" he asked.

"*Por dee* (just right)," I responded. It's the catch-all Thai phrase for moderation and contentment in all things.

Apparently my response on this occasion was to Luang Por's liking, as he broke out tea and sugar.

An American bhikkhu came by. While we were sitting there, he asked me if I'd finished learning the Patimokkha—Sinuan had told him I was studying it when he was at Wat Pah Pong recently.

I told him I'd already recited it. Luang Por immediately picked up his ears and said, "Patimokkha? Who?"

"Varapanyo, sir."

"I don't believe it," he said.

I replied that I really had learned the Patimokkha and had already recited it four times at Nong Hy. He asked if I would like to recite it for my parents on the upcoming Uposatha day. I replied, "I want to recite it for *you*."

Luang Por put in the order, and I managed to step out of character and do a good job of it. I think I had, for once, taken Ajahn Chah by surprise. Just as I had recited the last words of the Patimokkha and the Sangha responded with the required "*Sadhu*" ("well done"), he announced, "*Hy hoojuk Varapanyo* (You guys should know Varapanyo)!" He told me several times afterwards that my father gave a thumbs-up at the end, though I hadn't noticed.

After my successful recitation, Luang Por showed me his gentler side during most of my stay at Wat Pah Pong, and I felt a bit more at ease around him. But taking anything for granted was never a wise thing to do with him. One morning I overslept—I'd been burning it at both ends for several days and it finally caught up with me. I woke up in a panic, grabbed my robes, slung the alms bowl around my neck, and high-tailed it to the eating hall, hoping that not all the monks had left for pindapat yet. As I was stepping lively, who should I meet walking in the opposite direction but Luang Por, who looked at me with utter disdain and said fiercely, in Lao (which usually indicated trouble coming), "Someone who sleeps late can't stay here with us—get out!"

I knew he didn't really want me to leave the monastery right at that moment, but it gave me a jolt. Ridden with guilt, I picked up my pace even more. After a few more steps I tripped over a tree root and went face down, landing on the cast-iron alms bowl. I bruised my ribs and could barely raise my arms for the next week, struggling even to put on my robes.

My parents came and went from Ubon to Wat Pah Pong in a taxi until finally my father decided to rent a vehicle. All that was available was a pickup truck, which worked out well. The bed of the truck was covered and equipped with benches, so he was able to take groups of us out for day trips.

Because I was on *sattaha,* the seven-day leave that in special instances is allowed during the rains retreat, I had to return to Nong Hy for at least one night's stay. My father drove me there and spent the night too. Both my parents had stayed overnight at Wat Pah Pong after my Patimokkha recital, my mother staying with the nuns. That was quite enough roughing it for her, so she didn't come along on this trip but stayed in the hotel. At Wat Pah Pong she was given the kuti of Ajahn Chah's recently deceased mother, probably the best accommodations in the nuns' quarters; I'm sure the nuns' kutis at Sinuan's monastery must have been extremely basic.

My father and I had a pleasant chat with Ajahn Sinuan, during which my father revealed that he did his own meditation of sorts in his office before beginning the day. Sinuan asked how much he'd spent for his plane ticket to Thailand. We rendered the amount into Thai baht, and Sinuan suggested he could cash in the return ticket, buy a buffalo and a rice field, and stay in the neighborhood.

At the end of the evening, he showed my father to his quarters for the night, a new kuti that was the pride of the monastery. It was better constructed than any of the others except for the abbot's kuti and was freshly painted in bright colors. Sinuan grandly told my father, "Not many people around here get to stay in such a place!"

"Not many people where I come from get to stay in such a place either," my father replied.

***

By the end of the rains retreat, my third vassa as a fully ordained monk, I felt ready to move on, having stayed at Nong Hy some ten months. Luang Por Chah seemed to understand that I was finally able to fit in as just another monk and he accepted me thus as he received me back as a resident of Wat Pah Pong. I think that's what he'd hoped for when he sent me to stay with Sinuan. Drops fill a water barrel slowly, almost imperceptibly. The Buddha used this analogy for the way virtue is accumulated and the mind trained. Contentment to stay in a kuti and practice meditation grew while I was at Nong Hai, restlessness abated, and I was able to fit in and get along in ways that always had seemed impossible for one reason or another. The road was often bumpy, but I don't think Luang Por expected or wanted the ride to always be smooth.

***

I saw Ajahn Sinuan only a few more times over the following three years that I remained in robes. In late 1981, I made my first trip back to Thailand, and when shopping for gifts I bought something for Sinuan. It was more than a mild surprise to hear, upon meeting Luang Por in Bangkok, that Sinuan had disrobed.

When I got to Ubon, Ajahn Pasanno told me more about Sinuan. He'd been in robes from age twenty to age forty and probably was at a loss what to do with himself. Luang Por got him a job as a school custodian. But his tools were stolen one day and he was fired. Then he decided to raise chickens and sell the eggs, so Luang Por found someone to give him a stake to get started. He went to market, bought some chicks, put them in a sack, tied up the sack and put it on the back of his bicycle, and rode home. When he arrived home he opened the sack to find all the chicks dead. Luang Por said, "That's it. He's on his own. Giving money to Sinuan is like throwing it down a well."

A few years later I was at Wat Tam Saeng Pet, and Ajahn Vitun, the abbot, told me he'd been at a monastery in Sisaket province and Sinuan came to visit. He had a sister who lived there and he'd gone to stay with her, helping with the rice crop. "Your Ajahn was harvesting rice," Ajahn Vitun said, making a motion like swinging a scythe. I think he may have married by that time. He probably made a good father, as he was kind and patient with monks and novices in his monastery and often doted on the novices as though they were his children.

The time with Ajahn Sinuan was chronologically right in the middle of my monastic career. I often look back on it as the point at which things turned around, for which I have always given Ajahn Sinuan much of the credit, and of course Ajahn Chah for recognizing that Sinuan would be an appropriate abbot for me at that point, when it was looking questionable whether I would be able to hack it as a bhikkhu in Ajahn Chah's realm.

Part of that turnaround was just growing up and seeing things more realistically. When I was first at Wat Pah Pong, the senior monks and abbots of the branch monasteries seemed like such imposing, even ethereal, figures, but as time went by I got to know and observe them as real human beings, forging their paths much as I was, having their quirks just as I had. Still, Thai culture and monastic discipline called for a high level of respect and deference. But Ajahn Sinuan was someone with ideas of his own, a sense of humor, and an irreverent streak, and he stood on ceremony less than most other abbots. With my own brashness, insensitivity, and New Yorker's sense of humor, I even said and thought things about Ajahn Chah that I am in retrospect not proud of, so with the looseness that Sinuan allowed in his monastery and his personality I developed an often-irreverent attitude to him. And hearing what others had to say about him reinforced that. Indeed, it was well-known that Ajahn Chah said, "If Sinuan is suffering, I am happy; if Sinuan is suffering, I raise my hands in *anjali*." I first heard that from Sinuan himself, plaintively asking why Luang Por had it in for him. Even knowing how tough Ajahn Chah could be, I thought that was extreme and had to wonder if he had really said that. But a couple of years later I heard a layman who was one of Luang Por's earliest disciples repeat that and explain it.

"Luang Por says that Sinuan wants to have it easy," he said. "He feels that since he is now an abbot he doesn't have to practice hard. He tries to make everything as comfortable as possible for himself. He doesn't benefit from that and it's not a good example to set; so Luang Por says, 'If Sinuan is suffering I am happy'."

Luang Por also remarked, "Sinuan used to see me with the big cushion to lean on (one of the few perks of senior monks and abbots) and he thought that being an abbot would be really comfortable. He wanted to be a general without having been a foot soldier. But when he finally got the cushion, he realized it's not so easy to be an abbot, to guide people and take care of the monastery." Sinuan may have been one of Luang Por's favorite whipping boys, but that implied fondness, not disdain—which I think is characteristic of the resilient and forgiving Isan temperament and sense of humor in general. I never sensed rancor toward Sinuan from anyone, and while I probably held on to negative feelings longer than most Thai monks would, my overall feeling toward Ajahn Sinuan remained positive, and I've always been grateful to him for steering me through rocky shoals. I can't imagine what would have become of me if Luang Por hadn't sent me to a monastery where I could get a passing grade that year.

8

In Praise of Older Monks

Anyone can do what's easy, but what's the point?

—*Por Noo*

Wat Pah Pong and various monasteries, 1972-1977

The end of the year, after vassa and the subsequent ceremonies at Wat Pah Pong and the branch monasteries, was usually a quiet and relatively relaxed time in Ajahn Chah's monasteries. The weather cools off, which Westerners appreciate but which sends Thai monks into semi-hibernation. The schedule of group practice was usually minimal, and Ajahn Chah was often away at the branches and not teaching much when he was in residence. We could practice at our own pace, and we had more opportunity to get to know our colleagues.

The old monks were generally cheerful sorts, and several of them befriended me, the usual venue for conversation being the walk to and from the villages for pindapat. In my early days I mostly hung out with the teenage novices, but now, as a bhikkhu, I gravitated to the older guys. Ajahn Chah used to say, "Varapanyo has the mind of a seven-year-old child and the body of a seventy-year-old man" and interestingly enough I found my social milieus near those extremes of age.

***

If the morning meeting at 3:30 for chanting and meditation wasn't mandated, not many monks or novices would show up, especially on cold mornings. But I quickly noticed that the old monks were regulars. I also noticed some of them taking part in the all-night sittings on the lunar observance days that came four times a month. It wasn't an easy practice even for a youngster, so I started to wonder how people in the final decades of life could do that. Belatedly, as was often the case, I started to look around me, and to contemplate what I saw.

In Thailand, many fine customs are associated with Buddhism, which has been an integral part of the culture and daily life for centuries. Sometimes they are referred to as *ariya prapenie,* "noble traditions." One of the most wonderful, and most meaningful, is that of elderly men and women, people at what we would call "retirement age," taking ordination and going to spend the rest of their days in monastic environs.

There are many who use that opportunity to take it easy and pass their time enjoying good food, conversation, and the leisure of an undemanding life (and even so, they are removed from much of the frenzy, immorality, and deluded activity of the modern world and subject to virtuous influences). But for those who go to a place like Wat Pah Pong and its branches, and especially for those who submit themselves to the guidance of teachers like Ajahn Chah, it is anything but an indulgent way of life.

Luang Por Chah used to say that when he was young he liked to stay around the elderly monks, observing them and questioning them about what it was like to be old and near death. I always enjoyed the company of the older gents, maybe for different reasons: their easygoing dispositions, good cheer, and dedication to practice. There was something about them that said, I'm not struggling anymore; they weren't taking seriously so many of the things that present themselves with almost life-and-death immediacy to younger people. Many of my finest memories of the years I spent in Thailand involve some very lovely old gentlemen.

They grew up in a time and place where life was simple, where there was basic understanding and acceptance of the Dharma and genuine respect for the *sasana,* the institution of Buddhism that in all its facets was so integral to Thai society. There was also a concept of old age vastly different from ours. Aging wasn't denied or shunned, and the later years were seen as an opportunity for spiritual practice and the growth of wisdom. (It should be added that Ajahn Chah chided people who would say, "When I'm older I'll start practicing Dharma seriously," noting that the continuation of life from one year, day, or moment to the next is uncertain and urging us to "age before we age" by recognizing that we are every moment older than we were previously, and that if we continue living, aging and physical decline are inevitable.)

Several of the older monks became favorites of Ajahn Chah. They were of the same generation, for one thing, but I think the deeper reason might be that Luang Por really appreciated people who appeared ready to stay in robes for the rest of their lives. They'd had full lives in the world and were unlikely to have the restlessness and hankering that afflicts younger monastics. And they had a kind of street-smart quality that made them different from those who ordained young, and which made some of them colorful characters.

One got the sense that they were really there—their minds didn't seem to be somewhere else, there wasn't an air of wistfulness about what they might be missing. But of course Ajahn Chah usually wouldn't make such a big deal out of it. After visiting one of my favorites, Luang Por Laht, on my first trip back as a layman, I reported back to Luang Por my impression that "Por Laht's surrendered," to which he replied, "He's too feeble to go anywhere, so we say he's surrendered."

***

The only old monk I can recall disrobing was Por Sook. He was a sweet old gent, about seventy years of age, physically slight and quite humble. He was from the town of Wahrin and not one of the ex-farmers, though I never asked what he had done in lay life. His kuti was out in the open on the way back to mine, and I started striking up conversations with him. Like most of the old monks, he kept a low profile and strictly followed the routine in the monastery. He was there a little more than a year. After my second bhikkhu vassa, when I returned to Wat Pah Pong, he showed up on the observance day in lay clothes. He came to see me at my kuti and told me that he had been ill and his doctor insisted that he disrobe. An ex-farmer might never have gone to a doctor in the first place, but I guess Por Sook was inclined to accept medical advice. He told me that he shed tears when he gave his robes and vows back and took leave of Ajahn Chah. It was quite poignant. He invited me to go to his house sometime, but that's not something that junior monks normally do, so I didn't give it much thought.

I went off to stay with Ajahn Sinuan soon after and didn't see him until the following vassa, when my parents were visiting me at Wat Pah Pong. My father was there with his rented pickup truck on the day after Wun Pra, the lunar observance day. When he was taking me back to Nong Hy, Por Sook hopped in the back for a ride down the road. He plaintively said, "You still haven't come to my house." I apologized and said that I would try to do it in future. But the next I heard of him was one evening after the Uposatha ceremony the following year, when Luang Por was shooting the breeze with the monks. One thing led to another, and they were talking about an old monk whose lower robe came undone and fell off while on alms round in Wahrin, the nearby town.

"Who was that?" Luang Por asked, laughing, trying to recall. "What was his name?"

"Por Sook," someone answered.

"What became of him?"

"He died."

A few more laughs, and Ajahn Chah moved on to some piece of sangha business.

***

Por Put was another of the monks who befriended me when I was new to Wat Pah Pong. He was probably in his 40s or at most early

50s, not what we would now call elderly but then old enough to be my dad. He had just a tinge of grey in his hair, a reserved manner and dignified presence. He seemed serious about practice in a quiet way that didn't call attention to himself. One hot season, when Luang Por ratcheted up the schedule to include long hours of sitting and walking meditation, I would notice Por Put sitting silently on a bamboo bed in the dyeing shed late at night, after the evening's five or six hours of practice were done. Each day of that schedule required every drop of effort I could muster, and when the final bell rang it was all I could do to walk back to my kuti to sleep. But it seemed that Por Put couldn't get enough of it and wanted to push himself further. (One of the tricks of the trade was to not return to your kuti when you didn't want to give yourself a chance to change your mind and go to sleep, but rather to find a place inhospitable to lying down. Some monks might have chosen the sala, and when I saw someone sitting after hours I often had the sense that it was for show, but Por Put was sitting in the dark in an out of the way spot.)

He also tried to tutor me in Lao, though his diction was hard to follow and some of his phrases perhaps a little dated. He was one of Luang Por's favorites, meaning he was fair game as the butt of jokes. Once Luang Por was talking about inviting senior monks to give Dharma talks when he was away, and he did an imitation of Por Put sitting on the Dharma throne, petrified and unable to speak.

"The laypeople will ask, 'What's the matter with the venerable one?' You can tell them, '*Pra Pak Tai* (a monk from the south), he can't speak the Isan dialect.'"

Por Put went off on his own not long after completing five vassa. I met him at Wat Kow Chalak in Chonburi, in central Thailand, a few times over the years, both when I was still in robes and when I went back as a layman. He seemed calm and content to be continuing his practice there. Though I would give him a brief account of where I'd been and what I'd been up to each time I saw him, he was never particularly curious about any of it.

Luang Por Chai, the abbot, himself aspired to the hermit model and was happy to indulge those who wanted to spend most of their time practicing alone in the forest. He came in for some criticism for wanting to avoid teaching and dealing with people, but I really came to appreciate him. He always extended a hospitable welcome and appeared very bright and serene. I spent some time at Kow Chalak before I disrobed, and one evening after a Sangha function Luang Por Chai spoke about how he never wanted to be an abbot but figured it was his *vipaka,* which means the result of past actions but in common Thai usage usually refers to negative karma. But years later he was in charge of a much bigger community, with a large and devoted lay following, and he seemed to be doing fine with it all.

***

The elderly monk most known to the Westerners was Por Laht. Por Laht was always cheerful, and most things seemed to provoke delight and mirth in him. But when he was around Ajahn Chah, who clearly liked him, he was extremely humble and chastened, and quiet like a mouse. When Luang Por started going on a short alms round to the nuns' village, Por Laht was usually the only one who accompanied him, apart from an attendant novice. When I started walking again after knee surgery in 1976, I tagged along on that route. As much as I'd ever seen, Luang Por spoke with Por Laht simply one person to another, as men of the same generation, culture, and world-view. I think it was a sign of the respect he had for Por Laht. But in the assembly, it was a different matter, where Por Laht became the foil or the butt of jokes (as so many of us did), and sometimes the object of Luang Por's wrath, which may have been merely another of his acts but nevertheless could be quite intimidating.

Por Laht had lived all his life in one corner of Ubon Province, and at Wat Pah Pong. When he was getting near 70, he decided he ought to see the ocean before he died. He asked permission of Luang Por to travel to central Thailand, and after receiving his fair share of abuse, permission was granted.

Sometime later, there was Por Laht sitting in the fortnightly Uposatha ceremony. After the recitation of the Patimokkha, Luang Por zeroed in on him. In his gruffest Lao he asked, "So, Por Laht, did you see the ocean?"

With head bowed and hands in anjali, Por Laht meekly replied that he had indeed seen it.

"Well? How about it?" Luang Por demanded.

Even more meekly, probably with head bowed a little lower, Por Laht said, "Water."

Luang Por grunted, and that was that.

***

Por Laht was also one of an exclusive group of elderly monks who could do the Patimokkha recitation. I'm sure Luang Por really appreciated that, which would make the hot seat even hotter when the old-timers got up to recite. Once Por Laht was cruising along, and his mind suddenly seemed to go blank. He stopped reciting the Patimokkha but sort of hummed for a while until it came back to him, provoking some smiles and chuckles. Or as one Western monk remarked, "He forgot the words but he remembered the tune."

***

There were several other fine old gentlemen I had the privilege to meet over the years, but let me not forget an honorable mention for Por Noo, who was generally not loved. Thin, consumptive, and crotchety, without much in the way of social skills, he nevertheless had a good measure of Dharmic integrity, which may just become part of the territory when one submits to an authentic teacher and the Vinaya.

He was the nominal abbot during my first bhikkhu vassa, which I spent at the new branch monastery in the Detudom township of Ubon province. I don't think anyone cared for him too much, and he provoked a fair bit of ill will in me with his abrasive manner, leading me to take the diminutive *Noo* ("mouse"), which might have been a nickname for one small in physical stature or part of a longer first name, and dub him "Father Rat." But he also displayed understanding of Dharma and reverence for the monastic life that I couldn't deny.

When I told him, just after the start of the rains retreat, that I was going to leave, he held the rope firmly and wouldn't let me go. I can still remember the look of burning intensity in his eyes as he clobbered me with the recitation and translation of *"Acirang vattayang kayo, pathawing atthisesathi chuddho...,"* part of the funeral chanting that runs something like "Impermanent is this body, soon to be discarded upon the ground like a log of wood, bereft of consciousness." It made me feel that maybe the old codger knew more than I did and that I should cool off a little. In addition, when at the urging of Ajahn Anek, who did most of the teaching and task-mastering, I started performing the duties of a disciple toward an *acarya* (teacher) for Por Noo, I found I could swallow the resentment and transform my outlook considerably. So I always had some goodwill for the curmudgeonly old man after that, even though it seemed that nobody liked him wherever he went.

The last time I saw him was in my final year as a bhikkhu, when I had gained an enormous amount of weight after being almost as emaciated as Por Noo himself for many years. He was at Wat Pah Pong for a Sangha gathering, and when he saw me, he took hold of my meaty forearm and without saying a word chortled mightily, something no one may have ever seen him do.

***

At Wat Pah Pong after the vassa with Ajahn Sinuan, I finally had some sense of continuing with the practice without always feeling I was floundering around. After New Year, Luang Por sent me to a small but pleasant monastery, Wat Pah Klor, in Nam Yeun township, near the Cambodian border. I spent two months there, the only other residents being two old monks, Por Boon and Por Sieng Noi.

Por Boon was the most intriguing and inspiring of all the senior citizens I met in those days. He was a monk of the Dhammayut sect from another province in the northeast, soft-spoken, tall and thin, with a natural dignity that was accompanied by lightness of manner and a cheery disposition. When he first came to Wat Pah Pong his kuti was near mine, and no matter how early I rose in the morning I would always see a light on in his place. When Luang Por sent me and Por Sieng Noi to Wat Pah Klor a few months later Por Boon was there, holding the fort by himself. As hot season began, the two oldsters went on the longer pindapat and let me have the shorter one. In the afternoon, they would sweep leaves for hours while I gasped for breath. At night, Por Sieng Noi and I often drank hot, sugary tea, but Por Boon would abstain. "If I drink it, it just makes me hot," he explained.

I told him that I too got hot and sweaty from it, but at least it gave me a little energy for the long evenings of practice in my kuti. That led him to remark on the differences between the old and the young.

"An old person has aches and pains. He's tired. He feels that way today, he felt that way yesterday, and he knows he'll feel that way tomorrow. The old man sees home, he knows the end is coming, so things don't matter much to him. But to a youngster they matter a lot." Suddenly I understood how people who were no longer in the physical prime of life could practice so hard.

Por Sieng Noi was quite a comic talent, very lively, and he treated me pretty much as his buddy. He only spoke Lao, never Thai. He told me that he was from Pak Tai (the south), which had me a little confused until I finally figured out that he meant the south of Laos.

That was right around the time that Cambodia, Laos, and Vietnam fell to the communists, and sometime before I disrobed, two years later, I heard that Por Sieng Noi had gone back to his home and was executed. It's a not unlikely scenario, though one always has to allow for the exaggerations that creep in when stories get passed around.

Por Boon generally seemed aloof and didn't have much to say, though my brashness prompted a rebuke from him once. He referred to me as *Khun Look,* a phrase I hadn't heard before but which sounded to me something like "Son." When the time came to return to Wat Pah Pong I requested forgiveness for misdeeds of body, speech, and mind from the two old gentlemen. Por Boon spoke in a fatherly way, with a kindness and gentleness that made it clear he certainly had no hard feelings and was most understanding of a person from another generation and culture.

And when I met up with him a couple of years later at that same Sangha function where I made Por Noo laugh, Por Boon simply smiled sweetly, eyes twinkling, and asked, somewhat conspiratorially, *"Gin lai bor?"* (Have you been eating a lot?)

9

Wat Pah Nanachat

Don't ever expect anything from anyone.

—*Ajahn Sumedho*

The International Forest Monastery, 1975

In the early 1970s, there were usually only a handful of Western-ers at Wat Pah Pong at any given time. But by 1975 the numbers of American, European, and Australian men coming to train in the Forest Tradition had grown. With Ajahn Sumedho in residence at Wat Pah Pong, most of the Westerners stayed there. During the hot season of that year several of them were invited to Bung Wai district, about two hours' walk from Wat Pah Pong, to fire their almsbowls, a procedure that had to be done periodically, in the days before stain-less steel bowls became ubiquitous, to keep the bowls from rusting. It required copious amounts of rice husks and the right type of wood, and so had to be done someplace specific.

There were many long-time disciples of Ajahn Chah in Bung Wai, and they were happy to have monks come. The bhikkhus and novices set up their mosquito-net umbrellas in a forest about one kilometer from Bung Wai village and followed the usual monastic protocols for the several days they had to spend there.

After the bowl firing was completed, the villagers invited Ajahn Sumedho and the monks to stay in the area. I can imagine how joyful they must have been to see forest monks walking pindapat every morning. Ajahn Chah was consulted, the green light was given, and so was born Wat Pah Nanachat, the International Forest Monastery. Following local custom, in which monasteries are known by the names of the nearest villages or of the districts they are in, it was usually referred to by the shorter Bung Wai. Ajahn Chah soon started sending all the Western new arrivals there, and many of the veterans too.

I was at another monastery at the time, with Ajahn Jun, Luang Por Chah's second oldest disciple, when I heard the news. Another senior disciple was visiting one day, and when I went to pay respects he asked, "Varapanyo, do you know Bung Wai village?" When I said I didn't, he told me it was near the railroad line, which ran south out of the town of Wahrin, and that Ajahn Sumedho and some other farang were establishing a monastery there. Projecting my bleak world view, I imagined Ajahn Sumedho and the others living in a treeless expanse near the tracks, roasting in the hot season sun and enduring unspeakable privations. Little did I know that, as one of the Bung Wai monks told me later, "Every time you sit down someone hands you a cup of coffee." The area was an established forest preserve, having once been a crematorium and burial ground. Fear of spirits kept hunters and loggers away. And it was two kilometers from the railroad tracks.

When laypeople came to Wat Pah Pong, Luang Por would ask them if they'd been to "Sumedho's monastery" yet. The food offerings there soon became sumptuous, and the living became easy, at least from Ajahn Chah's point of view. A new bhikkhu, Gary (his Pali name never caught on), got cornered one day when visiting Luang Por.

"Gary, do you have coffee and sugar at Wat Bung Wai?" Ajahn Chah asked innocently.

Gary respectfully replied that they did.

"Oh. Do you have it every day?"

"Yes, sir, every day."

Luang Por got hold of some of the Bung Wai villagers and told them to cool it.

Unless one has lived in a monastery, it's hard to appreciate the importance things like coffee and tea can take on, especially in the austere monasteries of northeast Thailand, where only one meal is taken daily, often consisting mainly of rice and vegetables, and a warm, sweet drink might be available once a week. When I was living at Ajahn Sinuan's monastery, one afternoon he took a few monks to a nearby village to chant blessings for a newlywed couple. The next month he went to do funeral chanting in the same village one evening.

The following morning he asked if I recalled that they had gone to bless a married couple the month before: the funeral was for the bride, who committed suicide. My very first thought upon hearing this, fully sincere and totally free of sarcasm, was, someone who is a lay person has the freedom to drink coffee whenever she wants—why would she kill herself? When I told the story to Ajahn Sumedho, he said, "Maybe her husband wouldn't let her drink coffee anymore!"

Several Bung Wai monks got typhoid fever. One afternoon Ajahn Sumedho came to visit Luang Por. He told him about Pasanno Bhikkhu, who had developed stomach ulcers, lost weight, and was extremely run down, and shortly after became ill with typhoid. "He endures very well," he told Luang Por. "He never complains."

Luang Por got the gleam in his eyes, having been handed an opportunity.

"Not like Varapanyo. He complains about this, he complains about that, he complains all the time…."

***

The kutis, sala, and *bote* (chapel) at Wat Bung Wai were extremely basic. There wasn't much there, but there was an energy and spirit of common purpose that I hadn't experienced in the other monasteries. As Ajahn Sumedho put it, "We're not here because our mothers sent us."

Ajahn Sumedho set up a rigorous practice schedule for the vassa while always reminding us that the point of the practice was self-awareness, seeing the three characteristics of *anicca, dukkha, anatta*—

impermanence, suffering, and not-self—rather than becoming meditation athletes or trying to attain something.

His presentation of the discipline (Vinaya) was likewise practical, here-and-now. He had no patience for nitpicking and hairsplitting over rules, but he had great reverence for Vinaya as a tool for mindfulness and harmonious living, and there certainly wasn't any sloppiness. He explained that the rules weren't absolute principles that incurred punishment if violated. "It's not like God is watching over your shoulder, and if you pee standing up He calls out, '*Abat dukkot!* (*dukkhata apatti*, minor infraction).'" As also happened later on when the sangha went to England, occasionally some grumbling reached Luang Por's ears, so he would come to check things out and talk with Ajahn Sumedho, and decide that everything was fine.

***

Ajahn Sumedho had resisted the role of teacher for years, but at that point, he was ready and willing to surrender to Ajahn Chah's directives. He felt the way to freedom lay in giving up everything to do with self-grasping, including wishes about how and where he preferred to live. His example in this regard was impeccable and provided an ever-present standard and inspiration for us.

I noticed how his way of speaking about Dharma had changed. For many years, when explaining the practice he would tell us, "Ajahn Chah says..." But now there was usually no such preface. He was still enormously devoted to Luang Por as his teacher, but he was also clearly his own man, or his own lion, ready to roar the fearless sound of the teachings.

One night during meditation, he spoke about burning bridges. "You have it in the back of your mind that if things don't work out you can ask Dad for help. Then you can go lead a good life, having a nice house, doing yoga by the fireplace..." He wasn't promising anything in exchange for giving everything up, but instead wanted us to face the irrational fears brought on by the idea of giving up. He often reminded us that there was no excitement in our way of life. "Nobody's ever going to make a movie about sewing a set of robes and dyeing them in *gaen kanun* (jackfruit wood, which is boiled to make the dye)," he said. Still, his example and that of Ajahn Chah told us that staying the course and letting go was a safe bet.

During the first year at Bung Wai we started to get the idea that sooner or later some of us would go to the West to establish a monastery. "When we go to the West" often got inserted into conversations. Then in May of 1976, Ajahn Sumedho and I, accompanied by the layman Pansak as our steward, traveled to the United States to visit his family and mine.

During the trip, I got to see more personal aspects of Ajahn. He hadn't seen his parents for twelve years, and I think he felt some trepidation, unsure what it would be like.

At Los Angeles airport we were met by the parents of one of our comrades, who hosted us for a couple of days and then drove us to San Diego to the home of Ajahn Sumedho's sister and her husband. We stayed in a tent in their yard, and the next morning they took us to see his parents.

I felt some tension building as we arrived. We stood outside for a few moments and then his father came out, shuffled towards us, and said, "Hi Bob," as if his son dropped by every week and this was just another visit.

I was introduced and we shook hands, though he took my name to be "Warner Panyo." When he later introduced me to one of the neighbors, without batting an eyelash at the sight of two men in saffron robes the elderly gent said, "Hi Warner" and shook my hand.

His parents seemed pretty robust for their age, especially his mother. They offered us a meal and then left us to eat in silence. As we were finishing, Ajahn Sumedho turned to me and said, "My mother looks so old and shriveled up, it makes me want to cry."

Some old friends called on me, and Ajahn Sumedho got nostalgic and started thinking about looking up people. Then one day as we sat in the tent, he tore up his list and said, "Robert Jackman is dead!" But he also told me later on that when he took leave of his parents he told his father, with whom he didn't have as much of spiritual rapport as with his mother, that he loved him and appreciated him for being such a fine dad.

My high school friend Andy had driven down from Santa Cruz with a Zen buddy, and I went back with them, driving up the coast, camping out in Big Sur and meditating on a cliff overlooking the ocean, and enjoying coffee with refills the next morning. I spent a few days at Andy's hillside cabin outside Santa Cruz, and Ajahn Sumedho flew up to San Francisco later on.

However, I tore the cartilage in my knee while I was there and the joint swelled up badly, so after picking up Ajahn Sumedho at the airport we went to see a Chinese acupuncturist in San Francisco. He had an import shop, which was basically a front, as he wasn't licensed to practice; when a patient showed up he put the Closed sign in the window, locked the door, and pulled down the shade.

He greeted Andy sternly, seemingly taking no notice of the two monks.

"How you living these days?" he demanded. "Your mind like chop suey—too many things."

Then he looked at us. Andy told him a little about us and about my problem. He started talking about the times of persecution under Mao Zedong, how while the Buddhist monasteries got wiped out, the Daoists were more clever and went into hiding or melted into the lay population. He seemed to be weighing us up, maybe showing disapproval, but finally asked Ajahn Sumedho to hold out his wrist so he could take his pulses. He remarked that Ajahn Sumedho was quite a healthy specimen, and put some needles in his foot. Ajahn also managed to speak a few words of Chinese to him, having studied it in his Master's program years before.

He examined and treated me next. When we were done Andy asked what the fee was, but he waved him off.

Bhikkhus are always on the job. Spending time in idyllic locations in California felt almost like being on vacation, but still there was work to do. We maintained our code of discipline, and Ajahn Sumedho gave teachings, formally and informally. It was interesting to see him doing that outside of the traditional monastic setting, often with people who knew next to nothing about our way of life and sometimes were not very interested in Buddhism.

Ajahn Sumedho usually took a few minutes to warm up, getting a feel for his audience, but then out came the same clear explanations that I had become accustomed to over the years, in terms the listeners could understand. When we went to Santa Cruz, Andy had arranged for him to speak at the Zen Center at their Tuesday night practice, when the resident teacher usually gave a lecture after meditation and *sutra* recitation.

He began speaking with a big grin, talking somewhat aimlessly about how he was happy to be there. But then he got rolling and the packed room lit up with interest. He described monastic life and Theravada meditation practice, pointing out similarities with the Heart Sutra, a pithy exposition on emptiness that the Zen group had just recited. This and other experiences during the trip made me quite certain that Ajahn Sumedho was ready to be a teacher in the West, whenever that time would come.

After two weeks in California, we flew to New York. The original reason for the trip was my grandparents' 60th wedding anniversary celebration, to which my grandmother had invited me. We spent a few days at my parents' house, meeting old friends of mine and Thai people who had been alerted about our visit, and attended the party. Then Ajahn Sumedho went on to Massachusetts to visit Jack Kornfield at the newly established Insight Meditation Society, while I remained in New York to get my stiff and swollen knee examined and figure out what to do about it.

When it was time to go, I changed my flight so that I could stay in New York to have knee surgery, while Ajahn Sumedho with Pansak returned to Thailand via London. They stayed at the English Sangha Trust house in Hampstead. The Trust was set up years before to establish a monastic presence in England. The officers had been agonizing over how to find bhikkhus to fulfill their mission, and then all of a sudden Ajahn Sumedho was there and fit the bill perfectly. I stopped in a month later. Everything I said about Ajahn Chah's way of monastic life made good sense to them; it seemed to be exactly what they were hoping for. George Sharpe, the chairman, came to Wat Pah Pong a few months later to invite Ajahn Chah.

Ajahn Sumedho went to England with Luang Por and three other monks in May of 1977. To everyone's surprise, Luang Por left them there. Lucky for me: I had decided to disrobe while he was away, and I dreaded more than anything having to face Ajahn Sumedho with the news.

No doubt Luang Por would have evaluated the situation seriously before taking that step. But knowing the way he operated, it's unlikely he had a plan for establishing a monastery. He would have wanted to see the level of interest there, if there was a broad enough base to support a mendicant community and if people were sincerely interested in learning and practicing meditation.

And then there was the question of how the monks themselves would adjust to living in England. The climate was different, customs were different, it wasn't a Buddhist society like Thailand, where ordained people are treated with such enormous respect and deference and have all their needs cared for. And instead of living in a forest, they would be cooped up together in a house in the big city. Over the following years I heard many times from Ajahn Sumedho and others who lived there and visited in those early years just how difficult it was for them.

Once it became clear they were there for the long haul, their goal became finding a forest to live in, but there were no guarantees that it would work out as they wished.

Financial support was limited, among other things. But they went about doing what bhikkhus do, and as time went by people discovered them. They gave teachings, led sittings and meditation retreats, and also maintained a pindapat-like ritual. It had been determined that taking the almsbowls and going out to receive food was against the law, so they settled on taking a walk together early every morning.

On one of those walks, a young man approached and politely asked them what they were about. An earnest and engaged discussion followed. Ajahn Sumedho told the man they were hoping to find a forest in which to establish a monastery. The fellow said that was interesting, because he had a forest property, with a big old house on it, that he was trying to get rid of. That was the beginning of what was to become Chithurst Forest Monastery.

Chithurst is a quiet and remote location, ideal for a monastic retreat, though it took some years of hard labor for the monks to make it livable. As interest grew around England and continental Europe, branch monasteries were established. Ajahn Sumedho determined that a place was needed in central England that was more accessible to laypeople, and a few years later Amaravati was established, and Ajahn Sumedho took up residence there.

Ajahn Sumedho and Varapanyo, May 1976, Harrison, NY, at author's grandparents' 60th wedding anniversary celebration. It was Ajahn Sumedho's first trip back to the United States in a dozen years and Varapanyo's in seven. Photograph by Barbara Breiter.

10

Masters of the Isan

I went *tudong* in the Isan. The food was so poor that my stomach caved in and I ended up in a hospital.

—*Ajahn Pyrote, Doi Puey, Chiengmai*

Northeastern Thailand, February 1976

It was that ominous time of year when hot season could begin at any moment. I was lolling around the kuti, trying to shake off early-afternoon lethargy, when someone came to tell me to pack up my alms bowl, which doubles as the bhikkhu's suitcase. I was to accompany Ajahn Sumedho on a trip around the northeast of Thailand, an area known as the Isan. In an interesting few days, among other things I was to learn firsthand the sometimes not-so-subtle distinction between the two major sects of Thai Theravada Buddhism.

In the early 19th century Prince Mongkut, who at the time was an ordained monk, felt that Thai Buddhism had become lax and the monks had fallen away from the strict observances prescribed by the Buddha. The prince began the reform movement known as the Dhammayutti-kanikaya, or Dhammayut. All monks not recognized as Dhammayut— that is, most of the monks in Thailand—were classified as Mahanikaya.

The relatively new Thai Forest Tradition with its austere practices and strict observances has its roots in the Dhammayut sect.

There are many monks who ordain because it is a traditional thing to do and who aren't particularly interested in Dharma practice. There are also those who have turned away from worldliness and want to seek liberation, but don't really know where to go for genuine teaching and practice. Mahanikaya being the far larger sect, especially in the village monasteries that most farmers would go to for ordination, it follows that most of those monks will end up in Mahanikaya, as did Ajahn Chah. Some who go on to practice under Dhammayut forest masters eventually re-ordain Dhammayut, sacrificing their accumulated years of seniority and starting the vassa count all over again. But as in so many other things, Ajahn Chah took a different path.

For one thing, he felt that there should be Mahanikaya forest monasteries offering the same strict discipline as the Dhammayut places, so that Mahanikaya monks would always feel welcome and wouldn't have to feel like second-class citizens or think about re-ordaining. Ajahn Chah himself trained with accomplished teachers in the Mahanikaya tradition. And he often said that keeping the two sects separate, with many Dhammayut monks looking down on those ordained in Mahanikaya, amounted to *sangabheda*, schism of the Sangha, which is one of the gravest offenses in Buddhism and in the monastic code.

***

Every year Ajahn Sumedho traveled to Nong Khai province to pay respects to his *upajjhaya* (preceptor, the elder who gives ordination). In years past he went on foot, but now that he was abbot of a monastery he couldn't be away from his duties for so long. A lay supporter from town had offered to take him by car this time.

We did the afternoon chores and then had a high-spirited send-off, as the junior monks made coffee. Then we went to bathe and came back to wait for the car.

The "car" was a pickup truck; Ajahn Sumedho sat in front with the driver, Dong, a young Chinese man from Ubon city, and Tahn Jagaro and I sat in back with Dong's friend. By the time we left the monastery, evening was upon us.

It often happened that a slight break in the routine could trigger a huge change in my state of mind. The daily round involved, for me, a lot of plodding along, and I unmindfully built up a weariness of spirit, getting locked into a mindset of "Oh man, another day, let's try to get through it." When the routine suddenly changed, it momentarily knocked away the supports for that apathetic, sluggish mind so something positive and bright could occasionally burst through. On this occasion, as we drove out of the monastery I was looking out the back of the truck, and it gave me a feeling of leaving a lot of old stuff behind. I had recently emerged from years of physical weakness and emaciation. It was somewhat amazing to me to get my strength and weight (a lot of weight) back, and I still suspected I would wake up skinny and weak one day. One monk remarked that I must have finished with the karma that had debilitated me, so those physical problems might no longer be an issue. At that moment, I had a tangible sense of leaving that karma behind me.

***

We spent the first night at a city monastery in Nakorn Panom. The abbot was hospitable, the temple majestic, clean, and orderly. In Thailand, wherever a bhikkhu may be, at dawn he puts on his robes, takes his alms bowl, and goes out for pindapat (much as people nowadays rush to their cars and go for a latte and a muffin on their way to work)—and so we did. The provincial capitals in those days were simple places, more like small towns, and traditions were pretty well intact. It was Wun Pra, the lunar observance day, and a small group of middle-aged and elderly women (a fixture in Thai monasteries) had come to take precepts and hear the Dharma. Though they sat poker-faced, they must have been intrigued to see farang monks, as a few of them opened their purses and gave money to our lay attendants for our needs—we monks were not allowed to handle money.

On pindapat we'd also received ten-baht notes in our bowls, something that would never happen in the villages near Ajahn Chah's monasteries. Stainless steel almsbowls had just come into use, and after the meal I joked to Ajahn Sumedho that my stainless bowl had been stained, i.e., someone had dropped money in it. He gave me one of his terrifying scowls and reminded me about the foolishness of fixation on rules.

After the meal the abbot took us for a view of the Mekong River. On the other side was Laos, newly under communist rule. He told us the Lao border guards shot at Thai boats if they got too close, which had slowed down river traffic considerably. Then we took leave of the abbot and went on our way.

We stopped at the famous *chedi,* a revered shrine believed to be the oldest stupa (reliquary) in Thailand. It was being restored, slowly. Dong said the former abbot of the temple affiliated with the chedi had a mistress and that she absconded with the restoration funds. I accepted his words at face value then, but now the wisdom born of time and experience makes me realize there could well have been an element of exaggeration, or sheer fabrication, in the story. (Or as I once put it, someone says, "Did you hear? He said 'white'." The one he tells it to repeats it to someone else: "He said 'yellow'." That person tells the next one, "He said 'red'," until eventually it becomes "black.")

We traveled on to Sakon Nakorn province. Along the way we stopped at a small forest monastery just off the road. A novice led us to a kuti with a large porch, and then called through a door that had a handwritten sign on it saying "Do Not Disturb—Meditating." An older monk came out. He radiated the simple dignity, calm, and warmth of a seasoned meditator. He seemed very happy to see us— he may well have never met farang in robes before. Ajahn Sumedho spoke with him for a little while, telling him some of his personal history, of Ajahn Chah's monastery, and of the farang who had gathered under Ajahn Chah's wing. I mostly remember the monk looking at us with eyes of love rather than saying anything momentous or astonishing. This fellow was a disciple of Ajahn Mun, although of lesser renown than the other followers of that great master we would meet in the days to come. But of all the monks and masters we encountered on this journey, Ajahn Sumedho spoke most highly of this unknown bhikkhu, whose name I doubt any of us remember.

Then we stopped at Poo Tork, the monastery of Ajahn Juen. We were in hill country now, and this monastery was built high up on one large hill, what passes for a mountain in Thailand. The laymen dropped us off, showed us the way up, and went to eat. As the trip progressed, they did that several times a day. Dong often said he could never ordain because he was unable to go without eating more than one meal a day. Now we saw that he wasn't joking.

It was a killer trek, straight up. We had to stop to catch our breath along the way. When we got near the top, there was a clearing with some small kutis and an open-air sala set into a huge cave. We were greeted and taken to meet Ajahn Juen.

The sala was made of a gorgeous hardwood. Ajahn Juen welcomed us cordially and asked about the climb. We told him it was a workout. He said, "If you're not used to it, you can't make it without stopping." He also told us that foreign engineers had been consulted on building the monastery, and their professional judgment was that it couldn't be done in that location.

He invited us to go bathe and get set up in some of the nearby kutis. We joined the evening practice. After the chanting, which is similar everywhere in Thailand, Ajahn Juen gave a Dharma talk. He began by speaking about the snare of the hunter. It was heady, penetrating stuff; sitting there in the dim light and the stillness of the evening, I prepared to be inspired by some very high Dharma. But when he went into talking about meditation on the body, it let the air out of me. Later on, I returned to the kuti feeling kind of flat. But the next morning, Tahn Jagaro and I went to the sala to find out where and when to go on pindapat, and Ajahn Juen was sitting there alone, chewing betel nut. In the dim light he seemed so still, deep in the recesses of his being. We got the info from him, and as we left Jagaro asked me, "Don't you feel he's like Luang Por?" There was that same sense one often got from Ajahn Chah that he was presenting a persona, doing an act, while an unfathomable presence shone through from beneath the mask.

The pindapat was truly arduous, down the hill, through the village, and up again. It embarrassed me to watch the novices zip past as we panted and stopped for breath. Once back in the sala, we were placed among the bhikkhus according to our seniority, with no sec-

tarian fuss, something Mahanikaya monks usually face in Dhammayut monasteries. Ajahn Juen told us that we could have joined them
for the Uposatha ceremony the previous night—expecting that we
wouldn't be allowed, the three of us had done an abbreviated version
in a kuti. (Recitation of the Patimokkha requires a quorum of at least
four bhikkhus.)

We left after the meal and headed off to see Ajahn Fun. We had to
pause along the way while Dong and his buddy had lunch. When we
arrived at our destination later in the afternoon, they dropped us off
and went for dinner. Having lived on one meal a day for the last five
years, it was odd to see how often they needed to eat. It also got a little
irritating, as they sometimes left us sitting in the truck out in the sun,
without even thinking to get us a cold drink.

***

There was a nice easy feeling about Ajahn Fun's monastery. It
seemed like it existed mostly to make his wonderful presence available to the faithful, and that invisible waves of his strength and grace
carried everyone and everything along. He received visitors in the
daytime and spoke every night without fail, after chanting service and
meditation.

Dong had told us, in the touching, wide-eyed fashion of non-
practicing lay devotees, that in Ajahn Mun's monastery Ajahn Fun
and Ajahn Tayt were the senior disciples. When Ajahn Mun gave a
talk, those two sat by him and examined the minds of the monks
and novices as they listened. If anyone wandered off, they would catch
them and call them back. As we sat and meditated in the simple raised
wooden sala, I was uneasy about the glowing, mountainous Ajahn
possibly reading my thoughts.

After the meditation, Ajahn Fun took notice of us and engaged
Ajahn Sumedho in conversation. He asked him if his meditation had
been peaceful. Ajahn Sumedho replied that it had, and then Ajahn
Fun asked Tahn Jagaro and me the same question. Peaceful some, not
peaceful some, we replied.

"*Nae!*" exclaimed Ajahn Fun. "Why only peaceful some?" And then
he launched into the evening *desana*, which worked its way around to

his trademark theme, the repetition of "Buddho." Buddho, the One Who Knows, is a standard meditation in Thailand, but no one was more renowned for teaching it than Ajahn Fun. Bhikkhu Don, his one Western disciple, told me that Ajahn Fun taught on Buddho every night, and as I sat there I could well imagine that he did just that, presenting Buddho in a different way each time. Yet there was nothing contrived about it; his words had the authentic ring of someone who speaks from experience and has unshakable confidence in what he is expounding.

Later that night, Jagaro said he was thinking about coming to stay with one of these ajahns. When I later mentioned it to Ajahn Sumedho, saying I thought it might be good to wipe the slate clean and start in a new place, he said, "Don't ever think like that, Varapanyo."

Ajahn Fun was one of the most charismatic and widely loved of Ajahn Mun's disciples, more accessible to the laity than most of the other Dhammayut masters. He passed away not too many months after we visited.

***

The next morning they seated us at the end of the bhikkhu line for the meal. After eating, we visited Tam Kam, Ajahn Fun's branch monastery nearby. Ajahn Sumedho had been there years earlier. It was a cave monastery and had been a remote and austere place. When we arrived, however, we found the cave sala overbuilt, even a little garish. "They've ruined it,"Ajahn Sumedho said glumly. It looked more like a tourist attraction than a place of solitude—an unfortunate but frequent outcome for the monasteries of famous teachers.

Back on the road, Dong and his friend stopped for lunch, leaving us to bake in the truck. Then they picked up another friend. That friend wanted to stop in some market town to buy five-gallon cans of honey. It was getting crowded in the back of the truck.

While we were waiting for the laymen to conclude their business in the marketplace, an emaciated old man came to talk to Ajahn Sumedho. He had been a soldier and gotten addicted to heroin. Now the local heroin supply was controlled by an army officer who kept pushing up the price, and this fellow could no longer afford his daily fix. He asked

Ajahn Sumedho if he could intervene for him.

It took Ajahn a while to sort that all out and to realize what was being requested. He expressed sympathy but said that he didn't think he could do anything. At Wat Pah Pong, monks sometimes asked if I had medicine for hernia and other ailments. In those days, being from a Western country made one a superman in people's eyes.

In Nong Khai city we paid our respects to Ajahn Sumedho's upajjhaya. He was a lovely man, and it was touching to see Ajahn Sumedho's ongoing devotion and gratitude toward the venerable preceptor. We had a relaxed conversation and went to sleep soon afterwards. We planned to arise hours before dawn so we could be at Wat Pah Bahn Taht, the monastery of Ajahn Mahaboowa, in time for pindapat.

***

We arrived as the sky was showing first light. A monk came to greet our truck and took us to the open-air sala to meet Ajahn Mahaboowa, another of Ajahn Mun's famous disciples. We had our traditional offering tray with incense and candles. But when we approached the Ajahn, he ignored us. He was doing stretches as he sat on his seat, almost like yoga postures. He kept turning this way and that, as if he didn't see us. This went on for a good while, until finally he stood up and told us it was time to go on pindapat.

We followed him in silence to the village. We expected he would probably speak to us on the way back—we were farang, after all, and had been well received everywhere else so far—but right after we hit the last stop in the village a novice took his bowl, and Ajahn Mahaboowa was off like a shot out of a cannon. Everyone scurried along after him.

Back in the monastery, monks and novices rushed to get the food ready for the meal, emptying the bowls, sorting things into basins, receiving pots from the kitchen. Without ceremony, we Mahanikaya pariahs were seated apart from everyone else. Bhikkhus distributed the food and served us last. That was fine with us, but one dish came around late, and a young fellow brought it over and placed it on the floor near Ajahn Sumedho.

He and I looked at each other uncertainly. The fellow didn't look old enough to be bhikkhu, that is, a fully ordained monk. We wondered aloud if he weren't indeed a novice. Not wanting to chance it, we left the dish sitting untouched. Ajahn Mahaboowa was on record as saying that Mahanikaya monks aren't really bhikkhus, and it seemed we were being treated thus in that a novice was putting food *by* us but not offering it directly into the hand, as stipulated in the Vinaya, the code of monastic conduct.

Ajahn Sumedho was beginning to fume. We ate quickly, as did everyone, washed our bowls, and joined the others in the time-honored ritual of drying the alms bowl. As we sat outside on straw mats, Ajahn Mahaboowa came over. He was highly animated, chewing betel nut and stepping aside to spit it out again and again. He told us how necessary it was to be well prepared and firm in the practice if we were to go abroad. Ajahn Sumedho and I were planning to travel to the United States in a few months, though we hadn't mentioned this to him, not having gotten an opportunity to speak since we arrived.

After dwelling on that theme for a while, he gave us photographs of Ajahn Mun, reminding us to treat them with respect. He told of a man who put a picture of Ajahn Mun under his car seat and was killed in a crash. We listened respectfully, and then Ajahn Mahaboowa abruptly walked away.

I was merely wondering what was going on, but Ajahn Sumedho was livid. He told us to pack up the bowls and get ready to leave. Dong asked if we should present the customary offering tray to Ajahn Mahaboowa, but Ajahn Sumedho snapped, "Not necessary!"

Years later I was discussing famous teachers with some Thai men who'd come to see Luang Por Chah in Bangkok, and Ajahn Mahaboowa's name came up. I told them of our encounter with him. They laughed and said, "He was testing your minds."

Ajahn Mahaboowa always insisted on maintaining the separation of the two monastic sects, but in later years he visited Ajahn Chah when Luang Por was ill and also attended his funeral. He visited Wat Nanachat in the years after Ajahn Chah's passing, and he seemed to be caring for the farang sangha there. Today, the relationship between Wat Nanachat and Wat Pah Bahn Taht is amicable and sound.

I carried back to Wat Nanachat some strong impressions of the ajahns we had met, especially Ajahn Fun. A few days after our return a group of us went to see Luang Por Chah at Wat Pah Pong. He was extremely sharp and lively, and I suddenly found myself thinking those other guys had nothing on him. I asked someone afterwards if Luang Por seemed especially bright on this occasion, but he didn't think so—rather, he looked surprised at the question; it was just business as usual at Ajahn Chah's kuti.

***

Leaving and returning to Ubon province, we had traveled by the road that runs north from Ubon city to Amnatjaroen and then Nakon Panom. That road was a treasure trove of monasteries and teachers, some of them in Ajahn Chah's lineage, some unknown to most of us. Every so often I had the opportunity to stop in at one of those places— a small forest monastery here, an elderly disciple of Ajahn Mun there, and many dynamic teachers and meditators too. These visits led me to reflect on the pervasiveness of the living practice tradition in Thailand and made me wonder how much there was that remained unseen, how many accomplished monks and nuns there might really be throughout the Kingdom. In Ajahn Chah's circle, there was very little talk of levels of attainment, and looking at others with a judging mind was discouraged. "You don't gain wisdom by watching others," Ajahn Sumedho often said. But sometimes a little uplift was helpful for those of us deeper in the muck than Ajahn Sumedho was.

When we got back to Wat Nanachat from our trip around the northeast, I convinced some of the Bung Wai laypeople to organize outings to visit a few of the senior disciples of Ajahn Chah, specifically teachers that farang monks had stayed with. They hired a large truck and we went on two different occasions to offer food to Ajahn Sinuan and Ajahn Jun, the latter having hosted several of us over the years.

The ajahns received us warmly and gave Dharma pep talks to the laypeople. The sense of family and of mutual caring and respect that I felt on these occasions was always moving. But the most memorable meeting took place on our way back to Bung Wai from Ajahn Jun's monastery.

One of the laypeople suggested we stop at a monastery at Kilometer 29 on the north-south road to meet one Ajahn Pyrote. I had spent my second bhikkhu vassa a mile or so down Kilometer 30, literally around the corner from kilometer 29, but never heard of the place or the teacher.

Ajahn Pyrote was an outgoing fellow, maybe about 40 years old, obviously comfortable speaking to groups of people on the spur of the moment. Pleasantries were exchanged, and then there was a brief interval of silence. Por Yoo, the Bung Wai village headman, turned to the laywomen and said, "Do you women have anything to ask the Ajahn?"

"What's the matter, you men don't have mouths?" one of the women responded.

There was some laughter—I suspect as much at Por Yoo being shown up as at the humor of the response—and then Ajahn Pyrote began an informal, rambling discourse, much in the way that Luang Por would.

He urged the layfolk to practice correct speech. "The mouth is a weapon," he said. "Even though it's only sound, our speech can bring people happiness or pain. It can make us loved or hated." He covered a few other things, and spoke about perception: "Think about a flower. For a child it's an object of play. An adolescent will want to offer it to his sweetheart. For a grown-up, it's something to sell. And an elderly person thinks of offering it in puja. One flower, different meanings."

Thirty years later, those simple words still stay with me. It's a beautiful example of the Forest Lineage way of teaching Dharma, using the objects and vocabulary of everyday life to transmit the timeless truths that the Buddha taught. Luang Por Chah once told me not to think in terms of profound or shallow, and indeed it would be hard to pigeonhole such a teaching as Ajahn Pyrote gave as simple or profound, deep or common. There's not much to the words, but they get right to the heart of all our experience.

11

Varapanyo's Last Stand

*When you feel like you're beating your head against the
wall, you've just got to keep at it until one of them breaks.*
—*Varapanyo Bhikkhu*

Bangkok and environs, March 1977

The linchpin of Ajahn Chah's teaching was *mai tieng, mai nae:*
not permanent, not certain. For many years, the thought of disrobing was something I couldn't relate to at all, like leaving the
hospital in mid-surgery. But time flies and everything changes.

And it's not that I was enamored of the austere bhikkhu life. After
five years in robes, my "attainment" was finally feeling that I could
hack the lifestyle reasonably well. Some people take to monastic life
like fish to water, barely cracking a sweat from ascetic living and staying in robes for decades. I certainly wasn't one of them. Still, being in
robes seemed the only thing to do, and it made a lot of sense. It was
hard to conceive of how I would live on the outside.

One result of the training, something that has stayed pretty much
intact with me over the years, was being able to distinguish between

wants and needs. Buddhist monastic existence is based, physically, on what is called the four requisites: robes to cover and protect the body, almsfood to sustain life, a dwelling to protect against the elements, and medicines to alleviate illness. I explained this to my parents when they came to visit. My mother agreed with the concept, but added that "Some of us just do that in a more elaborate way."

As a bhikkhu, when I saw laypeople I mostly felt bewilderment. In their way of life, they carried so much that seemed unnecessary and complicating. There was an aura of heaviness about them. I had my own heaviness as well, and a lot of it was silly drama, but I think I was at least aiming in the right direction and not making things more difficult for myself through external involvements.

But everything is subject to change. In 1976, I traveled to the United States with Ajahn Sumedho. In California I saw that there were Buddhist groups studying under authentic teachers and practicing meditation. I stayed a few days with a friend who had a beautiful little cabin on a wooded hillside, and I imagined that lots of people were living that way (not exactly true).

Then came knee surgery and months of limited participation in the daily monastic round. I'd also been laid up with malaria and hepatitis for part of the previous two years, and in the following hot season, just as I was preparing to take a step into bhikkhu adulthood after completing five vassa by going on *tudong* (an extended ascetic walking tour), I fell ill while in Bangkok.

It turned out not to be anything long lasting or serious, but it dislodged a lot of thinking. I began to wonder if there was more to spiritual practice than enduring physical difficulty. I chewed over Doug Burns' phrase, "the point of diminishing returns." For the first time in my Buddhist career, I thought seriously about disrobing.

Ajahn Chah's training had changed me, I knew that. I felt in the tissue of my being that I could survive and take care of myself wherever and however I lived. Being in the United States and England had showed me that the forests of Thailand were not the only places in the world where Dharma was studied and practiced.

But the reassurance I got from considering those things paled in comparison to the turmoil I had thrown myself into by considering disrobing, and by the general insecurity of facing an unknown future. I realized it wasn't something to decide in the heat of the moment. And a close relationship with a teacher such as Ajahn Chah was not to be casually discarded. So I set my mind on going tudong and seeing where the chips would fall. I also kept it to myself. I realized no one else could tell me what to do, and there wasn't any point in stirring up talk and opinions, but it made me feel somewhat devious when interacting with others, who saw me as a bhikkhu and probably expected that tomorrow I would still be a bhikkhu.

Though I didn't succumb to impulsive decision-making in the heat of the moment, I had to endure the heat of the tropics. It was early April when I finally left Bangkok and headed south on tudong, and hot season was in full swing. "April is the cruelest month," I would recall every summer in Thailand, and I often wondered if that's what T.S. Eliot had in mind when he wrote those words. I started off by train to Prajuapkirikan province, a few hours south of Bangkok. A monk at Wat Pah Pong had told me about a small forest monastery near a waterfall, with an abbot who was a good practitioner. Falling water sounded good in hot season.

When I got off the train in mid-afternoon at the small station of Huey Yang, there were a few motorcycle drivers for hire, and little else. I asked where the monastery was. They pointed me to a dirt road opposite the station, on the other side of the main north-south highway. I asked how far it was.

"Oh, really far! Too far to walk! Maybe ten kilometers. Do you want a ride?"

"The monk doesn't carry money," I said, and shouldering my alms bowl in its cloth bag got ready to hike. But one of the drivers thought for a few seconds and invited me to get on the back of his motorbike.

The gents were drinking milk coffee and asked if I'd like a cup. "Monks don't take milk in the afternoon," I said.

"Correct!" said my driver, and got me a Pepsi instead. I gratefully drank it and off we went.

The monastery was indeed small, forested, and near a national park with a waterfall and large pond. The abbot, Ajahn Supan, was a serene and pleasant man who emitted the unmistakable quiet strength of a real practitioner. He invited me to stay with no strings attached. He remembered the monk who had told me about the place, and of course knew of Ajahn Chah.

I stayed a few weeks. The heat wasn't too terrible, and some afternoons I went to the park to bathe and even swim in the pond if there were no tourists about. I enjoyed the company of Ajahn Supan. The small group of laypeople who came regularly were curious about me in a respectful way. Ajahn invited me to speak to them at a funeral ceremony once, and another time in the evening of a lunar observance day.

They asked me about myself, about Ajahn Chah, and other topics. I spoke about the practice in Ajahn Chah's monasteries, remarking that laypeople and monks practiced through the night on observance day. They said they thought it would be too much for them—some were too old, the others had to work the following day. I suggested they could try doing a little more than they were accustomed to, maybe staying up until midnight. "The laypeople in the Isan have to work too, and a lot of them are old," I added. I was gratified to see them try it on the next observance day.

I also had good conversations with Ajahn Supan, which further convinced me of his genuineness. Maybe not a master, but certainly a good, solid person. And he did drop some hints when talking about meditation and Dharma in general that made me think there might be more than met the eye.

But I had the bug in my ear and felt I should be making a decision about my future. The prospect of disrobing started to tantalize, even as it made me uneasy. I didn't feel my practice was very dynamic, and I wasn't content to just keep on keeping on, which was Ajahn Sumedho's usual suggestion. So one day I packed up and announced to Ajahn Supan that I was heading further south, for the monastery of the renowned Ajahn Buddhadasa in Surat province.

I did the formal leave-taking, a brief but lovely ceremony that has always struck me as another wonderful example of the richness and integrity of monastic life. The Ajahn's forgiveness is requested for any offensive conduct of body, speech, or mind. Then he grants forgiveness, according to formula, and asks the same of the disciple.

I set out in late afternoon. Ajahn Supan had someone take me by motorcycle to the north-south trunk road, and I started hiking from there. The sun was sinking behind the trees, and it was a pleasant walk. After a couple of hours, I stopped in a field by the road, thinking to set up my mosquito net there. The net fits on a big umbrella, the *klot*, which is hung on a rope tied to two trees.

As I was sitting there drinking water, a man on a motor scooter stopped to talk. He asked where I was from and where I was going. I told him I was going tudong to Suan Mokh monastery in Surat and was planning to stop for the night in that spot.

He recommended I not stay there and said there was a monastery nearby that he could take me to. Southern Thailand in those days was known as being somewhat wild and dangerous, so I took him up on the offer.

It was a village monastery, not the kind of place I was accustomed to. Almost everyone stayed in one simple wooden building, and they were hanging out with the elderly abbot when we arrived. He was friendly, but he looked like Mr. Magoo and seemed absentminded. I even wondered briefly if he might be drunk. But he didn't occupy me for very long, letting me get set up in a cubicle near the meeting area.

I took the meal with them in the morning and hit the road. The sun was fierce, and after fifteen minutes, I was soaked with sweat.

Anyone who does something like this must be crazy, was all I could think. Years later, as a layman, I mentioned that to Ajahn Vitun at Tam Saeng Pet.

"It's true," he said. "Luang Por Chah was especially crazy." In other words, I might have been treading the path that Luang Por followed to enlightenment, but I gave up at the first hint of discomfort.

The day before I had refused the offer of a bus ticket, but now that sounded pretty good. After drinking some water, I trudged on and finally did get another offer of transport, which I gratefully accepted.

Well, Luang Por always said that the real asceticism of tudong was in the way one practiced, not merely in wandering around, and that it could be done very well in a forest monastery. So I thought that I would really get to work once I reached Suan Mokh.

The bus left me off at a train station after dark. I asked someone if following the tracks would take me in the direction of Surat. He asked what I was planning to do.

It just felt strange being in the South, I wanted to get to the forest monastery, and the relative cool of the evening felt like the logical time to walk. But the man was alarmed and pleaded with me not to walk. I had heard of the South's reputation for lawlessness, including stories of buses being attacked by armed bandits and foreign passengers being beaten up and robbed, but I thought that a bhikkhu was safe anywhere in Thailand at any time.

But after some back and forth with the gentleman, I began to think it might really not be the smart thing to do. I told him I didn't know where to stay, so he took me to a local monastery.

This place was much bigger than Abbot Magoo's. The main building was teeming with life, including radios playing loudly. The novices had a wild look to them. I couldn't imagine what might be going on there. Someone who wasn't aware that yellow robes were the sign of ordination in the dispensation of the Buddha would likely have gotten no idea that the place had anything to do with Dharma.

We found someone in charge and he gave permission for me to spend the night. But it was so ridiculously noisy that I took my gear outside and found a platform to sleep on. The man who brought me there came back in the morning, took me to a bus station, and bought me a ticket to Surat. At the time I didn't think much of it, but in retrospect I can appreciate how remarkable such generosity was. The guy certainly wasn't wealthy, he didn't know me and didn't owe me anything, he hadn't planned on any of this, but when he saw a robed stranger in a difficult situation he stepped in without deliberating.

***

In Surat, there were pickup trucks taking passengers to Suan Mokh and points along the way, and one driver offered me a ride. It was certainly a relief to enter the monastery and be in the forest once again. A monk took me to see Ajahn Buddhadasa.

After a few pleasantries, the renowned master told the monk to give me a kuti and said to me, "Come back in the evening for a chat." I did so, and found him talking with a few laypeople. After a moment he looked at me and demanded, "What have you come for?" Shades of Luang Por Chah! I mumbled something about paying respects, prostrated, and took my leave.

Suan Mokh was a real forest monastery, with real kutis, real wells, real pindapat, evening chanting outside under the trees, but somehow it didn't feel like what I was accustomed to in the northeast. Ajahn Chah's monasteries had a certain crackling energy from the group practice, the strict observance of Vinaya, and the proactive role of the Ajahn that I didn't notice in Suan Mokh or Ajahn Supan's monastery. A couple of Thai monks from Wat Pah Pong were there at Suan Mokh, and to me they looked a breed apart from the others.

So my practice wasn't particularly inspired or energetic there. One morning on pindapat, which was often the time of day when mind was clearest, I was able to note all the thoughts swirling around—*stay or disrobe, stay or disrobe, go back to Ajahn Chah or keep wandering, get out of Thailand and start all over or grit my teeth and hang in there?*—and the impermanence of it all struck me forcefully. What if I were to just make up my mind to simply see the three characteristics of impermanence, suffering, and not-self in all these mental productions, without letting them lead me by the nose? Having the resolve to see it through might well lead to a peace I couldn't imagine, I thought, and then I would be ready to utter the lion's roar. But that moment of inspiration too faded into the mists of anicca, impermanence.

Ajahn Supan showed up later on, as he had said he would. He came with a lay attendant and had the fellow get me a ticket back to Bangkok when I was ready to leave.

***

I kept floundering and wandering. I went to Chonburi province, a little east of Bangkok, to a forest monastery I had visited when first ordained. From there I went with another farang monk to a nearby island that featured a remote, abandoned monastery. The locals were glad to be able to feed monks again. It was certainly peaceful there, but I wasn't peaceful.

I carried my burdens to Chiengmai, in the north. I'd given up on the idea of walking and was able to procure a bus ticket at Wat Boworn, where I was the abbot's guest because of having helped complete the translation of an important text on monastic discipline.

Some people had told me Chiengmai was cooler in the hot months, so I thought I should check it out, "just in case," but it turned out that was only true if you got out of town and up into the hills—the north is home to the highest peaks in Thailand (which are still not very high). I met up with two older monks who had been at Wat Pah Pong briefly, and one of them took me to Doi Puey, the second highest mountain in Thailand. There was a small monastery above a Meo hill-tribe village, at an altitude of 6,000 feet.

Finally I had found a temperate climate, but I still couldn't find clarity of mind. One night I confided in the abbot, Ajahn Pyrote, that I had been thinking about disrobing for a few months and was probably going to do it.

"You're like a calf that's just left its mother," he said. "You completed five vassa and set out on your own, without the teacher to guide you, and now you are meeting perils." He told me that thinking about disrobing was common for monks, even for someone like himself, ordained for nineteen years. After all, he said, the life of a bhikkhu is not easy. We accept that there is something urgently needing to be done, that we are suffering and in need of a cure. But, he added, you could say that being ordained is like being in a hospital. "No matter how good the conditions are in the hospital, no one wants to spend a whole lifetime there."

Ajahn Pyrote also told me that he once heard Ajahn Chah teach. "His words still resound in my ears," he said.

***

When I returned to Bangkok, I was certain it was time to say goodbye. I got fitted for pants, informed the abbot of Wat Boworn that I planned to disrobe—which news he received with a chuckle, having seen it all in his forty-plus years in robes—and told him that I would go to Wat Pah Pong to take leave of Ajahn Chah first. Disrobing in Ubon was unimaginable, so I planned on doing it at Wat Boworn, where my saga had begun some seven years previous. It also seemed a good idea to be as close to the exits as possible.

I suppose I should have known that Luang Por Chah wouldn't let me go easily and that I would be hard pressed to deal with his wily ways. But he knocked me off guard and kept me in a suspended state for over a month, even getting me to sign up for one more vassa, while my pants, and my plans, languished in storage.

Luang Por only had my best interests at heart—that I knew. He said he was afraid I might be acting prematurely and wanted me to be really certain about what I was doing. In a few brief moments at his kuti, he made everything that had transpired in the previous few months vanish. I had the sensation of standing at a crossroads, but all the signs and markers had been removed and it was only me in an empty landscape—an unsettling feeling.

So after a brief trip back to Bangkok to undo my arrangements, I entered vassa at Wat Nanachat. But I remained mostly uninspired. It was a hot, dry rainy season. There was talk of drought and a failed rice crop. One day I said to Ajahn Pabhakaro, who had recently been installed as abbot, "It looks like you guys might not have any rice to eat next year." It took a few seconds for that to sink in, and then he raised an eyebrow. "You guys?"

After a month I was more certain than ever that it was time to go. Leaving during vassa was bad form, and Luang Por didn't make it easy, but finally he gave his blessing. We had a touching farewell, in which he said he felt like he was losing one arm. He had received with skepticism my assurances that what I intended to find was a more suitable situation in which to continue Buddhist practice, but now he sincerely said, "Keep only the good. Discard all your suffering—throw it in the ocean."

***

Luang Por occupied my thoughts much of the time after I returned to the United States I got to see him two years later when he came to

Seattle, New York, and Massachusetts for a visit and I had the privilege of being his attendant, chauffeur, and interpreter. He seemed genuinely curious about my experiences. He specifically wanted to know how I was applying the Dharma to lay life. Although I tried to convey that I was studying with another teacher, he generously set me straight when he saw the need.

Driving him through the bowels of Brooklyn one day, I said, "People in these parts aren't very attractive." Without missing a beat, he came back with "Where are people attractive?" Even in Luang Por's presence, I easily slipped into my habit of complaining about the shortcomings of others. He would patiently hear me out and then bring me up short by saying things like, "There are no good people—if we are not good," repeating it to make sure I got the point, and asking if I understood.

He asked how I was doing in keeping morality. I told him I thought I was doing pretty well with the basic five precepts of virtuous conduct. He laughed and said, "You don't steal from others, but you're still stealing from yourself." It was a unique take on *sila* (virtue, morality), but the idea has kept me looking over my shoulder through the years.

Part Two

Riding the Great Vehicle

12

Kobun

When the great Zen masters went into action, they were dragons galloping and tigers charging; heaven and earth turned, and nothing could stop them from revivifying people.

—*Yuanwu*

Santa Cruz, California, 1976–81

o outside and pray."

The soft-spoken little Japanese priest was talking to his young daughter. I assumed he meant, "Go outside and play," though I figured it could have been either.

I was visiting Kobun Chino Sensei (who was actually a *roshi,* someone certified as a master by his or her own master, but never used the title, preferring the humbler *sensei,* which simply means "teacher") at his home in Los Altos Hills in 1976. Ajahn Sumedho and I had come to the United States to visit our families, and while he was in San Diego I came north with Andy, an old friend who was now Kobun's student. Ajahn Sumedho was to give a talk at Kobun's Santa Cruz Zen

Center after flying up on a Tuesday. On Monday, Andy and I took the drive over the Santa Cruz Mountains to Kobun's house.

Roshi Kobun Chino Otogawa, May 1976, Santa Cruz, Calif.
Photograph by Bob Shamis.

It was an upper-middle-class neighborhood on the outskirts of what was to become Silicon Valley. Kobun had a spacious home, though it looked like he had just moved in and was waiting for his furniture and possessions to arrive. The walls were nearly bare, the rooms sparsely furnished, the floors uncarpeted. He served us coffee and we talked about monastic life.

Mostly, he asked questions and listened, maybe accurately sizing up someone who couldn't see very far past his own nose. I was a Theravada forest monk and wasn't all that curious about Zen. Friendly but unassuming, Kobun didn't make much impression on me one way or the other. Little did I know he would soon become the most important influence in my life.

***

Almost a year and a half after that casual visit with Kobun, I left the monastic robes and Thailand and found myself once again in Santa Cruz. Although I had disrobed, Buddhist practice was still my primary concern. I usually attended the Tuesday night meditation with Heart Sutra service and lecture at the Santa Cruz Zen Center. Kobun sometimes came to the adjoining house to have tea with the community afterwards.

I lived a few miles outside of town with no public transportation and had to depend on others for rides to and from. One Tuesday night when I was at the *zendo,* which literally means the meditation hall but was the way we usually referred to the center, Kobun offered to drive me home.

He came inside after we arrived, sat down, picked up one of the big apples I had brought from my fruit picker's job at Happy Valley Farm, and bit into it. He asked me how I was doing in my new life.

To my surprise, I had found myself getting a little distracted on city streets, and seeing how easily I could lose my focus was unsettling. I anxiously conveyed this to him.

But all Kobun said was, "It's very good to have you here."

In time I discovered that his approach was unrelentingly positive. He once began a Dharma talk by saying, "I congratulate you." To him it seemed to be an immeasurably great thing for people to be doing sitting meditation, even if only once a day or once a week.

Still, it wasn't easy for me to get used to the idea of a married monk and a sangha of lay meditators. After I got closer to him, Kobun told me that if he weren't married, many of the people who came to sit with him wouldn't be there. I wasn't sure what to make of that statement at the time—I thought he was referring to his Los Altos sangha, which had a much higher percentage of people with families, homes, and careers than the ragtag Santa Cruz bunch—but he may have accurately seen that aspiring Buddhists in California at that time, especially the freethinkers in the Zen tradition, wouldn't be attracted to celibate monks. Andy said that Kobun seemed to be enlightened and neurotic at the same time. Looking back on his compassionate activity, I suspect his way of being was intentional. Perhaps it was a means to help make it easier for people to relate to him.

After arriving in California, I wrote to Jack Kornfield. He wrote me back, one of his short letters in his big cursive hand: "Kobun Chino at the Santa Cruz zendo is great! Very funny and gentle." But it took me a while to appreciate Kobun and warm to him.

After a year in Santa Cruz, I went to visit my grandfather in Miami Beach. There wasn't a whole lot for us to talk about or to do together, and it was hot and humid outside, so in the afternoons I started hanging out in the nearby Americana Hotel coffee shop, where I would down two or three cups of coffee for sixty-five cents, plus a quarter tip for Otto the waiter, and work on translating one of the few talks of Ajahn Chah that was in print, which the compiler had entitled "A Dharma Reception."

I mention this because it was a profound and powerful informal talk that Luang Por gave to a visitor, in which he spoke about how some people learn quickly, taking a teacher's words to heart, while others have to take their lumps repeatedly before they get it—"life has to teach them all the way to the end"—until finally they are like a buffalo that has been tied down firmly by all fours and can be castrated: "Then if you want to cut, you can go ahead and cut."

(To my chagrin, in the book of Ajahn Chah's talks called *Still Forest Pool* this became "if you want to give it medicine," which seemed awfully watered down and evokes for me an image of a buffalo sitting on a stool, an ice pack on its head and a thermometer in its mouth, its hind feet in a bucket of hot water, and someone spoon-feeding it medicine.)

When I went back to Santa Cruz, I was finally ready to hear Kobun's teaching, and in retrospect I can see I was a fine example of the slow learners Luang Por talked about. But of course while translating it I thought it referred exclusively to others.

When I heard Kobun speak one Tuesday night in the fall of 1978, everything he said not only made sense, it was also quite moving. He was always trying to bring his students down to earth, here where other beings live. "The way you relate to others reflects how you treat yourself," he said. He didn't want people to proclaim themselves as bodhisattvas of vast intention. "At this point, no one wants to be saved by you," he once remarked in response to a lofty question. Instead, he said, people should see what was right in front of them and deal with it with care and respect. "In some cultures, people call each other 'brother' and so on," he said. "This comes from a time when people really felt that they were a family."

It was as if my ears had been unplugged. It was a long talk but I was enraptured throughout. Finally, there might be some refuge for me in lay life. Seven-day *sesshins* (intensive meditation retreats) in country locations, weekend sesshins at the zendo, and Tuesday night lectures became high points in my existence.

Kobun seemed a mixture of traditional and unorthodox. He didn't use koans at all, though his teaching style left you feeling there was "no place to put your hands or feet," as is said about koans. Widely used as a meditation object in Zen Buddhism, a koan is a statement or question whose meaning cannot be discerned by reason but only by intuition.

The *kyosaku,* the stick for whacking drowsy or slouching meditators, was not used either.

He once related how he saw his wife standing over his two young children as they sat in zazen (meditation), holding a kyosaku and ready to strike at the first sign of imperfection. "I felt very sad," he said.

He discussed it with his wife later, and she asked, "Don't they use the kyosaku at Tassajara (Zen Mountain Center)?"

"Ah, yes," he told her. "But they are all confused."

Kobun's elder brother Keibun, abbot of their home temple in Japan, came to visit in 1978. Although his English was limited, one night he gave a brief talk. He was the picture of seriousness, but I got the impression that a big sense of humor lay just below the surface.

"As you know," he said, "Kobun is a very strange person. I feel that I myself am more wise than Kobun. And in Japan, people respect me. But there is something strange," he continued. "Everyone respects me—but everyone loves Kobun."

When Kobun lectured, he spoke slowly, in a hushed voice, usually holding his Zen master's stick, leaning forward slightly and straightening back up throughout the talk. I began to feel that his talks were akin to performances by a master musician and so it would be good to request him to play something. I became insufferable with questions about scripture, enlightenment, koans, and other arcane topics. When I once remarked that enlightenment seemed so close, he said, "That is really good luck! Usually it is very far away." I was unaware that Kobun compared a person seeking enlightenment to someone with shit on his nose: Everyone sees it but the person himself.

His take on precepts was different from anything I'd heard in all my years as a monk and brought a new dimension to morality in the context of the five precepts. These are the five most basic guides for virtuous behavior: refraining from killing, stealing, sexual misconduct, harmful speech, and the use of intoxicants. He spoke about the third precept, the prohibition against adultery, in terms of spiritual promiscuity, going from one teacher to the next without commitment. In his vow ceremonies, the words he used for this precept were "No attaching to fulfillment." And his version of the fifth precept was "No selling the wine of delusion." The first was "No killing life," and among other things, he applied this to the practice of *shikan taza,* "just sitting," saying that as we sit, our past existences express themselves through us, and that rather than repressing anything we should just let be.

Kobun was one of those teachers who sometimes seems to be speaking just to you in his lectures and is no doubt tuned in to the minds of his listeners. Once he started talking about our constant need for attention. "Even if no one is interested in you, you will say, 'Here I am! Here I am!'" He said it in a small, lonely voice that precisely evoked the feeling of someone in a distant corner desperate for human attention. He was constantly telling us to take care of ourselves and to accept and be kind to others in the most ordinary ways rather than setting ourselves up as saviors. "It might take 300 years to change one person. Do you really want to try?"

Sitting sesshins also led to my feeling that I was once again a legitimate member of a sangha. The biggest event of the year was Rohatsu, the early December sesshin commemorating the Buddha's enlightenment. I first attended in 1978. For the occasion, we rented a ranch in the outskirts of Santa Clara County. It was freezing cold, a good time to bundle up and sit still, especially as there was no way to warm up, no heat anywhere on the ranch. During one sitting, I became aware of breathing and small movements in the room; it felt like we were one organism. Everyone started to appear as old friends. After sesshin was over, we had an informal lunch outside. One fellow introduced himself to me, and I thought, why does he need to introduce himself, I feel like I know him so well already.

Compared to the way other Zen groups practiced, our sesshins weren't overly demanding, but still, sitting some ten periods a day was not easy. Kobun said that he had pain in sitting sometimes, but no tension. When we went to the high mountains with him once and I massaged him, it was striking how soft his muscles were. He said not to be concerned about getting rid of pain: "If you have no pain in sitting, you forget there are hungry people in the world."

***

The zendo in Santa Cruz was a simple affair, with an austere, dignified beauty. Bare white walls, *tatami* (straw mats) covering the floor, black sitting mats (*zabuton*) and cushions (*zafu*), a small altar that didn't even have a Buddha statue. There was some sort of stick with calligraphy on it, the meaning of which I never learned. I assumed that the altar being set up that way was a statement that the Buddha has no form. One side of the altar had a seat for the teacher, the other side for the person who beat the drum and rang the bell during Heart Sutra service.

We recited the Heart Sutra, in English, every Tuesday evening after zazen, and every morning during sesshin, with the occasional rendition in Japanese. Kobun's teaching style was informal, and I never heard him give commentary on the Sutra, but one night he mentioned the mantra—*Gate gate paragate parsamgate bodhi svaha*—and said what it really meant was "Falling apart, falling apart, everything is always falling apart, nothing you can do about it, that's the way it is," and he explained that the final word, svaha, was sort of like swearing "Jesus Christ!"

We sat facing the wall, in Soto fashion. Forty- or fifty-minute sittings were broken by ten minutes of very slow walking (*kinhin*) in a circle around the zendo. Meals during sesshin were formal, *oryoki* style: three bowls that were kept wrapped in a cloth, a spoon, and a cleaning stick. Outside of sesshin, the residents of the zendo usually had breakfast and dinner together, and others often joined in. It was the cheapest dinner in town, seventy-five cents, substantial though simple vegetarian fare.

The first time I went there for dinner, shortly after I had disrobed, Andy introduced me, telling people I'd been a monk in Thailand. One woman asked if I lived in a monastery there. It seemed a strange question—where else would a monk live?—but I answered yes. Sensing my hesitation, Andy explained that many Zen monks in the West don't live in monasteries.

Though not a by-the-book Zen teacher, when Kobun was in full regalia, wearing his black robes and holding his staff, he fairly reeked of tradition. And he was well-versed in many of the art forms long associated with Zen. One night he played a recording of *shakuhachi* (flute) solo music after the sitting. It had that Japanese quality of clean, ascetic stillness, and even though I had long before lost my taste for music and generally found it annoying, this was not bad, almost meditative, you might say.

After it concluded, someone said he wasn't sure how he was supposed to be listening to the music.

Kobun replied, "Like hearing a dog barking in the street."

The people Kobun ordained were an interesting bunch, maybe not the ascetic, renunciate types you'd find in a forest monastery in Thailand, but somehow removed from the mainstream of American life by a step or two. Robes were usually only worn to group events. It was a challenge for me to expand my horizons to be able to take all this in. And after less than a year of serious involvement, one day at *dokusan* (private interview) in the spring of 1979, Kobun said to me, "I have to do something to take care of you. Do you want to become a monk?"

Though I liked and respected Kobun a lot, I thought maybe he wasn't in the top tier of Zen masters. I wondered if I shouldn't be looking for a more spiritually advanced teacher to study with. But whenever such thoughts started to gel, Kobun would surprise me and make me realize that he was always several steps (or light years) ahead of me, that he was paying attention to me and ready and able to help.

Still, monkhood again? I knew that it wasn't the same kind of monkhood as I had experienced in Thailand, more like a statement and commitment. But I needed time to think about it. (When I finally decided to go ahead with it, Andy's father said, "He's served his time! Why don't they leave him alone?")

***

At sesshin in May of 1979, I got a message to call Western Union. Ajahn Chah was coming to the United States in the end of the month, with Ajahn Pabhakaro, and Jack Kornfield had arranged for me to travel as their attendant. After the sesshin, I got hold of a suitcase, threw a few items of clothing and a zafu in it, and took a bus to San Francisco airport for the flight to Seattle.

Luang Por gave me such a hard time in the first days of that visit that I actually began to wonder if the great, wise, compassionate master I spent years with in Thailand was nothing more than a product of my imagination. He kept telling me I was wasting my time as a layperson and ridiculed everything I tried to say about Zen. He was so unrelentingly cantankerous that the last thing I wanted to do was go back to Ubon and be a monk again, and I felt more than ever that I was following the right course. And then after several days of this psychological pounding, everything changed and he became the Ajahn Chah I used to know. Once again, he was showering down amazing and insightful teachings, once again he was making me laugh and radiating his matchless warmth and magnetism.

When I related this to Kobun later, he immediately said, "He was reflecting your divided mind." That rang perfectly true. I got the feeling that he and Luang Por drank from the same pristine spring of wisdom. Though Kobun often warned us against flitting from teacher to teacher, when in 1981 I told him I was going back to Thailand for a visit he said, "A fortunate person can have many teachers."

Still, I kept in mind what I told a friend: "Ajahn Chah saved my life; Kobun saved me from Ajahn Chah." As much as I loved Ajahn Chah, he was not an easy master, but those first years back in lay life I was often haunted by the feeling that somehow I would end up back in the tank under Luang Por's thumb again. Kobun validated my choice to move on from Theravadin monkhood by showing me there was a genuine and complete way to practice as a layperson.

***

In the brief period I spent studying with Kobun, I didn't hear much about his own training, but he did drop little pearls now and then. When he was a young monk in Japan, one of his teachers called him in. They sat at opposite ends of a long table. Kobun spoke about the episode in his usual slow manner, with a minimalist description of what was probably a very simple and quiet setting. The master said to him, "I am eighty-six years old. You cannot imagine how precious the time is to me now." Kobun told us, "Compared to him, I felt I had no appreciation of my life, that it was just something worthless to me—like toilet paper."

He also said that his teacher used to confess every time he thought in terms of self and other; on another occasion he mentioned that his teacher took a vow that nobody could lie to him. This was a theme Kobun used often: If you really pay attention to people, they are always telling you something true about themselves.

Later on I sometimes felt Kobun was a Tibetan *tulku*, a reincarnate realized being, who had somehow taken birth in Japan. His view seemed close to the Tibetan Mahamudra and Great Perfection teachings, and he once said, when talking about how he didn't see himself as separate and distinct from the rest of existence, that there was no specific moment when his experience changed to become like that.

He was extremely humble and never tried to promote himself. He once met Jerry Brown, at the time governor of California, at Zen Center of San Francisco. The governor had his feet up on the coffee table but quickly sat up straight when Kobun entered the room where he was waiting to see someone.

Brown asked Kobun about himself. "How many disciples do you have?" he inquired.

"I don't have any disciples," Kobun said.

Governor Brown was taken aback. "Baker Roshi (head of Zen Center, Suzuki Roshi's Dharma heir, and Brown's teacher) has hundreds of disciples."

"I have many friends," Kobun said. "But no disciples."

Talking about Dogen Zenji, the founder of Soto Zen in Japan, Kobun said he was awestruck when reading his words and felt he was by comparison just some kind of insect, "chewing on Dogen's toe dust." On another occasion he said, "You don't need to give me any title or fancy name… Something like 'Dirty Kobun' is good enough." But he never seemed to see others in that way. He was always uplifting, praising good qualities and intentions, which in my own case I usually felt were nonexistent.

We were at a sesshin in the Santa Cruz Mountains in 1979 when the Dalai Lama came to Santa Cruz on his first visit to the United States. Several of us, including Kobun, drove into town to see him at the university. He spoke on what was to become one of his standard themes, universal responsibility and the good heart. His Holiness was on an extremely tight schedule and kept glancing at his watch, so there was something of a hurried feeling. But the local Buddhist community was floating on air to have him there. That evening Kobun remarked on the event, noting how at the very beginning of his talk His Holiness prostrated to the throne that had been set up for him and then pulled up a folding chair to sit on. "When I saw that, for the first time I felt maybe there is something good about Tibetan Buddhism," Kobun said.

Avalokiteshvara (*Kannon* in Japanese) and Manjushri are familiar bodhisattva heroes in Japanese Buddhism, but Kobun said that for us the ideal is Maitreya, the future Buddha. Rather than being someone on high who looks down on beings with pity, Maitreya stands shoulder to shoulder with you, like a friend. The root of his name is *maitri* (*metta* in Pali), translated as love, loving kindness, and sometimes friendliness.

That kind of equality and respect for all beings summed up Kobun's approach. The way some students interpreted his teaching led to a lot of flakiness, rejection of any sort of discipline or hierarchy, with the predictable result that the simplest things were often impossible to agree on, the practice schedule fell apart, the house and zendo weren't maintained properly. But I think Kobun's message was really an uncompromising way of telling people that ultimately they were the only ones responsible for themselves, and for others too. "Making yourself happy is easy," he said. "You can go eat ice cream. Making others happy is more difficult."

***

I did finally take ordination, in February of 1980. Perhaps reflecting my last-minute decision, Kobun rummaged through his stores and could only find a robe that was many inches too short and a set of little *oryoki* bowls that seemed made for a Japanese pre-teen.

At the end of the ceremony I read a windy statement I had prepared, praising Kobun, proclaiming my shortcomings with my trademark false humility, and promising to try harder to put into practice what Kobun taught. Then Kobun invited sangha members to have their say, and in conclusion, he asked me to thank everyone, which was one item I had overlooked. But in the following months, when Kobun was away on the island of Dominica with his family, the sense of gratitude, towards both Kobun and the sangha, started to grow in me.

In a teaching I read by Ajahn Sumedho, he said that gratitude became a major catalyst in his practice. I mentioned that at a community meeting. One person replied that at some point gratitude becomes action. We were all struggling to keep things going with Kobun gone indefinitely, and that was helpful to hear.

Kobun's return kept getting delayed. His wife, Harriet, had always wanted to travel. They probably had little time together as a family, and this might have been the chance of a lifetime. The first time I met Harriet she was planning to work in a refugee camp in Thailand as a nurse. Kobun asked me to come to their home to give her some idea of what to expect in Thailand. She told me she was doing it in part for the opportunity to go abroad. Turning to Kobun, she reminded him of his premarital promise that they would travel the world.

Kobun permitted himself the slightest look of sly satisfaction. "Ah, but that was a trick."

What was to be a month in Dominica turned into almost half a year. Then one night in late spring of 1980, there he was in the zendo, in his robes and with hair almost to his shoulders. It was a strange sight, but when he began speaking it was certainly the same Kobun.

His marriage got rocky during the following year, and we saw him only sporadically. His Silicon Valley sangha, which met at the Los Altos zendo and had many members dating back to the days when Suzuki Roshi was alive, purchased an old church and a house across the street from it in Mountain View. For twenty-five dollars a month, I rented floor space for a place to sleep, as I had a job in San Jose working with Indo-Chinese refugees, my first full-time employment since disrobing. But we rarely saw Kobun, since he had appointed a teacher for the group, Sensei Les Kaye.

Kobun's centers in Silicon Valley and Santa Cruz were managed independently of each other. Relations were good and we basically considered ourselves one sangha of Kobun's students, though the older students, and most of the money, were in the Silicon Valley area. In summer of 1979 they had bought a large property in the Santa Cruz Mountains for a country center. A dead-ender hippie community was squatting there. Everyone assumed they would have to go, but Kobun said it wasn't right to evict people from their home. We tried coexistence but it didn't work very well; among other things, they had a rock band and especially liked to practice during sesshin. Our neighbors gave off a feeling of leftovers, like food that had been sitting in the refrigerator way too long. Only two or three of Kobun's students took up residence, and Kobun and the sangha gathered there only for sesshin and the rare special event. Most of the sangha eventually gave up. After a few years of frustration, during which period Kobun began spending more of his time in New Mexico, Angie Boissevain, one of Kobun's senior students, took charge. In 1983 some of the land was sold off and the hippies evicted, and Jikoji Zen Center was up and running.

***

At the end of the summer of 1981, Andy got the idea that a few of us should take Kobun hiking in the high Sierra Mountains. He'd been living alone for a while—Harriet had moved out with the children—and appeared to be in a funk. We cleared it with his secretary, who promised to tend to all his affairs. Then we prepared a backpack and sleeping bag for him and went to fetch him in the predawn hours one morning.

He clearly didn't want to go. "What about...?" he protested.

"We spoke with your secretary and she will take care of it."

"But I have to look after...."

"It's all arranged," we assured him.

"I don't have things for the mountains."

"We've got everything you need," we told him.

Finally he looked at us like a little boy and said, "So I really must go?"

But once we were up in the mountains, Kobun was ecstatic. We had some of his items in our own packs so he wouldn't have too much to carry, and he was practically flying up the trails.

Sitting in the high mountains was exhilaratingly calm and settling for me. In the morning, we did zazen with Kobun. After breakfast Andy and our other traveling companion, an old mutual friend who was a part-time Zen sitter, took him on day hikes, where they said he was leaping from boulder to boulder, while I stayed to mind the camp and continue sitting. After dinner we would sit around the fire, Kobun smoking Camels and drinking coffee. One evening he picked up the coffee pot to pour himself another cup and discovered it was empty. "Oh! Did I drink it all?" he said reflectively, and paused. "Don't tell anyone."

Those evenings sitting around the campfire with Kobun were the most intimate time I had with him. They were typical in that he showed the completely ordinary behavior of someone who liked cigarettes and coffee while at the same time he inspired us with words that showed his transcendent, unfettered view. It left no doubt that he was someone with a vast and unfathomable mind.

***

Before I left for Thailand in the fall of 1981, a trip I had started planning as soon as I got the job in the refugee clinic, Kobun invited me to his house one evening. He didn't often invite students there, so I assumed he had something in mind to discuss with me, maybe some important parting advice. I dropped by to find him with his attendant, inspecting long rolls of brush paintings. I didn't know this side of him and I wasn't much of an art buff, but I marveled at the yards and yards of his work.

"This is amazing, Kobun," I said.

"Yes, I know," he replied.

Then his face lit up and he asked, "Would you like to have some?" I gratefully took a piece that he cut off and brought it to my parents' home.

We never discussed anything that evening. After a while I let go of expectations and figured he had just invited me to hang out.

***

I went to Thailand in December of 1981 and spent about eight months there, with a month's interlude in Sri Lanka, living in Ajahn Chah's monasteries and becoming immersed in Theravadin ways again. Towards the end of my stay, I heard the call of Vajrayana and decided to give the tantric preliminary practices (*ngondro*) a try when I returned to California. I still loved Kobun, but it seemed my Zen career had run its course. And Kobun was spending less and less time in our area and more in New Mexico, where he had a small group; in Colorado, teaching at Naropa University; and points unknown to any of us in Santa Cruz.

During those golden days of 1977 to 1980 Kobun was a fixture, and barring special occurrences we could count on him showing up every Tuesday evening in Santa Cruz, Wednesday in Los Altos, and at sesshin for both groups several times per year. It's always been my tendency, once I'm involved with a group and a teacher, to start thinking such is the way it is and always will be. But as we know, the good fortune to meet such special beings and drink the nectar of their instructions involves the expenditure of massive amounts of merit, and can end abruptly and unpredictably. But for me, a casual attitude usually takes over and I only appreciate my good fortune after it's too late.

I saw Kobun only twice after that, very briefly each time. The first time was at Jikoji in fall of 1983, when I briefly held a sinecure as unpaid caretaker—though I wasn't interested in Zen practice at that time, the place being remote and mostly inactive suited my need for an opportunity to work on the tantric preliminary practices. Kobun came one Saturday for an event. I sat next to him for a while. He was quiet and reserved, even more so than the way I remembered him. He asked if I went to Japan on my trip to Asia. I told him I hadn't gotten there and was now signed on with the Tibetans. He didn't react one way or the other; I felt he wasn't completely there in spirit and was just putting in a ceremonial appearance.

He was often in my thoughts in the following years, but I lost track of his whereabouts and activities until I returned to Santa Cruz in 1997. An old zendo friend told me Kobun was staying at someone's house north of Santa Cruz. She gave me directions, and one Saturday I bought a huge melon, a traditional Japanese gift, to offer Kobun, and went to find him.

I located the house, a beautifully constructed Japanese-style abode, but no one was in. I left the melon and a note by the front door and went back to town. Not long after, I stopped in a market on my way home from work one day and there was Kobun at the checkout counter, with his new wife, Katrin, and their baby. Kobun recognized me and said hello, catching me by surprise.

"You came to the house?" he asked.

It was a real treat to see him. I said, yes, I'd been out to his place, and asked him how he was.

"As you see," he said.

We spoke for a little while. I wondered if he'd had a stroke, he was so restrained and spoke so slowly, but then I remembered he'd always been like that. He was noticeably older, which wasn't surprising, as it had been fourteen years since I'd last seen him.

He paid for his groceries and was ready to leave. I said goodbye, feeling it probably wasn't appropriate to ask about visiting him, and told his wife, "Please take good care of him." She looked at me with dismay and asked, "Who's going to take care of me?"

***

I didn't hear anything of Kobun for several years after that. When I visited Abhayagiri Monastery in northern California in 2002, Ajahn

Pasanno told me Kobun had died in Europe, by drowning. He was sixty-two years old.

It's a tragic story that left many people grief-stricken, yet in a way a signature act by Kobun. He was at the home of a student in Switzerland. There was a pond on the property, and his little daughter, Maya (who must have been the baby on Katrin's shoulder in New Leaf Market five years earlier), wandered in and went under. Kobun, although unable to swim, jumped in to rescue her. Father and daughter drowned together.

Kobun often said that he wasn't going to live very long. When he was forty, in the Zendo one night he stated, "I feel my life is about two-thirds over." And someone recently told me that Kobun had actually said sixty-two was the age he would live to. In life he was an intriguing figure. Much of the time exhilarating to be around, he still sometimes gave off an air of quiet resignation, even perhaps melancholy—if it sounds like I'm hedging my bets here, it's because he wasn't easy to pin down or pigeonhole. When I heard about the way he died, it seemed to fit in with the mood and trajectory of his bodhisattva faring in this life. It also left me regretting that I hadn't gotten to know him better, but it was a grand reminder of impermanence and the necessity of cherishing what is truly important.

13

Monk

This precious jewel of your mind, do not throw it in the river like an idiot.

—*Naropa, to Marpa*

Santa Cruz, June 1978

n Thailand, there is little talk of yanas, spiritual "vehicles" to awakening. In contemporary Buddhism, there are three such vehicles: *Hinayana, Mahayana,* and *Vajrayana.* The form of Buddhism generally practiced in Thailand and other parts of Southeast Asia is *Theravada,* the "Word of the Elders." It is usually what is being referred to by the term Hinayana, the "lesser vehicle." Theravada is the sole survivor of some eighteen earliest schools that fell into the Hinayana category. Its source of instruction is the Pali Canon, the earliest Buddhist scriptures.

Mahayana, the "great vehicle," came later in the evolution of Buddhist scholarship and practice. Zen and the various other Japanese forms are Mahayana, as are Ch'an and Pure Land Buddhism (focusing on Amitabha Buddha) in China and Soen in Korea.

Strictly speaking, Hinayana refers to the motivation of one's practice being primarily for one's own liberation. Mahayana, on the other hand, is aimed at the liberation of all beings. The devoted practitioner is considered a *bodhisattva*, a buddha in the making who would forego complete enlightenment until it can be attained by all. The term Hinayana is used only by way of comparison to the later-appearing Mahayana, so it's understandable that it is taken as a pejorative. Some contemporary Mahayana teachers have taken to referring to it as the "foundational vehicle."

There are a few Mahayana temples in Thailand, mostly belonging to Chinese lineages and not frequented much by ethnic Thai. In America the names of the yanas are bandied about, carelessly it often seems, and I couldn't help wincing whenever I heard someone use the H-word. I also questioned if there were real differences, or if the differences were enough to warrant the terminology. It is certainly possible to practice with a Mahayana approach while maintaining the moral discipline of Theravada; in his classic, *Zen Mind, Beginner's Mind,* Suzuki Roshi said that the Zen practice he taught was Hinayana discipline with Mahayana mind. And many aspiring to the bodhisattva path have noticed how much kindness and compassion is displayed by veteran Theravadins, Ajahn Chah being a prime example.

The third school is Vajrayana, the "diamond vehicle." Like the others, Vajrayana has its roots in India. In the eighth century, the adept Padmasambhava brought Vajrayana Buddhism to Tibet and its environs. Today, Vajrayana and Tibetan Buddhism are practically synonymous in popular usage, though the latter actually includes the teachings of all three vehicles, and Vajrayana practices are also found in the Japanese Shingon and Chinese Mi Tsung lineages. Padmasambhava—better known as Guru Rinpoche (Precious Guru)—is considered the Second Buddha.

Vajrayana is also a Mahayana tradition, bodhisattva motivation being considered indispensable for anyone aspiring to follow that path. Sometimes Vajrayana is referred to as *tantra* Mahayana, the resultant path based on the scriptures known as tantras, as opposed to sutra

Mahayana, the causal path. And Vajrayana can be subdivided into four or six vehicles, as lower and higher or outer and inner tantra.

With all the spiritual activity in Santa Cruz, where I went to live after disrobing in Thailand, I couldn't help but notice the strong Vajrayana presence, with the Gelukpas leading the pack. Lama Thubten Yeshe taught a class at the University of California that was open to the public, and the auditorium he spoke in always had big crowds—after all, it was free, and a lot of young people had time on their hands in that laid-back town.

Tibetan Buddhism has four main lineages. The followers of Padmasambhava are known as Nyingmapa, the "ancient tradition." The Kagyu, Sakya, and Geluk came afterwards and are called the "new schools." They rely on later translations of different sets of scriptures, though elements of Nyingmapa have been incorporated into all of them. In general, there are more similarities than differences among the four lineages, and it is customary for followers of one school to study the teachings and practices of the others.

Gelukpa was established by the master Tsongkhapa in the early fifteenth century as a reform movement. The world's best-known Vajrayana Buddhist, His Holiness the Dalai Lama, is ordained in Gelukpa and is generally associated with that tradition, though he stresses nonsectarianism and studies widely in the other lineages. Lama Yeshe, one of the seminal figures in transmitting Tibetan Buddhism to the West, was also a Gelukpa monk.

In the spring of 1978 one of Lama Yeshe's teachers, Song Rinpoche, came to lead a retreat on *lamrim*, the graduated path to enlightenment, at Camp Kennolyn in the Soquel Hills. Lama Thubten Zopa, Lama Yeshe's junior partner, would be translating. The fledgling Vajrapani Institute, north of Santa Cruz in Boulder Creek, was running the retreat. The cost was thirteen dollars per day, which sent a lot of people scrambling to get up the money for the ten days.

One afternoon I visited Edward, a friend and former novice at Wat Nanachat who had immersed himself in Tibetan Buddhism. All his money, including the pennies, was laid out on his kitchen table, and he was counting it to see if he could afford the whole retreat. He gave me a sales pitch, insisting it was something not to be missed. And, he said, George would be there. So I planned on going for a few days.

Edward tended to well over with enthusiasm about whatever spiritual activities he was involved in, and everyone who knew him heard plenty about George. He was a mysterious monk, an older man who'd done all sorts of things worldly and spiritual and had realized the meaning of the Buddha's teachings. Edward painted him as a fierce and intimidating fellow who brooked no nonsense.

***

The lamrim was my first in-depth exposure to Tibetan Buddhism. The scholarly, methodical approach of the Gelukpa lineage overwhelmed me, yet like my first meeting with Buddhism in Bangkok years before, it made a lot of sense. And the broadened aim of practicing to develop *bodhicitta*, the awakening mind of compassion that maintains the wish to attain enlightenment in order to liberate all beings, was uplifting. The point of the teaching and practice was still elimination of suffering, but with the understanding that "I am one, while others are many," that others likewise wish for happiness and don't want to suffer but because of their ignorance only find unhappiness, and are thus deserving of compassion. And it was pointed out that we suffer because of the self-centered pursuit of happiness, termed "self-cherishing," and that Buddhas and bodhisattvas realize ultimate happiness through giving up self-cherishing and putting the welfare of others first.

It did seem like an awful lot to take on, what with all the classifications—six of these, four of those, thirty-seven of that—the step-by-step meditations, the visualizations, the prayers. Like many a newcomer, I wondered if it was really necessary to do all those things. Theravadins and Zennists seemed to do fine without them, after all. And there was a moralistic overtone to it, almost like a Judeo-Christian good-and-evil orientation. But that old foreboding was upon me once again, the suspicion that this was something I might not be able to wiggle out of.

Song Rinpoche presented voluminous material every day, all of it new to me. When I paid to attend a retreat, I expected long hours of silent meditation. But apart from quiet time in the early morning, there was an atmosphere of activity—especially during the teachings—with some brief guided meditations, also something new for me.

One evening, Edward alerted me to George's arrival, and the next morning I saw him in the shrine room. Red robes, Tibetan style; a shaved head, just like he was supposed to have; and a bushy grey beard. (George later told me that when he stopped in Bangkok on his way home after ordaining in India, he stayed at Wat Benchamabopit, the Marble Temple, which hosted a couple of Tibetan lamas at the time. When he was taken to meet the abbot, who was having a smoke, the abbot said, "I've never seen a monk with a beard!" to which George replied, "I've never seen a monk smoking a cigarette!" And that was the end of the conversation.)

Over the following years, I found George to be knowledgeable about almost any subject I brought up. Edward later told me he'd been a symphony musician, fought with the Polish underground against the Nazis, practiced Zen and Hinduism, and instructed students in Christianity. George told me that as a youth he'd travelled to many countries around the world because of his father, who I guessed to be a British civil servant or army officer, though no one was certain about his origins. A few of Edward's friends had discovered him in Southern California in the late 1960s, when he was known as "the old man" who rode his bicycle by the beach. In the mid-'70s, he went to India and took ordination with the Dalai Lama, telling his students that there comes a point in practice where you realize that you need some help from outside, that continuing on your own strength isn't enough.

Edward said that George preferred to be called "Monk." That sounded a little funny—like the big guy in the group who's called 'Tank"—but then, he was the only monk around in those earlier days.

Most of us retreatants camped out on the property, others stayed in dormitories. But Monk had a cabin to himself. One evening I had the opportunity to pay him a visit.

Expecting his reputed ferocity, I knocked on the door of the cabin. He bade me to enter and sit down on one of the beds.

"Well, how are you?" he greeted me warmly. Seeing his beard

and his gracious smile made me think more of Santa Claus than Bodhidharma, the sixth century founder of Zen Buddhism who is usually represented as a forbidding figure—the latter comparison had immediately come to mind when I first saw him in the meditation hall.

Edward had told him something about me, and I think he was pleased to meet a former monk. He asked about forest monastery life and listened with genuine curiosity. At one point, he interjected a brief comment in the form of a question. "So, the basis for the way of life is the Vinaya, is it not?"

I confirmed that it was, and he continued, "It teaches mostly on the level of conduct, but it doesn't talk about impulse origin, does it?"

Obviously (obvious to me now, so many years later) he was pointing at Vajrayana teaching, but at the time I thought he was referring to the mental defilements and ignorance as the originating place for our impulses. So I mumbled something in assent—his terminology had thrown me off.

I'd been out of robes some nine months. It already seemed like a pretty long time, and I was starting to feel I needed to determine a new direction for myself. But Monk had the long view, telling me that I was in a transition stage. When I disrobed I did have something like that in mind; I thought that much as I had committed to a minimum of five years as a bhikkhu with Ajahn Chah, I should be prepared to patiently learn what I needed to learn and not rush into any major decisions such as career or marriage—or re-ordaining. But now there was some bewilderment as I met unexpected bumps in the road.

I told him I'd been shopping around at centers and events in Santa Cruz and that the lamrim teachings, especially the *tonglen* ("taking and giving," meaning mentally taking on the suffering of others and giving them happiness), made a lot of sense, but were also overwhelming, and I wondered if it was really necessary to practice in such an elaborate, conceptual way.

"What's going on here," he explained, "is that these fellows are saying, 'Now listen: Everything is fine, and you're really OK. But we have to give you something to do.'" In a similar vein, during a later conversation he pointed out how monasteries and ashrams gave people a sanctuary in which to live that out, especially people who'd had transformative experiences and didn't know what to do next.

He spoke about the approach of using all the facets of our existence, including the conceptual mind. "You've got this mind that is always busy thinking," he said, "so why not put it to good use?" He explained the steps in the practices, sometimes in terms I could readily understand, sometimes alluding to other practices I knew nothing of, such as the seven-branch service and *mandala* offering.

His reasoning was flawless, his exposition crystal clear. Over the years, I saw him many times, and I got the sense that he was someone who'd developed the ability to transmit the meaning of the teachings over many lifetimes through aspiration and hard work, that is, through developing his paramita, or spiritual perfections (*paramita* is the Sanskrit term used in Mahayana, while Theravada uses the Pali *parami*).

In Tibet, Monk said, Dharma teaching was the only real education available. Such courses of study as we were getting a small taste of at the retreat were the means to develop people's intellectual faculties. But more than that, the practices could bring specific results that were difficult to achieve otherwise.

We talked about different Buddhist traditions and teachers. I told him I had read some of Trungpa Rinpoche's books and liked Lama Yeshe a lot—he was almost a dead ringer for Ajahn Chah in many ways.

Monk said that Asian teachers were trying to find avenues to reach Western seekers. "Trungpa thinks, 'They're all psychologists,' so he uses psychological language. Lama Yeshe thinks, 'They're all businessmen,' so he entertains them." Then he added, "But for me, the teacher I most prefer to study with is Kalu Rinpoche." I heard Kalu speak the first week I was in California—he was the first Tibetan teacher, or *lama,* I ever saw—though he didn't make any particular impression on me with his low-key style. Monk praised Kalu Rinpoche's vast experience, teaching ability, and nonsectarian approach, noting that he was a holder of several lineages.

He mentioned some other teachers. The names didn't register with me, but I've always remembered the vignette he related about the sixteenth Karmapa.

The Karmapa incarnation is one of the most important figures in Tibetan Buddhism and the head of the Karma Kagyu, which is probably the best-known of the Kagyu sub-lineages. Monk went to a public event given by Karmapa, and at the end, everyone was invited to file by His Holiness's throne for blessings. When Monk reached him and bent his head in respect, Karmapa took his head in his hands and rolled it around in his lap. "I'm not the mushy sort, but I started blubbering like a baby," he said.

The hours passed. I asked questions about the life I had become enmeshed in. He wasn't at all hesitant about going into details of lay life. He had ordained relatively late in life so had plenty of familiarity with worldly matters. Though he very rarely spoke about his own experiences, he obviously wasn't merely theorizing but spoke as someone who'd been in situations similar to what we were going through.

A monk or nun, he said, is like a fighter performing within the well-defined boundaries of the ring, with rules on what can and cannot be done. A lay practitioner, on the other hand, has to take the whole world as his arena. A daunting challenge, but one that provides vast opportunity for spiritual education.

I described my work as a hospice volunteer. I'd gotten involved with hospice through my association with Stephen Levine, who led weekly meditation classes in Santa Cruz. I was intrigued by his work with the dying, as well as his solid presence, and he encouraged me to join the fledgling Hospice of Santa Cruz as a volunteer in their first group of trainees. There was a great deal of sincerity, flakiness, and murky feel-good spirituality in those early days of the Santa Cruz group—Stephen Levine wasn't actually involved with it, and there was no real Buddhist or other spiritual influence—and I wasn't really sure what we were doing.

With the mention of Stephen, Monk said, "Yes, one hears this name."

I described what we were trying to do, along with some of my experiences visiting terminally ill people. Finally, Monk said gravely, "As I listen to you, a word rises up from inside me. Now this is no reflection on you, but the word is 'ghouls.'"

Monk said that there is an ego-dissolution that takes place during the dying process. He feared we might be interfering with it with our good intentions. When I saw Ajahn Chah the following year, he said we were unlikely to affect the dying very much, either for good or for bad, as the intensity of their experience would outweigh anything we might present to them. Looking back on several such discussions with Monk over the following years, I think that such statements as he made about hospice were more to provoke investigation rather than to be taken as the way things are—which was similar to how Ajahn Chah operated.

We sometimes had guest speakers at our hospice trainings. One month we had a rabbi and two ministers. The rabbi said something intriguingly close to the Buddhist view. When asked about the view of rebirth in Judaism, he said, "We don't talk about rebirth, but if you believe you will be reborn, then you probably will." One of the ministers presented his fundamentalist view and didn't generate much interest. The other one, a younger man who looked more like a football player than a cleric, had gone through a near-death experience in Vietnam. He said that as he felt himself outside of his body, he had a panoramic view of the world. When I related this to Monk, he cut me short.

"Please," he said. "If you are going to speak with me, you *must* refrain from using Trungpaisms." I told him "panoramic" was the exact word the minister had used, but he said, "It doesn't matter. Please don't use Trungpaisms with me."

(Reflecting on this after years of speaking and corresponding with Monk, I don't believe his comment indicated skepticism about Trungpa Rinpoche; like a good copy editor, Monk was extremely careful in his use of words and demanded the same of others. And he had no patience with jargon, catch-phrases, and anything with the remotest whiff of New Age.)

My first hospice assignment was a young Canadian man dying of leukemia who had somehow ended up in Santa Cruz. After we got to know each other he told me that someone had given him several doses of LSD, and he asked if I would like to try it with him. That certainly took me by surprise. After I'd been a monk for a short while, I just assumed that everyone else had also stopped doing such things; by now, surely, psychedelics were consigned to a dead and ancient past.

I demurred, but the prospect of expanded consciousness had some appeal. On one of my visits to Los Angeles, I asked Monk, "For someone who's been practicing meditation for a few years and has the commitment to continue, could taking psychedelics be useful?"

He appeared to mull this over for a few seconds, and then said, "Someone who's been practicing meditation for a few years.... You wouldn't by any chance be talking about yourself, would you?"

I had to admit that it was indeed I. I told him of a life-changing acid trip in 1968 and my suspicion that it was a precipitating factor in my eventually getting ensnared in Buddhism.

Needless to say, he'd heard many such stories, of people seeing God, realizing they were Christ, or whatever. "In the 1960s I met more Christs than you could shake a stick at," he said. "My question to them always was, if you say you are Christ, then why don't you live like Christ?" He said that insights and experiences from taking drugs can be valid, and he didn't doubt the veracity of what I was telling him, but he added, "You have to understand that in a way, such experience is still a delusion, because it wasn't preceded by the gradual dissolution of ego that occurs through practice." He continued, "And no, it's not really necessary for someone who has been meditating for a few years and is committed to practice to take psychedelics."

***

On that first evening with Monk, at the lamrim retreat, I had a lot of questions about the bodhisattva ideal and about the concept of different vehicles within Buddhism. It would be several years before the pieces fell into place for me, and Monk probably sensed that a comprehensive explanation wouldn't have been appropriate or helpful at that time, but what he did tell me was clear and practical.

Monk compared the three vehicles to education, saying that the approaches telescoped into each other, with each one providing a foundation for the next. "You can think of Hinayana as high school," he said. "Now, people can get a high school education and do well in the world, but there's always a certain narrowness about them: 'I never went to college, but...' Mahayana is like university. And Vajrayana is post-graduate."

The following year (1979) Ajahn Chah came to the United States. He grilled me about my Buddhist studies and practice as a layman, and when I started talking about Zen and the motivation to liberate all beings, he said, "The bodhisattva!" and went on to compare the arahant to a high school graduate, who can do just fine with what he's learned, and the bodhisattva to a PhD, who can do greater things. But I doubt he had conferred with Monk to prepare for discussing the Dharma with me.

Monk also said, when I told him how overwhelming and even bewildering Tibetan Buddhism could be, that so-called Tibetan Buddhism is basically Indian Mahayana, and that furthermore all the vehicles are the teaching of the Buddha, so the common ground is far greater than the differences.

During the retreat, two young fellows who managed the Karma Kagyu center in Santa Cruz were asking theoretical questions about yanas and other topics. Monk heard them out and said, "You don't really know yourselves at all, do you? You were born and you don't know why. You are going to die and you don't know what will happen. You have thoughts and feelings and you don't know where they come from. Please just let go of all this thinking, and you will feel a lot better."

Soon Monk warmly bid me good night, taking my hand in both of his.

***

I saw him frequently after that, at his home in Hermosa Beach, in Santa Cruz when he came for mind-nature teachings, and at summer retreats. Each meeting clarified whatever I was involved in at the time, showed me unseen dimensions, and planted seeds. No matter the topic, he always seemed to know a great deal about it.

The teaching that especially grabbed my attention during the lamrim retreat was that of tonglen, the practice of taking and sending.

One visualizes taking on all the sufferings of others, breathing them into one's heart and extinguishing the flame of self-centeredness, while sending back one's own happiness, good fortune, and wellbeing. It was an intriguing form of meditation on compassion, and I was eager to learn more. Vajrapani Institute announced that a transcript of the teachings would be available in a few weeks, so I ordered a copy.

Weeks became months, and the teachings became a distant memory. Finally the transcript did arrive, unedited and replete with "you knows", broken English, and painful repetition. Still, it revived my interest, and as my reeducation at the hands of an undisciplined world went on and I continued to take my lumps, I felt some urgency to change my approach to practice and living.

Around that time the Zen Center of Los Angeles expressed interest in publishing teachings of Ajahn Chah that Jack Kornfield and I had compiled. I met Jack in Los Angeles and we went to discuss business with the folks at ZCLA. Staying with a friend in Santa Monica, I was just down the road from Hermosa Beach, so one evening I took the bus to visit Monk.

As was his custom, after welcoming me inside and passing a few pleasantries, he made tea for both of us, his signature blend of half Earl Grey, half Darjeeling, in large glasses. We sat at his kitchen table and talked. This priceless scenario was repeated many times over the years, and even though he moved to new quarters twice, the feeling was always the same.

I was back in Los Angeles a couple of months later. Eagerly looking forward to another visit with Monk, I called him to ask for some of his time. On the previous visit the conversation, though inspirational, was fairly general. I hadn't asked much about tonglen, maybe because my suffering in lay life hadn't festered long enough to provoke me into taking the step of making a commitment to such a new way of practice.

But this time, when I asked about visiting, Monk said with typical bluntness, "It would be best if you prepare your questions so we can get right down to business; otherwise you tend to come with a mind that is somewhat limp."

I got the message and arrived better prepared. Monk encouraged my desire to practice tonglen and gave practical instruction on it. Everything he said was reasoned, though often he would challenge me to look deeper. When explaining that the seven-branch service is done preliminary to practices such as tonglen, he went through each item: prostration, offering, confession, rejoicing, requesting teachings, beseeching the teachers to remain, and dedication. And to each he tacked on the question, "But what does that mean?"

During our discussion I proffered the idea that the lamrim teachings were a sort of trick to help put the mind in order, to renounce, to develop positive qualities. He saw my logic and said there was something to it, but he went into a fuller exposition of the way it worked on the mind and concluded by saying, "No, it's not a trick." When I asked him about teachings on the six realms of existence, he said, "Such things mean exactly what they say—but they don't mean *only* what they say."

I asked if it were possible to just practice tonglen on the spur of the moment, as needed, rather than as a formal meditation. He replied that a doctor doesn't simply set broken limbs on the spot, but must have a thorough training beforehand.

Over the years, we covered a lot of ground, but he always brought me back to the basis of bodhicitta. He spoke from the point of view of renunciation too, but sometimes advised me to focus on talk of love and compassion with people who showed interest in Dharma, and to leave the "Hinayana stuff" for later; I think he also sensed that such an approach was appropriate in instructing me at the time.

When I told him I often felt it wasn't in my nature to be able to develop compassion, he said, "Oh, come now. What makes you think you're such a hard-hearted fellow?"

I often saw Monk before leaving on my many trips to Asia in the following years and wrote him when I was in new situations. He urged me above all to be kind, and not to be judgmental about people. That was an insidious, uncompassionate habit he was easily able to discern from my correspondence, even when I thought I was merely giving an unembellished account of my life and practice in the various places I lived in. Monk was uncompromising but also had the ability to tailor his advice to people's needs. In his last years, he started grilling me on my understanding of bodhicitta. Bodhicitta is taught as having a relative aspect, love and compassion, and an ultimate aspect, emptiness. Most of us Zen types—when I first heard the teachings on bodhicitta I wasn't yet deeply involved with Kobun or the Zen center but was at that point more connected to Zen than to anything else, maybe because I felt it wasn't demanding too much of me—figured we could jump straight to the latter, but Monk early on gave me an appreciation for the benefits of consciously working to develop the former. Later on, however, he didn't distinguish the two but seemed to be pointing at the Big Picture, and he dropped tantalizing hints about what it was like to experience bodhicitta.

But when I was in transition from Theravadin monastic life, I couldn't help approaching other ways with a certain amount of skepticism, often of my own motives. I once told him I thought that my taking up a path like lamrim might be a rationalization.

"A rationalization for what?" he demanded.

I told him I suspected myself of ulterior motives, something along the lines of telling myself I was staying in the world to help others while simply following my desires.

"If a man stops you on the street and asks for directions," he asked, "do you question your motives before you answer him? You just respond and help the fellow out, and that's all there is to the matter."

14

Lord of the World

Karmapa, Lord of the World, think of me.
    —*From* A Far Reaching Cry to the Guru, *Jamgon Kongtrul*

Santa Cruz, California, 1980

Freshly out of monastic robes but still basically homeless, I went to Santa Cruz, where I stayed for a time with Andy, a childhood friend.

Two days after I arrived from Thailand, in September of 1977, he and I attended a talk by the venerable Tibetan Lama Kalu Rinpoche.

A monk gave a brief introduction in broken English, telling us that "the truly realized being in the world" was Kalu Rinpoche. I was fascinated by the monk's big wristwatch, something Thai monks don't wear, and also thought he sounded a little like a TV commercial.

Kalu Rinpoche was elderly, thin, and soft-spoken. He taught on the four thoughts that turn the mind from *samsara*—the preciousness of human rebirth, the certainty of death, the uncertainty of when death will come, and the infallibility of karma—which I appreciated, though it didn't sound like earthshaking news. Afterwards he gave refuge to those who wished to participate. I wasn't sure exactly what that meant, since in Thailand it's common for laypeople to take refuge frequently, when they go to a monastery or even invite monks to their home or business for a meal offering. And I was in no hurry to take on new commitments.

After everything was done, Andy offered to take things back to the Dharma center in his truck. While waiting for the signal to remove the throne we perused a table with religious articles and photographs for sale. Andy picked up a small photo, examining it intently.

"Who's that?" I asked.

"That's my hero," he replied, "His Holiness the Karmapa."

***

As time went by and I dabbled and window-shopped among the various spiritual offerings in the area, I often heard the name Karmapa. But the mystique of Tibetan Buddhism hadn't grabbed me yet. The simple, minimalist approach of Zen started to speak to me, and I felt I was broadening my horizons under the tutelage of Kobun Chino.

In early summer of 1980, the news came around that the sixteenth Gyalwa Karmapa would be making a visit to Santa Cruz as part of his upcoming tour of the United States. At the zendo, we heard that volunteers were needed to help at the Karma Kagyu center across town, Karma Theksum Choling, or KTC. I got a job in the kitchen.

The day before Karmapa and entourage rolled into town, Andy rounded up the crew of his on-again, off-again landscaping business. Mostly a group of over-educated and under-employed Zen students who devoted more time to the big questions than to matters of livelihood, and so were readily available when such events occurred, we sat in the back of the truck with flats of flowers and headed over to KTC, where we tidied up the yard and planted flowers of various colors in the shape of Tibetan mantric syllables.

That evening we had a meeting at the center with someone from the Karmapa's center in San Francisco. She told us to expect a frantic time, especially in the kitchen, and to be ready for the pushiness of the Vajradhatu people—though apart from the high-handed head cook, Trungpa's students were easier to deal with than the Karmapa's. She

explained protocol. When His Holiness arrived we would line up outside the house to welcome him with ceremonial scarves, while his
monks would be blowing Tibetan trumpets. Then she added, "You
don't have to try to control your emotions when you see His Holiness.
It's all right to cry."

***

The grand arrival
next morning, a pha-
lanx of luxury cars and
the procession of la-
mas issuing forth, was
almost a side event to
the chaos in the kitch-
en. We rushed outside
to line up. The monks
had their horns at the
ready as soon as they
got out of the cars, and
the sound of Tibetan
trumpets filled the
street. His Holiness
greeted everyone as
he walked the gaunt-
let into the house, and
then we rushed back
into the kitchen.

"What is this?" the
head cook scornfully

Karmapa XVI, Rangjung Rikpe Dorje, Santa
Cruz, Calif., 1977. Photograph by Bob Shamis.

demanded, holding up a package of meat wrapped in Styrofoam and
plastic. The threadbare ex-hippies and recent University of California
graduates who were the mainstays of KTC Santa Cruz had scraped
together money to buy a supply of steaks from Safeway, but the cook
would have nothing of it. He rattled off a list of what we needed to go
out and buy. "Seven-Up?" he sputtered, looking at the beverages on
hand. "Jamgon Kongtrul likes Sprite!" The beleaguered director of the

center managed to come up with more cash, and I volunteered to go do the shopping, at that point just wanting to get out of the kitchen and away from the house. Another assistant cook offered to help me out, and off we went.

We went to Shopper's Corner, an upscale supermarket with a renowned meat counter, and rushed back to the house. Lunch was finally served. His Holiness ate in his room with Kongtrul and Ponlop Rinpoche, who was a teenager at the time. "He's a little naughty, so His Holiness keeps an eye on him," someone said. "He doesn't eat his vegetables and he drinks too much coffee." The other lamas ate together at a long, low table set up in the dining room. None of us dared to ask about having any lunch ourselves, so we busied ourselves cleaning up and keeping out of the cook's way.

After an hour or so, the dishes were brought back to the kitchen, and a little while later the woman from the San Francisco center offered us some of His Holiness's leftovers. "There's a blessing in it!" she said glowingly.

"Yes, especially when you're hungry," was all I could think to respond.

That afternoon most of the lamas and laypeople went out somewhere. I was alone in the kitchen when His Holiness walked in, holding an empty pitcher and looking very somber. I wasn't aware of his history, but he'd had a stroke a year or two previous and had Bell's Palsy, a condition that leaves one side of the face paralyzed. "Drog," he said, handing me the pitcher.

Not sure what that meant, I followed him back to his room, where I saw a puppy in a large cage. I filled the pitcher with water and brought it back. His Holiness lit up and put his hand on my head.

Recently I've pondered that moment over and over. How often in the succession of lifetimes does a person get to be alone with a Karmapa? Sometimes I think I should have cut off my head and offered it to him on the spot, as aspiring bodhisattvas do in Buddhist mythology.

Later in the afternoon there was a group interview in the backyard. A throne was set up, but His Holiness sat on the edge of it rather than climbing onto the seat. People of various Buddhist persuasions showed up, and the questions ranged widely. Someone asked, "You are said to be the incarnation of Avalokiteshvara, the bodhisattva of compassion. Can you tell us what that's like?" The Karmapa's reply was brief.

"His Holiness says please don't ask him anything about himself, as he doesn't have anything good to tell you," the translator supplied.

Another questioner asked about the principle of the Adibuddha. I'd bet most of the people there had no idea what that referred to—I sure didn't—and His Holiness simply said, "This is a profound concept that can't be explained briefly, and even if I were to explain it you probably wouldn't be able to understand it."

One of the features of Dharma life in Santa Cruz was the frequent presence of colorful, mentally disturbed individuals. I thought it a sign that a center had come of age when such people showed up. They usually drove teachers and Sangha members to their limits with broken-record questions and convoluted reasoning. Some of those folks were present on this occasion, and one said, "In place of wars, I would like to see boxing matches between world leaders." His Holiness replied with enthusiastic applause.

***

The Vajra Crown ceremony was held that evening at a large auditorium downtown. It was one of those events I was sure I ought to attend even though it didn't mean anything special to me at the time. Always looking for a chance to expose worldly-minded friends to something meaningful, I bought a ticket as a birthday present for one of them. She was an aspiring symphony musician. During the preliminary ceremony, when the Karmapa is in the process of actually becoming Avalokiteshvara (the Bodhisattva of Compassion), she remarked with awe about the trumpeter monks holding their notes for a very long time while employing what is called circular breathing.

After the ceremony, the translator announced that His Holiness would be giving refuge. "Those wishing to take refuge should come up here now. The rest of you can split," he said in his immaculately clipped tones.

At least I had enough sense to betake myself to the stage and join the group seeking refuge with His Holiness. I provided him with a giggle when he tried to snip the required bit of hair off my freshly shaved head. The refuge ceremony was brief, and at the end, we received certificates saying that we had taken refuge with the Karmapa and giving each of us a refuge name.

***

The next day I went back and forth to the center. In the afternoon His Holiness and entourage went out to visit pet stores, one of his favorite activities. There was a Milarepa empowerment that evening.

In an empowerment ceremony (*abhisheka* in Sanskrit), a master generates the state of a particular enlightened being, which could be the historical Buddha, a deity from the tantric pantheon, or an enlightened master such as Milarepa—all of whom are considered Buddhas, or wisdom deities. That awakened energy is transmitted to the mindstreams of those present. It blesses the minds of the recipients, helps purify their karmic obscurations, and authorizes, or "empowers," them to do the meditation of the particular deity. Sometimes it is compared to planting seeds in the mindstream. But whatever the case, I had only a vague idea of empowerment then, and also felt I'd had enough for the time being and went home to relax, not thinking even for a moment that it was a once-in-a-lifetime opportunity. I went back to the center at night, after they had all returned.

That morning while out shopping for dinner I decided to eat lunch rather than go back and wait interminably for handouts. I ate at the Bagelry and also got a garlic bagel to offer His Holiness. When I saw him sitting in the living room that night, I went into the kitchen, sliced the bagel and buttered it, put it on the nicest plate I could find, and approached on my knees to offer it, turning my head and looking away as we'd been instructed to do.

His Holiness accepted the plate. I backed away, sat down, and watched. He looked around the room as if to ask, "What am I supposed to do with this?" and then started kneading the butter into the bagel with his thumb and breaking off pieces to eat. He polished it off, which gave me a great feeling and led me to plan on going to the Bagelry at dawn to get more bagels to offer for breakfast. (I got a dozen, for the whole crew. When I told the proprietor the bagels were for the

Karmapa, he said, "I didn't know he liked bagels" and refused to take money for them. Santa Cruz was like that.)

But there was serious deliberation going on. They needed to find a pond in a hurry. His Holiness had bought hundreds of goldfish, probably sold as bait. He was leaving Santa Cruz in the morning and had to find a place to release the fish.

Something scratched in the recesses of my mind. Fish pond, fish pond. Somewhere there was a pond, I just couldn't think of it. I sat there and followed the discussion, hoping they didn't call it a night before I could remember.

Finally I recalled that during the winter we had gone to Kobun's house to help him landscape his yard, the centerpiece of which was a koi pond. I spoke up.

His Holiness was thrilled. But it was getting late. Kobun was away and the only person at his home was his mother-in-law, who lived in a separate unit in the backyard. I called a friend who lived near Kobun. He said that Grandma, as she was known to us, stayed up late, so he would bicycle over there and talk to her and then call us back.

Lewis called after a little while; everything was good to go. When we informed His Holiness he was really happy, and he kept putting his hand on my head and blessing me.

The next morning we offered a breakfast of bagels and Danish pastry, after which the Karmapa gave some final advice to the center members. He told them they were representing the Dharma now, so they should not appear to be bums but should dress neatly and behave well. One of the long-haired members arrived just then. As he did his prostrations, the Karmapa started giggling. "His Holiness says you look like a girl," his translator told the young man, and just in case he didn't get it, added, "You need to get a haircut."

He also told them not to engage in politics, though I wasn't sure if he meant center politics or the politics of American society. "Do your practice. Take care of your responsibilities. I will come back in three years," he said. After he passed away in November of the following year and nothing was heard about his reincarnation for a long time, I often wondered if there was a hidden meaning in that pronouncement, that an infant Karmapa might be living in Santa Cruz, unknown to the world.

Finally he spoke about the fish. Looking at me, he said, "I am appointing you the parent of these fish in my place. I will check on you to make sure you are taking care of them." I have always thought that someday I will meet the Seventeenth and maybe he will remember me, the guy he put in charge of the fish.

Then the entourage packed up, their limos waiting outside. I had talked a few of my fellow Zen practitioners into going, so we went ahead in a van and waited for the Karmapa.

When we got to Kobun's house we let Grandma know we were there. She came out to have a look. Soon after, Karmapa and retinue arrived. His Holiness was still ecstatic over finding a home for his fish and continued to pat my head. Meanwhile, the lamas walked to the pond holding large bags full of water and goldfish.

Lewis rode up on his bicycle. I told His Holiness who he was and his crucial role in the operation. The Karmapa put out his hand to bless Lewis' head, but instead of bending to offer his crown, he shook hands with His Holiness. Fair enough, I thought.

The Karmapa surveyed the pond. He noticed something floating on the surface, a flat piece of wood with a metal cross on it. He asked Lewis if that was a religious symbol.

"No, it's a toy boat," Lewis answered with a poker face.

His Holiness started laughing uncontrollably and finally had to cover his mouth with the corner of his robe.

Then the lamas encircled the pond, knelt at its edge, and started chanting while opening the bags and releasing the fish, the Karmapa standing behind them and reciting. It was funny and touching at the same time. Just as they were finishing, a young couple pulled up in a car and got out. They were going to rent the house while Kobun was away. I explained to them that what they were witnessing wasn't an everyday occurrence at Kobun's place.

***

His Holiness went on to San Francisco. He was gone but not forgotten. He started appearing in my dreams and overwhelming me during waking life whenever I thought of him. I was planning to visit New York while he was in Boston and hoped to bring my parents to the Vajra Crown ceremony there, but it was not to be.

I did drive up to Woodstock one day to Karma Triyana Dharmacakra, his main seat in North America. There wasn't a lot there in those days. Someone gave me a quick tour. The main house contained the residences, kitchen, office, and shrine room. There were a few cabins on the property. I still have the image of one small cabin, not very far removed from the rest of the buildings, with smoke coming from the chimney. A woman had begun a three-year retreat there and after some time at it requested to stay longer. She was going on six years and planning to stay for twelve. It felt like looking at another world, right there in the midst of our own yet separated by an almost unbridgeable gap measured in light years. Here was a person undertaking what many of us feel is the greatest endeavor for a human being, but which we lack the auspicious coincidences, or maybe just the courage, to do ourselves.

In the shrine room there was a large framed photo of the Karmapa on his throne. I stood and looked at it, transfixed. The eyes seemed to look back at me, so much so that I felt he was really there. I had to remind myself that it was a photograph. Years later, long after the death of His Holiness, I received a photograph of the seventeenth Karmapa, a very mature-looking twelve year old at the time, and his eyes had that same living, piercing quality.

***

In the three-plus years since disrobing, work had never been a high priority. Like many young people in Santa Cruz, I felt there were more important things to do, and so I got by on occasional employment, doing whatever jobs I could find—picking fruit, landscape grunt work, home aide. But that winter I made use of my one professional qualification—speaking Thai and Lao—and got a full-time job in a refugee clinic in San Jose. The pay was quite modest, but it was more income than I'd ever had, and I started planning a trip to Thailand and possibly other Buddhist countries in Asia. Going to see the Karmapa in Sikkim—a small state in northeastern India —appealed to me strongly. I wasn't yet interested in practicing Tibetan Buddhism, but he exerted a pull that went beyond lineages and practices. "Ajahn Chah at one hundred and ten percent," I sometimes thought of his presence. Everything else aside, it was no small thing to find someone with even more spiritual charisma than Ajahn Chah.

At a small gathering at KTC in Santa Cruz, a layman who translated for visiting lamas told us of the many illnesses the Karmapa bore as part of his bodhisattva activity of taking on the suffering of sentient beings. But I didn't realize he was critically ill at the time. Before leaving for Thailand, in November of 1981, I went to New York to visit my parents and sat for two weeks of the fall retreat at IMS in Barre, Massachusetts. Late one night at the tea table I met Jack Kornfield. "HH Karmapa died three days ago," Jack informed me. I was deeply saddened. I told him about the connection I felt with the Karmapa and that I'd been thinking about going to Sikkim.

"Impermanence," Jack reminded me, that old Theravadin standby that you just can't get away from.

***

"Karmapa, Lord of the World, think of me," begins a stanza in a prayer to the Karma Kagyu lineage masters. Having met a Karmapa in the flesh, I could well understand why he was referred to in such a way.

When I did finally begin practicing Vajrayana seriously, three years after meeting Karmapa, I signed on with the Nyingmapas, another of the Tibetan lineages. I didn't know that going back to at least the Third Karmapa, Rangjung Dorje, the Karmapas were considered lineage gurus in the *dzokchen* tradition, which is the crown jewel of Nyingmapa practice. Still, along with millions of others in Tibet, India, and the West, I longed for the Karmapa's return in his seventeenth incarnation.

Like all things, remembrance of the Karmapa faded from my daily consciousness. But occasionally I was reminded how deeply he had affected me. In 1998 I was watching a video about the Karmapa. When Osel Tendzin was interviewed after His Holiness's funeral and talked about what he was like, I suddenly found myself sobbing.

Karmapa, Lord of the World, think of me.

15

Lama Gonpo

Think about your good fortune in meeting a lama… There are many lamas, but not many like Lama Gonpo.

—Lama Tharchin

Santa Cruz, 1980

One day in early 1980 I visited Edward. He was enthused over a lama who had recently arrived from India and was staying at Yeshe Nyingpo, Dudjom Rinpoche's center in Berkeley. Edward had invited this lama to give "mind-nature" teachings in Santa Cruz. Those teachings were of utmost profundity and were rarely given, Edward said. They belonged to the highest class of teachings, *dzokchen* or Great Perfection, that were exclusive property of the Nyingmapas.

Out of curiosity, I went one afternoon to hear Lama Gonpo Tseten Rinpoche. Although I didn't get any special impression of the teacher or the teaching from this first encounter, I continued to dabble and usually dropped in for a session when Lama Gonpo came to Santa Cruz, mostly to keep Edward off my back—or so I thought. I figured it couldn't hurt, and I did have plenty of free time.

Lama Gonpo, left, and Monk at unidentified California airport, circa 1982.

Monk, too, came to the teachings with a couple of his students from Los Angeles, two big guys someone called "Monk's henchmen." The first series was at the University of California Santa Cruz campus, a stunning hillside location. The vast campus was graced with stands of tall redwoods and adjoined a state park. During breaks we would go outside and walk around. One afternoon Monk was out with a small entourage. When he spotted me, he genially said, "Well—come to do some window shopping?"

Lama Gonpo's visits continued, at various venues in Santa Cruz. Whenever Monk came, I tried to visit with him. The Mahayana ideal was still something I was struggling to piece together, and now Vajrayana was in the mix. While still emphasizing bodhicitta, Monk started to shift the perspective. The answers to many of my questions, he said, would become clearer once I heard mind-nature teachings. "When you have the opportunity to receive such teachings, run, don't walk," he insisted.

***

Lama Gonpo was pushing *ngondro,* the tantric preliminary practices. I didn't know much about it, and I told myself that such things weren't necessary. A few months later, though, I found myself doing Zen-style prostrations to start the day out. But I didn't yet suspect it could be Lama Gonpo's influence sending me in that direction.

He seemed nice enough, but he didn't project great charisma. When, at the conclusion of one weekend of teachings, enraptured, beaming students requested him to come back, I wondered if I had missed something.

Still, I kept dropping in. "The most secret teachings…rarely given… not many lamas are qualified to give these teachings…his realization is equal to the Karmapa's." And the empowerments: never before given outside of India or Tibet; perhaps half a dozen lamas in the world who can give this. Edward was relentless.

After the empowerment for the hundred peaceful and wrathful deities, an occasion much hyped by my friend, Lama Gonpo brought out a *phurba,* a ritual dagger that symbolizes cutting through obstacles on the path. This one had belonged to Guru Padmasambhava, the main importer of Vajrayana Buddhism to Tibet. It was given to Lama Gonpo by the Dalai Lama in appreciation for teachings—Lama Gonpo, I learned as time went by, had given Great Perfection instructions special to his lineage to several of the super heavyweights of Tibetan Buddhism. When we filed by for the traditional post-empowerment blessing, we received a touch on the head with the phurba as well.

One time, after the teachings were over for the day, invitations went around privately to meet back at the Karmapa center in Santa Cruz for a most special empowerment. I had a long way to go to get home to my cabin in the Felton hills, and I thought I'd had enough Dharma for one day. But before I could slip away Monk caught hold of me and asked if I was going. The way he asked it clearly meant I should go.

As he was my most reliable advisor in such matters, I asked, if this is such a rare empowerment, usually only given to people who had practiced certain things, why was Lama Gonpo bestowing it on this ragtag bunch and on people such as me, who had no particular interest in or commitment to Vajrayana?

"He's very kind," Monk said with an understated smile.

So I drove into town to the house on Belmont Street. Everyone who'd been at the teachings was there.

The proceedings were a little unusual, but having been to few Vajrayana empowerments and ceremonies and not knowing what to expect, I didn't think much of it and just tried to contain my restlessness until it was over. But with Tibetan Buddhist ceremonies, just as you think they're finished there are always more things to be done, prayers, dedication of merit, final advice, and filing past the lama for blessings. Edward said it was good to offer something to make auspicious connection, so I peeled a dollar bill out of my wallet. It seemed like an expensive day, the teaching having already cost me a whole five bucks. Little did I realize the pricelessness of the life-changing empowerment I had just received and the immense offerings Tibetans, and Indians before them, would traditionally make to receive such a transmission.

***

One evening after Lama Gonpo's teachings, which had been given in the living room of the house where Monk was staying, several of us remained to hang out with him around the kitchen table. One fellow recently graduated from University of California was pondering his future. He was thinking of nursing, but Monk said that if he was truly interested in medicine he ought to consider becoming a doctor. I saw over the years that he often gave such advice, urging people to think big in whatever they were pursuing and make full use of their potential. Years later I was considering paralegal work and mentioned it to him. He asked, if I really wanted to go into law, why not become a lawyer; but he also advised me to try to first get into a law office in any position I could, to find out if that's what I really wanted to do. "After all, in the practice of law, everyone is lying about everything," he said.

The discussion went on to careers and work in general. But he never let it get too far from a Dharmic context. He said, "Actually, I don't believe in work." A few people snickered, but he elaborated, "I believe in activity, but not necessarily work," and pointed out how we needed to find what we really want to do and then do it with commitment, focus, and energy.

One of the people there that night was a regular at local spiritual events. He was a great skeptic and resisted committing himself to anything, but he did have a lot of respect for Monk, having known him for a long time. As we discussed the teachings, he kept raising questions, and objections to the answers, that weren't really to the point. I started to feel sorry for him and his *shtick,* which I thought he took pride in maintaining; it seemed he could go on forever asking the same sort of questions without really wanting to get meaningful answers.

Monk said to him, "It's all right to question; but you have to question more deeply."

Without a pause the admission just popped out: "I don't know how."

***

Months passed. I went on with Zen practice and involvement in the Zen center. The following year (1981) I was preparing to go to Thailand to spend some time in the monasteries, and Lama Gonpo wasn't in my thoughts much. I did attend some teachings, partly to see Monk. He was clearly keen on Lama Gonpo. He wasn't trying to sell me on anything, but the hints he kept dropping got harder to ignore.

The Mahayana teachings of Chinese and Japanese origin were not that great a leap from Theravada, but much of Vajrayana was new territory—deity practices, devotion, the sheer number of meditations and classifications, for instance—and took considerable time to digest. The secrecy was another unique aspect of Vajrayana I had some difficulty accepting.

In Theravada scripture, the Buddha compared the way he gave teachings to an open hand, with nothing hidden and everything presented clearly, for all to see equally. But of course in the Pali Canon there are discourses the Buddha gave to ordained people, those he gave to the laity, and meditation instructions of different depth that were geared to the level of the recipients—and the Pali scriptures were not committed to writing until centuries after the Buddha's passing. Lama Rinchen, the resident teacher at Yeshe Nyingpo in New York, said, "Some people will say the Buddha never taught some things, or the Buddha didn't give secret teachings. Maybe His Holiness (Dudjom Rinpoche) comes here and gives teaching to a few people. Afterwards they are talking about it and someone who wasn't there says, 'His Holiness never taught that. I never heard it.' But the others did hear it, and it really was the teaching of His Holiness." I found that simple explanation satisfactory, and it pretty much settled the issue for me.

One mutual acquaintance in Santa Cruz had a different take on the matter. "Those Nyingmapas are really clever," he said. "They say they have the most profound, secret teachings, so they attract all these proud people to the Dharma."

***

In between his visits to Santa Cruz, I also corresponded with Monk. I told him that having a regular job often left me longing for the forest monasteries. The first few years of sporadic employment and relative isolation in Santa Cruz were something of a cocoon-like existence, where I met mostly other spiritually minded individuals and usually had all the time in the world to go to centers, retreats, and teachings. Just the amount of time spent commuting and working now, along with the diverse and generally worldly people I met, had me much more involved in worldly life.

Monk acknowledged the many benefits of monastic living, but as always tried to refocus me on the present and encourage me, saying I certainly was well enough trained to maintain my practice in any situation, and that "as we both know, it's possible to maintain a most urbane mind while living in a forest monastery."

Indeed, my ongoing education was showing me that *samsara* is never perfect, and that being alive in the human realm is often a case of "pick your poison." When I was scraping by with occasional work, usually hard physical labor, I depended on food stamps, low rent, and dicey transportation, and I never considered that a day would come when I might not be fit enough to pick fruit, dig trenches, plant trees, or move large rocks. I bought a used car for two hundred dollars, which meant that I was often involved in getting it repaired and seeing what miniscule savings I had evaporate as a result of that. One Tuesday my home-based mechanic, who worked for five bucks per hour, told me I needed a new brake drum. That night I went to the zendo for zazen, sutra service, and lecture, and for most of the sitting period I found myself thinking, "Brake drum, brake drum, brake drum."

When I got a full-time job working in a refugee clinic in San Jose, I upgraded to a $500 car. It removed the constant worry about every little sound coming from the vehicle, I spent fewer weekends getting repairs, and I was no longer being gassed by exhaust fumes, but the trade-off was that there wasn't much time for anything beside work and commuting, short zazen morning and evening, and a weekend of sleeping in and doing laundry.

On the other hand, I was able to save money. Working with Southeast Asian refugees felt like being back in the game. I was speaking Thai and meeting people from the old neighborhood, and it awakened enthusiasm for going back to Thailand.

Paul Breiter and Lama Gonpo Tseten, Sebastopol, Calif., June 1983, at the now-defunct Muktananda rural center, where Lama Gonpo was teaching a summer retreat.

Part Three

Still Wandering

16

Again within the Culture of Generosity

Do you want to be happy? Do things for others.

—Anando Bhikkhu

Wat Boworn, Bangkok, 1981

To save a hundred dollars, I took a marathon flight from Newark to Bangkok via Oakland, Anchorage, Tokyo, and Hong Kong on the now-defunct World Airways.

Jack Kornfield had prepped me for my first return trip since disrobing four years previous. Jack had taken temporary ordination the winter before, staying at Wat Pah Pong.

Being a timid sort, the privations of forest monastery living were much on my mind. Of course, I looked forward to seeing Ajahn Chah, but I also knew his surprises could be more difficult to deal with than hunger, snakes, and hard floors. Jack had composed an A-to-Z guide: Aches, Bugs, Cold showers, Diarrhea, Endless Dharma talks, and so on. But he wasn't aware of Ajahn Chah's recent illness and surgery.

Luang Por was in Bangkok, which I learned when I visited Wat Boworn and spoke with Western monks staying there, though not in a monastery. I tracked him down at the home of a wealthy couple who had built a luxurious kuti on their property, and I became a regular visitor for the week that I remained in Bangkok.

There is some value in being un-nuanced and naïve. I showed up daily in well-worn jeans, one of my father's old sport shirts, and a straw hat, not thinking I might be out of place among Bangkok's upper crust (the Queen of Thailand even sent a delegation there to offer food one morning). After brief greetings to the servants, I would enter Luang Por's kuti and hang out in the sitting area downstairs with him or his attending monks. When the woman of the house, Mrs. Kesree, or lay visitors came in to see Luang Por, I would be introduced and received with smiles and anjali.

Interestingly, it was only Ajahn Chah who remarked on my humble appearance. I told him, "I have new pants and shirt, but I thought that if I wear them on the streets of Bangkok I might attract thieves."

Without missing a beat, Luang Por said, "When the thieves see you in these old clothes, they'll think you're a thief too and do you in."

If I went in the morning, after the monks finished eating I assisted in emptying and washing the almsbowls. Then someone would invite me to have food. I was probably a curiosity, a foreign layperson with experience in monasteries who could speak Thai. My being a layman allowed them to converse at length without the constraints they might feel when talking to monks.

Being in Thailand as a layman, and spending most of my time there in monasteries and around monks, I quickly started to appreciate a lot of things that passed me by when I was hanging on for dear life in Ajahn Chah's rehab program.

In my appearance and socio-economic situation, I was not much better off than the servants, but I was always treated with respect and consideration at Mrs. Kesree's home. Showing up as a disciple of Ajahn Chah, my resume of having been in robes and my friendship with the Western monks present certainly helped, but when other Western laypeople came to see Luang Por they too were graciously received. And later on, when I was staying in the forest monasteries again, I observed similar interactions between the farmers who were the daily patrons and visiting government officials, generals, tycoons, and society ladies. I didn't think much about it at the time, as it was just the way things are done, but in retrospect it seems remarkable, as do many other Buddhism-influenced aspects of Thai society.

I had brought some humble gifts for old teachers and companions, one of which was a can of ground coffee, quite the luxury item in those days. I presented it to Ajahn Pabhakaro, who was attending Luang Por. A couple of days later I noticed an electric coffee maker in the kuti, and when the can was empty, more ground coffee was provided. For a forest bhikkhu that's heaven-realm treatment, but it also points out the sensitivity and awareness of people with truly meritorious minds, always looking out for what they can do in service to others.

***

The late Robert Aitken Roshi, an American Zen teacher, said he was often asked why he taught so much about generosity. His answer was that all other positive qualities, all the spiritual perfections, grow out of it.

Generosity, or *dana,* is explained as having several facets or levels: giving material support, giving freedom from fear, and giving the gift of Dharma, for example. For Westerners who aspire to the Buddha's way, the first of these often means parceling out donations to a teacher, sangha, or worthy project. These days many people are living on tight budgets and struggling just to pay bills without getting submerged in debt or losing their homes, so it seems like every material offering has to be scrutinized for its affordability and worthiness—especially as it often comes in addition to hefty fees charged for teachings and retreats.

Westerners sometimes have a dismissive attitude toward the practice of generosity: Asians do it because they want to get better rebirths; as laypeople who avoid the hard work of meditation and renunciation, they try to buy their way out with offerings; they are just following cultural norm; and so on. Yet who could fail to notice the easygoing nature of so many people in Asian Buddhist countries, the selfless helping and hospitality that are practically a reflex, the way that meditation seems to come so easily to those who do practice it—this compared with the difficulty in practice and the tense, uneasy character of many of us long-time Western meditators, who find it so hard to take our focus off of "How am I feeling?" and "What do I need?" I am probably not the only person who has had the notion that I would need to practice for a long time just to get to the "level" of so many Asian Buddhists who rarely, if ever, sit down to meditate.

The nineteenth-century Tibetan master Patrul Rinpoche said, "A spark of merit is worth more than a mountain of effort." Dana is taught as a way to reduce self-centeredness and possessiveness, which seems like an excellent route to the avowed goal of all Buddhists, recognizing the nonexistence of self. And obviously, if there's no self to protect, there is no basis for fear. In the various presentations of the Buddha's way, dana often is the first factor. For example, there is the progression of the parami; the summary of the path into generosity, morality, and meditation; and the *nekhamma gatha,* beginning with generosity leading to celestial results, then the shortcomings of the heavenly states of sensual pleasure, and the blessings of renunciation.

***

As in the monasteries, most of the laypeople congregating to see Ajahn Chah in Bangkok were women. But there was one poker-faced Chinese man who frequently stopped in on his way to or from work. One morning he and I were washing almsbowls, and when I had a soapy sponge in one hand and a bowl in the other, he put some hundred-baht notes in my shirt pocket.

I looked at him quizzically and could only think to say, "Why?"

"Disciples of Luang Por should help each other," Mr. Manun replied.

"That's not necessary," I tried to protest, but he just gave a nod and went back to cleaning up.

We got to be friends in the days and months that followed. His expression never revealed any emotion, but he truly had a heart of gold. I received mail at his place for a few years, and whenever I went to pick it up he insisted I join them for dinner. It was quite a production every time: five or six children, his sister and mother who lived there, he and his wife, with the servants and the women of the household constantly cooking and bringing out one dish after another. "This one's really tasty," he would say with each new platter put on the revolving table.

I started going in mid-afternoon, fearing I was imposing on them. But when I showed up outside of meal times, whoever was there would insist I wait while they sent out for food. So I went back to visiting at dinner time and made sure I brought an empty stomach so as not to disappoint them. Occasionally I would bring some dessert, which the kids liked, but Manun or his wife would admonish me that I didn't need to do that.

He pressed money on me occasionally. Finally I became aware of when he was reaching for his wallet and was sometimes able to stop him. Once I brought a friend who had been at Wat Nanachat and was thinking about staying in Bangkok to teach English, and as soon as I introduced him Manun asked with concern, "Does he need money?" and almost had his billfold out before I assured him my friend was fine.

The way I was treated as a layperson in Thailand came as quite a surprise. Of course it was due to the deep and widespread reverence for the yellow robe, not because of my personal charm or virtue. As with the tradition of giving, this may be something that Westerners think of as not really having much to do with the essence of Buddhism, yet it isn't difficult to see how it creates a harmonious social structure that supports the continuation of the sasana and also helps create people who are nice to be around.

***

But it was still puzzling that even in my lay attire, some Thais seemed to mistake me for a bhikkhu. And some considered my past sufficient to give me a free pass in the present. While I was visiting Wat Nanachat, I became aware of a hole in a wisdom tooth and thought that a filling had fallen out. Not trusting provincial dentists much, I waited until I was back in Bangkok and went to the Thai Army hospital, which was walking distance from Wat Boworn, where I was staying.

Tourists in Thailand, if they get up and out early enough, can see people putting food in monks' almsbowls every morning. And in rural areas decades ago it was no small thing for subsistence farmers to be sharing their food daily. But the support of the laity goes far beyond food. The four requisites of ordained persons are robes, food, dwelling, and medicines—in other words, their very lives are in the hands of lay supporters. When you have an infected tooth, it has to be taken care of. Medical care wasn't always the best, but it was offered freely and sometimes alleviated a lot of pain and suffering.

When I went to the Army clinic as a monk, I found the dentist competent, though stingy with anesthetic. On this occasion the dentist—the same guy, I think, though he didn't recognize me—asked me how I found the place, as it was unlikely any Western laypeople were going to walk in off the street, much less know of its existence. I told him I'd been there when I was in robes several years before.

He examined me and said the hole was from decay and that the tooth should be pulled. He gave me a shot of Novocaine this time and yanked it. The fee was a whole forty baht (a dollar and a half, which could buy three square meals at that time), but he absolutely refused to let me pay.

"You were a monk," he insisted.

"But I'm not a monk now," I replied.

"It doesn't matter. You were ordained."

***

The layperson I spent the most time with in Bangkok was Pansak, also an ethnic Chinese. A junior officer in the Thai Air Force, he lived in Ubon city when I was a bhikkhu and came to Wat Pah Pong and Wat Nanachat regularly. He spoke some English and knew Ajahn Sumedho, but we suspected him of wanting to con us into giving him English lessons, something we tried to avoid. But as months and years went by I started to appreciate him as a pure-hearted person, and also noticed him showing up at the most fortuitous moments, usually with a jar of instant coffee and a box of sugar cubes.

He left the Air Force under circumstances rumored to be less than favorable and after that was always busy with some big idea that was going to make him rich. One American monk compared Pansak to Sergeant Bilko, the central figure of an old TV sitcom who always had money-making schemes brewing. He did well with nightclubs in Ubon city, but Luang Por told him it wasn't good livelihood so he turned them over to his brother. He started a restaurant that was going gangbusters, but then his brother started one across the street and ran him out of business. Next was dogs: he got the idea to raise Afghan hounds, thinking he could corner the market in Thailand. But they couldn't take the heat, and he ended up spending a fortune on steak dinners and vitamin injections for them and soon gave that one up. After that came bean sprouts, and who knows what else.

Pansak later told me that in desperation he went to Bangkok with his oldest son and was riding around town on a motorcycle to cut people's grass for twenty baht a house. Yet through it all, he came to the monasteries regularly to offer food, and was available to run errands on the way home, with repeated offers to supply the Pra Farang with anything they needed.

Pansak finally moved his family to Bangkok, where he had his ups and downs for a good while. When I returned in 1984 and went to visit him, his wife told me he was in Samrong Hospital with hepatitis. I took a bus out there one evening. Soon after I arrived an Indian man came in, handed him a roll of five-hundred baht notes and asked after his health, and departed. Pansak lifted up his pillow and added the wad to a big stash he had there. "Everyone is bringing me money," he said. "When I get out I'll give it back." Then he said something I'd heard from other Asian lay Buddhists: "I've made offerings, I've helped others when I could, so I'm sure I will be taken care of."

That was the second time he'd had hepatitis, and the doctor told him that if it happened again he'd be a goner. Sadly, that did happen fifteen years later. But one other thing he said to me then was, "I'm prepared. I've trained. Luang Por has taught us to think, 'If I get better, that's OK. If I die, that's OK.'"

With his wife and five children, he lived in a rented shophouse near New Road. She sold rice and curry downstairs in the daytime, and he got a regular job as personnel manager in a factory in Samutprakan, well outside of town, which meant a few hours a day commuting by motorcycle, often in the rain.

It was tight quarters, but whenever I visited there was always a feeling of spaciousness and family harmony, and of course the usual hospitality. His children were just plain good kids, though each with a distinct personality.

One time he told me that one of his wealthy friends had taken him to the lunch buffet at the Royal Orchid Sheraton. He couldn't get over the lavish spread and the beautiful surroundings, all for some ten dollars. "Just to see the ice sculptures is worth the price," he said. And he offered to "sponsor" me for lunch there on Sunday, only requesting that I first spend a little time to help his older daughter with her English homework.

So we went, and it certainly lived up to his description. Still I felt a little funny being hosted by someone who lived hand-to-mouth.

Through the years the trips to restaurants continued. My offers to take him out were never accepted. His family all called me "Ajahn" and my ex-monkhood probably put me on a special footing with them, but he was quite open with me about most things. We usually spoke as good friends. He often voiced regret about not having the opportunity to practice and taste the truth of the Buddha's teachings.

"You're lucky you never married. What a burden it is having children," he would say.

He wasn't the only Thai layperson I heard this from. I usually answered him with something like "Who forced you into this? Did someone threaten to kill you if you didn't get married and have children?"

Once when he was complaining about some specific family incident, I said, "That's samsara—dogs bite cats and cats bite rats."

He thought for a moment. "And who do the rats bite?"

"Rats bite pillows," I said.

But later on he got some land in a remote spot in Hua Hin, a few hours south of Bangkok, and used to go there to retreat. I was happy to know about that, though I had little contact with him after the early 1990s.

***

Giving Dharma and giving freedom from fear are intertwined with giving provisions. In Thailand, it is considered that ordained people follow the highest calling, renunciation of the world and the quest for enlightenment, and their part in the interaction with lay supporters is to practice to attain enlightenment and to give teaching. Selfless action on any level is a form of teaching; when I see a Buddhist helping others without self-concern, I feel it speaks volumes about what that person has learned and put into practice.

Dharma points out the way to reducing and eliminating fear in our lives. Taking it a step further, anyone who has been around a teacher like Ajahn Chah has a very tangible idea of what refuge means and knows how the presence of an enlightened being can dispel anxiety and fear. "Safe" was the word that most often came to mind when I first found myself under Luang Por's wing, and it was pretty obvious the way people flocked to him that he instilled similar feelings in them. And the kindness of legions of lay donors also gives a feeling of safety, not simply through being fed and housed, but because you become aware of being part of something meaningful and of the fact that there are others who care about your existence.

While Luang Por's reasonable words and wise counsel were always illuminating, it was his being, more than anything else, which gave comfort. He offered his whole life, first to incredibly diligent practice and a willingness to undergo any hardship for the sake of enlightenment, and later to guiding people and making himself available without conditions or time restrictions, even to the detriment of his own health.

The Dharma is always given free of charge in Thailand. No one could conceive of charging a fee for teachings or for staying in a monastery. There is also the fine tradition of printing Dharma books for free distribution, usually with great and small donations from large numbers of patrons.

We experience fear because we are afraid of harm coming to ourselves. If there were no sense of self, no self-cherishing, how could there be fear? And what better and easier way to begin turning the tide of me-focused living and undoing the painful knots of self-concern than to make the habit of giving rather than holding and grasping?

For Western Buddhists, it seems the approach we usually follow is to carefully construct a fortress to protect ourselves, making sure we have provisions, comfort, money, freedom from irritating factors, and so on, so that we can undertake spiritual practice. In defense of my fellow lay aspirants, I will note that monks and nuns don't have to worry about rent or mortgage, taxes, insurance, and inflation; but at some point I think we need to let go and trust the Dharma, trust "the way things are" enough to stop worrying about what might happen in the future. As a layperson doing meditation retreats, I sometimes feel that I practice Dharma like a politician, always negotiating (albeit with myself) about how much I am willing to give up or do, always trying to protect some territory. I think it means an inability to fully practice renunciation, which is the foundation of the path; the habit of generosity, which after all is a very concrete form of giving up, is in turn a foundation of renunciation and greases the wheels for traveling the Buddhist path.

The best wealth empowerment I ever received in the Tibetan tradition was the simple reminder of the Buddha's promise that none of his followers would ever starve to death. Luang Por Chah said similar things to monks, nuns, and laypeople. And during the first vassa at Wat Nanachat, Ajahn Sumedho said that real vipassana meditation means to be able to face any conditions, observe your mind, and let go, and that trying to create a perfect environment so as to make every meditation session just right is "cheating."

Alms round in Bung Wai village, near Wat Nanachat, Ubon Province, December 2010. Photograph by Paul Breiter.

Back Inside

Associating with the wise brings happiness,
Like a gathering of relations.

—Dhammapada

Ubon Province, Northeast Thailand, 1981-82

After a week and a half, I had my fill of Bangkok, never imagining it would be the last opportunity, ever, to hang out freely with Luang Por, to see the Ajahn Chah I used to know. I took a train to Ubon, this time saving a little money by not going overnight on the express. The "rapid train" stopped in the tiny station near Bung Wai village around five o'clock in the afternoon. The young stationmaster was a regular at the monastery, and as soon as he saw me alight, he greeted me and offered to take me to the wat on his motor scooter. A job is just a job, but a visitor is something special.

Being an alumnus, I probably got special treatment from the monks and laypeople, which made me sometimes feel like I was observing safely from the sidelines. But once I was in a kuti, it felt very much like before. The peace of the forest was nourishing. There was a certain timeless quality to staying in a kuti in a forest monastery, meditating at night and hearing the sounds of the forest denizens. Worldly concerns were so far away, and so unnecessary.

When I was a hungry bhikkhu, laypeople who came to the monastery were basically objects, those who fed me. I felt we were supposed to interact with them as little as possible, which may be an accurate interpretation of the rule for junior monks in Ajahn Chah's monasteries. There can be a difference between keeping distance and being indifferent, I suppose, but previously I didn't contemplate it too finely. Now, however, the virtuous atmosphere that pervaded the interaction between the monastics and the laity struck me full force.

In the morning I usually hung around the kitchen to help with whatever I could, occasionally cooking something, and to chat with people I knew from five years previous. Most of them being middle-aged or elderly may have lent an even more unhurried, untroubled air. To me the atmosphere was one of family, people harmoniously joined in doing good. Thai Buddhist teachers often begin a sermon by addressing their listeners as "friends and relatives in birth, aging, illness, and death." No one could argue that we as humans have at least that much in common. The Buddha's teaching was compassionately given to help us out of that predicament, and when we start observing, it becomes obvious that we are not the only ones experiencing dukkha.

To be sure, in monasteries there are disagreements from time to time, squabbles and suspicion and all the other foibles of humans, among laypeople and among the ordained. But it generally takes place within the safe container of Dharma. Resentments don't fester, and most everyone recognizes a purpose beyond their own interests and viewpoints. Those laypeople who don't will usually stop coming; those monks, nuns, and novices who don't will usually leave. It's not that people are all saintly there, or that they are exclusively good. No one expects that—if everyone were perfect, there would be no need for training. But the good side of people is encouraged and reinforced, repeatedly pointed to as that which makes life meaningful.

I soon started to think of the monastery as a center for world peace. But the hardships hadn't gone away, and my reveries were as impermanent as anything else. The floors were hard. I was often hungry. Getting up at 3 a.m. was not easy. The many poisonous critters—scorpions, centipedes, snakes, huge spiders, and weird, creepy things like leaf insects and stick insects—required heightened mindfulness and provoked frequent, though not required, unease. And ants and mosquitoes were still out in full force.

***

When I wasn't contemplating creeping crawlers, I was practicing in the sala with the monks, sweeping leaves like in the old days, and sitting in my kuti and doing walking meditation in the forest. After a few weeks, I took to the road to visit branch monasteries.

But that layman's burden, the future, kept me occupied too: It's peaceful in the forest, maybe I should think about just staying here; but maybe I couldn't hack it; I should pursue Zen more seriously and go to Japan; while I'm in Asia, I should go to practice in neighboring countries. There were questions of livelihood and how I would survive if I went back to the United States. Then I would come full circle and think, If I were a monk I wouldn't have to worry about any of those issues.

Ajahn Sumedho used to say, "There's no need to force hardship on Varapanyo; he torments himself with his own thinking."

One morning at Tam Saeng Pet, sitting silently in the open-air sala before the food was distributed, I was just gazing into space when I felt my chest open. All of a sudden I was breathing freely. The baseline anxiety, the constant undercurrent of mental activity that I'd gotten accustomed to as a layman, subsided for a moment, and again I had to ask myself what was the point of going back to lay life and not just staying in a place like this instead. Why not let dukkha wear itself out and stop making fresh causes for more dukkha? What was to be gained by going back into, what was for me at least, the maelstrom?

Such insights and inspirations don't take place in a vacuum, or a resort environment, however. The living wasn't easy, never was, and probably never will be. You get hungry; you are fully exposed to the harshness of climate. In the afternoon, I would steel myself to get into one of the shower stalls after thinking each day, "Maybe today I can skip the shower, I haven't been sweating much." The water was in stone barrels, which kept it even colder than if it had just come out of the ground. I rubbed a little on my arms and chest to get used to it, but the first scoop I threw over myself was always electrifying. It also cut right through any discursive thinking, good or bad.

There was also my hypochondria. I had experienced plenty of real illness during my years in robes, as had many other monks, and now every time I felt a little bit sick or run down I started imagining I was coming down with some dread disease. A ditty I composed in the previous decade often came to mind:

Hepatitis, meningitis, malaria and worms;
Living in the tropics you can get all kinds of germs.
Dysentery, beri-beri, typhoid and the flu;
Living in the tropics makes a mess of you.

But nothing serious befell me. The side effects of the probably useless and unnecessary malaria preventatives I took were the worst symptoms I experienced.

Lay Westerners kept showing up at Wat Nanachat. Some were just curious, some had experience in meditation, some wanted to ordain. I was close to a lot of the monks I'd known in the past, and got close to several new monks—I generally felt more compatible with ordained people—but I struck up friendships with some laymen too.

One was a Zen practitioner from Colorado. He'd trained at Shasta Abbey in Northern California with the Englishwoman Jiyu Kennet Roshi and recounted the strict practice there. Richard had also gone to vipassana retreats, which was when he got the idea to travel to Thailand and ordain. He came with his wife, who like him was wearing white. There were three or four such nuns (*Mae chee,* who keep eight precepts but apart from cooking and handling money live much as the monks do) at Wat Nanachat at the time.

"Some of these senior monks have a real quality of selflessness," Richard said. "You can't fake that." He was about 40 years old and seemed a steady person. When I came back in April after time in Bangkok and Sri Lanka, he was still there, this time in yellow robes as a novice.

Then one morning he came to chanting in lay clothes. When the morning meditation concluded and we got up to clean the sala, a Thai novice looked at him quizzically, and Richard told him with a smile, "I'm washing my robes."

Soon he and his wife were gone.

When people leave the monastery, traces of them disappear quickly. There wasn't much talk of Richard or his epiphany, but at the fortnightly gathering Ajahn Pasanno, the new abbot, remarked about "insight without wisdom." It was an interesting phrase and seemed to fit the bill. Ajahn Pasanno was new on the job but he was no pushover. He kept a sharp eye on things and, much like Ajahn Chah, would wait for the appropriate moment to admonish people. Chronic complainers didn't get any slack from him. One young American, a student at Harvard, wrote to say that he wanted to ordain and meditate during his summer break. Ajahn Pasanno wrote back to welcome him, explaining that he would be allowed to wear white robes, keep eight precepts, and live and practice as the rest of the sangha does.

He flew to Thailand and came straight to Wat Nanachat. After three days, he was ready to leave. Ajahn Pasanno took it in stride, but without rancor said to the young man, "You're just running around like an idiot. You made a plan to come here, you spent your money and traveled halfway around the world, and as soon as things don't meet your expectations you want to go somewhere else. You might want to cool off and think about it first." But the fellow had made up his mind and that was that.

For me and others who kept coming and going, he gently suggested that we could save ourselves a lot of trouble by making a commitment. "We've got plenty of yellow cloth," he reminded me once.

Being a layperson and thus only qualifying for two- or three-month visas, I had to leave Ubon frequently to renew my visa in foreign lands. On my peregrinations, I visited friends from California who worked in refugee programs, and I started to think about doing that. But the frenzy of the cities aggravated my inner turmoil and made me want to hurry back to the forest to do more serious work.

The seasons changed, I had my ups and downs. I kept telling myself

I was a Zen practitioner and kept trying to fight off internal and external hints that maybe I should hunker down for a long stay in the tank.

But the thought of taking robes started to become a more serious option as the months rolled by. The intensity of monastic life in a genuine practice environment was a crucible, and slowly my path was being forged. As if in a Buddhist morality play or *Pilgrim's Progress,* the first milestone that had to be passed was a sincere attitude of renunciation. Being in the company of people who have renounced the world, and following a rigorous routine that doesn't allow much room for indulging bad habits or much time for daydreaming, tend to move one in the right direction, taking practice out of the realm of theory. My priorities were being realigned, and in retrospect it seems that the more I was able to let go of, the more the horizon widened.

The thoughts of ordaining, born of a combination of inspiration and desperation, dissolved into the mists as I slogged through hot and humid days of summer and rainy season. No matter how you slice it, monastic life is not easy, and the northeast of Thailand is an often-harsh environment.

One of the English bhikkhus at Tam Saeng Pet said to me, after I told him my plans for the immediate future, "Good luck...with whatever it is you're trying to do." As I kept questioning what to do next those words often repeated on me. I wasn't sure where I stood with Zen practice. Kobun had moved to New Mexico and the California sangha seemed to be in disarray. And the practice of *shikan taza,* "just sitting,"which was the mainstay of Kobun's Soto Zen, was producing mostly knots in my back and sore knees.

***

My shopping in the spiritual supermarkets and department stores of California had tilled the soil of my mind and planted many seeds. Toward the end of the trip, I started to feel a pull to learn about the tantric preliminary practices, or ngondro, taught in Tibetan Buddhism. Lama Gonpo Tseten especially came to mind. The seeds he had sown may have been the hardiest.

A few months before I left for Thailand, *Rain of Wisdom,* a collection of songs of realization of the Karma Kagyu lineage masters, was released. It was deeply inspiring and also seemed to be seeping into my consciousness and affecting my view. When I was meditating in a cave at Wat Tam Saeng Pet, I felt that something had changed: the mahamudra-flavored songs made good sense, and I connected dots and felt that the empowerment I had from Lama Gonpo almost two years previous had something to do with it.

As months went by in Thailand, I started to hear the call. I wrote to Edward with questions about doing ngondro. He'd said before that the dzokchen empowerment Lama Gonpo gave in Santa Cruz allowed one to hear all tantric teachings and do all practices. But among other questions, I wondered if it was like a driver's license that needed to be renewed periodically. He wrote back saying that when I returned he would help get me started; it wouldn't do merely to send me a text and have me try it on my own. Little did I know what was in store for me.

18

Heeding the Vajra Call

Although the goal is the same, in tantra there is no ignorance.
There are many skillful means and less hardship.

—*Lamp of the Three Vows*

California, September, 1982

Through a strange set of circumstances, I landed in Los Angeles on my return, even though I was booked for San Francisco. I stayed at Zen Center of Los Angeles for a few days and managed a visit to Monk.

I hadn't seen him for a while. When he answered the door, with a twinkle in his eye he said, "You haven't changed a bit." We chatted for a while over tea, and then got down to business. I told him of my Vajrayana urges and the difficulty I had with "just sitting."

"Zen is the hard way," he said. "Tantra is the easy way." I hadn't heard Vajrayana described thus; it always overwhelmed me with all the detail and the innumerable practices presented. "In Zen, it's pretty much the sitting—either your shikan taza or employing a koan—and if you can't do that, there's nothing else. But in Tantra, you have a whole armatorium to choose from to find what suits you."

I did have some idea of the huge number of practices in Vajrayana. But how does one know where to begin and what practices to do?

"That's where the teacher comes in," he said. I asked about Lama Gonpo.

"Lama Gonpo is in Tibet."

"Not India?" Very few teachers had returned to Tibet at that point. Monk assured me that Lama Gonpo was indeed there. But he said I should be able to start the preliminary practices in the meanwhile.

I went on to Santa Cruz, got instruction in ngondro, and then traveled to New York, as I had planned to do. I lived with my parents in the suburbs, working as my father's dental assistant, and began ngondro. I did it in fits and starts. My life was as unsettled as ever, but I had it in mind to attend half of the three-month retreat at Insight Meditation Society in Massachusetts and then continue working for my father while I began studying *shiatsu*, Japanese therapeutic massage, in Manhattan in the hope of securing a dependable means of livelihood.

∗∗∗

After a few false starts with ngondro, I got hooked while at the three-month retreat. Doing it with a more focused mind, the visualizations came to life, and the practices generally made the mental dust settle quickly. I wasn't sure why that should be, but it was happening. I began to believe that all the big statements and claims about Vajrayana just might be true.

I called Monk from the retreat one night and told him what was going on. "I feel like I've been kicked upstairs," I said—unable to hack Theravada monastic life or Zen sitting, I seemed to find myself suddenly promoted to the highest echelons of Buddhist practice.

"Well, that's the way it is, isn't it?" he responded. "If you'd been happy and successful in worldly things, you would still be stuck in the pleasures of the senses and would never have gotten interested in Dharma."

Ajahn Chah's physical condition had deteriorated during the months I was in Thailand. By the time I left he had stopped speaking, and the illness progressed rapidly after that. It appeared that he wouldn't live much longer, and I was certain I would never see him again (though the old trickster lived another ten years after that, and I got to pay respects to his nearly inert body many times). As I became more committed to Vajrayana practice, Theravada practice and monastic life became a distant memory. Or so it seemed.

***

My worldly circumstances remained precarious. Shiatsu hadn't worked out, but at least instead of doing manual labor I started getting jobs that provided more income for less sweat. I began studying with Lama Gonpo in earnest. The idea that he instilled in me, which reinforced already-existing tendencies, was that work was for the purpose of saving money for retreat.

When I surveyed the possibilities for doing retreat, practicing in monasteries in Thailand looked like the best option. Apart from buying the plane ticket, there was little expense. I would be able to practice in the company of people keeping pure morality, and while monasteries are not exactly retreat centers, distractions would be limited.

So I was back in the loop again. I was able to find monasteries where I could practice on my own with a minimal amount of group activity. Luang Por had described me as *kon nork bunchee,* "someone off the list," and again here I was outside of standard classifications, not completely a part of the Theravadin environment I was living in, while practicing Vajrayana in an environment foreign to that tradition.

***

After a few years of practicing in Thailand for several months at a time and then going to work elsewhere, I was able to do a retreat at Vajrapani Institute in California. It went smoothly and was an eye-opener—no visa hassles, no swarms of insects, no hunger. So I started to migrate my retreat time to that new venue. Once again a backwards man, while Dharma friends worked at home to save money for trips to Asia, I worked in Asia, teaching English in Japan and Taiwan, and retreated in the United States

Visits to Thailand became fewer and far between, and I thought that this time I had really reached a parting of the ways. My comparatively luxurious retreats were getting better and better, and during one particularly inspired session I even thought, "Watch out, Chah, I'm gaining on you!" (He was just a little guy, after all, a teacher of the "lesser vehicle.")

If I actually was gaining on Luang Por, he probably only slowed down to let me get close enough for him to get his hooks back in me. In 1994, I was teaching in Taiwan. There wasn't much work, and I didn't want to spend another hot, humid summer there. I still can't reconstruct the chain of thought that led me to it, but one day I had the idea to visit Amaravati monastery in England.

Ajahn Sumedho and company had taken monastic life to a new level, it appeared to me. I was treated like an honored guest and given comfortable accommodations, which made it easier to appreciate what others were doing. But the energy of the practice in Amaravati was clearly evident. Being able to receive teaching and training and to communicate in one's own language makes it easier to get down to business. Those who came to train and ordain were not necessarily confused wanderers at the end of the hippie trail or shell-shocked Vietnam veterans, as was often the case with farang showing up in Ubon in the 1960s and 70s, and there weren't a bunch of people merely ordained out of tradition. And the buildings were much sturdier than the simple northeast Thailand constructions, complete with electricity and even kettles for boiling water anytime one fancied a cup of tea. Everything was maintained immaculately.

I visited two other monasteries and some old monastic friends who had disrobed. Though I mostly kept to myself outside of meal times and didn't really feel a part of things, it was an uplifting and peaceful time, and I expected to return before long. But Ajahn Chah brought the mountain to me.

***

After circumambulating the world for fifteen years, I ended up back in Santa Cruz, California, in 1996. I'd heard previously of a group in San Francisco sponsoring visits by Ajahn Chah's monks, and I learned at this time that they had just established a monastery in Mendocino County.

Ajahn Pasanno was coming from Thailand to serve as co-abbot, and he would be arriving on New Year's Eve. With nothing else to do, I drove to the airport to greet him. His host in San Francisco invited me to stay the night and join in a meal offering the following morning. Though I told myself I was participating with the status of outsider, I was soon back in the mix, and the newly established Abhayagiri Monastery became a place of refuge. I should have known Luang Por had plans for me.

***

A teacher like Ajahn Chah once encountered is never forgotten. Since then I have studied with several wonderful Buddhist masters, but I never had the same close relationship with any of them that I had with Luang Por. It was close, but in a framework of distance: the Vinaya provides a hierarchical structure for monastic life, for one thing, and Ajahn Chah, while extremely human and humane, was so obviously on a different plane from the rest of us that it was difficult to think of anyone calling him a friend.

Ajahn Chah was no longer my only teacher and spiritual friend, but still he remains a towering (all five feet and two inches of him) and unique figure. Months can go by without me thinking of him, but then every so often something reminds me of what he was like and the full depth of feeling returns. I still dream of him, usually healthy and active. Now, many of his disciples are called "Luang Por" in their own right, having aged chronologically and matured spiritually, but I don't think any of them are considered able to fill Ajahn Chah's shoes, and for me the name Luang Por only brings to mind Ajahn Chah.

19

Thailand, and Me, Forty Years Later

Friends and acquaintances are like passers-by in the market-place—meeting is temporary, but separation is forever.

—*Milarepa*

Thailand, December, 2010

Thailand is changed, Thailand is unchanged. A lot of toothpaste is out of the tube and has been for some time now. But priorities are still in order for a lot of the populace.

Last time in Bangkok was 1996. Today, in the taxi from the airport, speeding along the new system of expressways, I gawk at new high-rise buildings in every direction. A far cry from my first arrival in 1970, when farmers tending their fields could be observed on the way into the city. And from what people will soon tell me, it is a far cry from the city skyline of even five years ago. It looks uncomfortably like a gritty futuristic movie. A couple of days of traveling around town in the comparative luxury of taxis and the new Skytrain system are exhausting. The Skytrain and the subway system can certainly get you to the parts of town they service a lot faster, but there are a lot of stairs to climb and few escalators. The heat from street level rises to the platforms. Travel in daytime means standing all the way. The elevated line takes up a lot of space, making the roads look and feel even more cramped.

How people can endure such living conditions is a mystery, and it's not hard to start thinking that the end of the world has begun. When I see those Thais who are "making it" in the brave new Siam and affecting all the modern ways, the words "displaced persons" come to mind. But it's also not hard to see that many people have retained their grace, good natures, and kindness.

Everyone's got cell phones. I get one on my first night, at a stall in a Skytrain station. A very pregnant lady sells it to me after I say, in my best Thai, "I want the very cheapest phone you have. I'm only going to use it for a month and then throw it away." She patiently sets it up and tests it for me. So for twenty-five bucks I've got a new phone with SIM card and fifteen baht of airtime. I buy another 200 baht worth. Calls in country are about six minutes to a baht (a half cent per minute), international about ten cents a minute.

Ajahn Pasanno arrives the day after me. We'd already planned on traveling to Wat Nanachat together. For him, starting a busy schedule twelve hours after arriving from the other side of the world is no big deal.

I buy postcards in the hotel gift shop to send to people at home. After addressing them I go to the counter to buy stamps.

A receptionists looks under the counter and in drawers. "Sorry, there are no stamps." As I start grumbling to myself, she says, "I can stop at the post office and mail them on my way home." I try to imagine a similar scenario with surly clerks in an American mid-range hotel.

As the days unfold and I spend more time in the monasteries and on the streets, the infectious good nature of the Thai people works its magic on me. Even taxi drivers, an old nemesis, start to appear like great beings. I used to view them as crooks, weasels, and worse, a bunch of rough characters who all exist solely to criminally over-charge me. But now they turn on the meter so there's no haggling. I sit

back and admire them patiently wending their way through the hor-
rific traffic of Bangkok, and often get into friendly conversation. Almost always there are amulets hanging from the rear-view mirror and
Buddha statues and pictures of venerable ajahns on the dashboard. I
find myself adding a tip to the fare, something I never would have
considered before. "He really earns his money," I can't help but think.

Vendors line the sidewalks everywhere, especially in the tourist areas. For non-food items, haggling is expected, but the mood is light
and amicable. It seems a wretched existence, sitting or standing day
and night in the heat and smog, the traffic noise deafening, trying
to earn a pittance. Yet I can't help but notice that people are generally much more cheerful and pleasant than people back home. Maybe
we've got something to learn from these "unsophisticated" folk.

Plenty of beggars too, just as before, cripples, amputees, grandmas,
ladies with small children, small children with puppies.

And 7-Elevens are everywhere, two or three to a soi, on some streets
one every twenty or thirty yards. One can't help but wonder why so
many of those establishments are necessary; but once in action, walking down the street and pouring sweat, it is a great relief to be able to
immediately duck into an air-conditioned shop and get a cold drink.

***

I take Thai Airways to Ubon with Ajahn Pasanno and a Canadian
monk coming to train in Thailand after several years in Canada and
California. There is also an American monk on the plane with his
parents. He looks like a boy, but is the abbot of a branch monastery.
His parents are about my age, maybe younger.

After one hour, we are at the humble Ubon airport, greeted by a
boatload of bhikkhus, several laypeople, and three vans to take everyone to the monastery. We get to Wat Nanachat after dark.

It's not only Bangkok that looks different. The road to the monastery is lined with shops and houses where previously was empty land.
Construction materials are piled outside the sala. We go to sit in a
building that didn't exist last time I was at Wat Nanachat. Vehicle
noise from the highway, once an unpaved and little used road, pen-
etrates into the monastery. The now-ubiquitous fluorescent lights at-

tract swarms of insects. As the monks pay respects to Ajahn Pasanno and exchange small talk with him, I notice it doesn't feel like winter. Still jet-lagged and woefully short of sleep, my knees and back start to protest the reintroduction to sitting on hard floors. How long will the reception last?

Ajahn Pasanno, perceptive as ever and even more sleep-deprived than I, skillfully steers the conversation to accommodations for the visitors. Junior monks snap to, and soon I am ensconced in the VIP room above the kitchen.

It feels like midnight, it's morning in Florida, but it's only about eight-thirty in Thailand when I fall asleep, expecting it will be a chore to get up by dawn. But I wake at 1:30 a.m. After a little while I realize I won't be falling asleep again, so I get off the bed, exercise, and start practicing.

The feeling is at once familiar and dreamlike. The highway has quieted down, the insects are serenading. Meditation is calm and happy, if a little on the spacey/discursive side. At first light I hear the sound of someone sweeping leaves. It goes on and on but fits into the peaceful atmosphere.

When I used to visit as a layman we were expected to be available to help in the kitchen. As the sun comes up a great throng of laypeople appear, arriving on foot and by every sort of vehicle. The monk who showed me to my quarters the night before told me it wasn't really necessary to help out in the kitchen. I can see I would just be in the way.

I look for familiar faces. I've been told that most of the old-timers had passed away. Then I see Por Som. Once the youngster in the group of regulars from Bung Wai village, black-haired and strong, now he is the elder, stooped, thin, and graying.

He is thrilled to see me. We talk for a while and a few other villagers gather. Some recognize me.

"Long time, Ajahn!"

"Yes, fifteen years," I answer.

The women ask if I remember them. I stall for time and say I'm not quite certain, something like, "I *probably* remember you, but not completely sure," the kind of hedging that is acceptable in polite Thai discourse. They explain who is the wife, daughter, or sister of whom.

"How old are you now, Ajahn?"

"Really old—sixty-two."

"What do you do in America? Are you working?"

Paul Breiter with Por Som, one of the elders of Bung Wai village and one of the original supporters and builders of Wat Nanachat, December 2010.

"I just hang out," using that wonderful Lao phrase, *"yoo seu-seu,"* which can cover the whole spectrum of inactivity from base idleness to detachment. They laugh.

Then I notice what must be the primary reason for the legions of food donors: Ajahn Sumedho.

What a wonderful surprise. I had no idea he was there. I knew he had "retired" from the abbotship of Amaravati Monastery in England, but I wasn't aware of his plans or activities.

He is standing near the kitchen, talking with Ajahn Pasanno and the new abbot of Wat Nanachat, Ajahn Kevali. He looks radiant and smiles broadly when he sees me approach. Holding a cane, he appears older than when I'd last seen him (who doesn't?) but looks gorgeous.

We exchange pleasantries and catch up on mutual acquaintances. His plan is to retire in Thailand. Ajahn Kevali says, "We are trying to make Luang Por comfortable here." With a conspiratorial smile, he adds, "We hope he will stay."

It's time for the meal. What a production. The monks take their seats on a raised platform by the kitchen. Ajahn Sumedho says a few words, then Ajahn Pasanno, then the blessing is chanted. The food has been placed on long tables, and on this day, the tables stretch a good twenty yards. Laypeople offer each tray, pot, and basin to junior monks, and then the whole sangha lines up with their alms-bowls to help themselves. Resident laypeople follow them. There is so much food, most of it enticing, but I have to take tiny amounts of each item or my basin will soon be overflowing. Six varieties of rice, noodles, curries, fried and roasted meat, chicken, and fish, chili sauces, raw and steamed vegetables, the usual mysterious-looking items, some local specialties, a huge bowl of salad, mounds of fruit, Thai sweets, cookies and cakes, drinks in containers. The monks go to their eating hall, a new building behind the sala, and the resident laypeople sit in a separate area behind a wall at the end of the kitchen. The rest of the laypeople help themselves to the remaining food, which is still plenty.

I haven't been looking forward to eating one big meal again. I eat what seems reasonable, though by afternoon I will be hungry.

Workers arrive for the rebuilding of the sala. It gets noisy, but I fall into a faint soon after the meal and catch up on sleep.

In the afternoon, I walk around the forest. I'm home again. No matter what changes take place, the forest remains the forest, and the feeling is always the same.

Raised paths have been built, lined with bricks and the earth mixed with gravel, which would make the paths much more passable in the rain. There's similar attention to practical detail everywhere I look.

An outer sala was built in the early 1990s, an open-air building where the sangha can meet to practice without being impacted by visitors in the main area. Like most of the newer structures, it has a tasteful elegance and beauty to it, enough to be uplifting without being excessive. The ubiquitous skeleton-in-glass-case is there, the non-negotiable reminder of impermanence.

That evening Ajahn Pasanno, who is on something of a whirlwind visit of six days before returning to Bangkok to lead a retreat for the Young Buddhists Association, is going to Wat Pah Pong to pay respects to Ajahn Liem, now the abbot. He invites me, and the monastery van takes us with a few others.

Hard to recognize anything on the way to Wat Pah Pong. There are new roads in addition to all the shops, businesses, and houses, and I soon lose my bearings. Ajahn Liem's kuti is near the wall of the monastery. As we speak with him, trucks occasionally thunder by.

Like so many other monks I knew before, Ajahn Liem is now called Luang Por. He had gone from quiet, mindful role model to Ajahn Chah's right-hand man to reluctant and sometimes cranky caretaker abbot during Luang Por's illness, and now a man at peace, and the one the farang monks and other Thai abbots look to as leader and guide.

In the first year at Tam Saeng Pet and after that at Wat Pah Pong, Ajahn Liem was an intriguing figure to most of the farang. His deportment was impeccable, everything done with ease and gracefulness. Ajahn Sumedho, who didn't go in for observing others, said, "Whatever he's doing, he doesn't waste any energy. Once I was trying to cut jackfruit chips for washing my robes. I was hacking away and not getting much done. Ajahn Liem came along and took the machete from me, and he cut a big pile of chips in no time. Then he left without saying a word." Another time Ajahn Sumedho was trying to put together a broom for sweeping the grounds. It kept falling apart when he swept. Ajahn Liem noticed his travails and with a few flicks of the wrist had his broom in good working order.

After my first bhikkhu vassa, I was at Wat Pah Pong and one night dreamed of Ajahn Liem saying that he had no more suffering. I took it as shorthand for saying he had reached the arahant level.

The next morning I followed Ajahn Liem out on pindapat. Walking behind him, I related my dream.

"A person with knowledge doesn't have suffering," Ajahn Liem replied. Then, in the manner of Ajahn Chah, he asked a question and repeated the statement: "Do you understand? A person with knowledge doesn't suffer."

Since I had his ear, I asked more questions about theory and practice.

"People say they can only do what their karma allows them to. Sometimes I wonder if I have suitable karma for being ordained."

"Do you know what karma is?" Ajahn Liem asked. "Maybe I feel like going to Luang Por's kuti"—a pretty good example, since many of us often wandered over there in the afternoon to no particular purpose except to avoid being alone with ourselves—"but I can decide not to go. That's karma I create by my decision."

In Ajahn Chah's tradition, there is little talk of levels of attainment. We were discouraged from watching others, which can easily become another way to avoid paying attention to our own minds. But with that comes an understanding that you never know who might be highly realized. Now that so many monks have ripened after years of good guidance and genuine practice, the cat is out of the bag, the good qualities of many of them obvious without labels needing to be affixed.

***

Next day's meal is another big production. Reflecting on the ocean of virtue, the generosity and harmony. There's nothing to fight about here. It's almost unreal—aren't people supposed to be always contending and squabbling?

Looking from the outside, it can appear that there's not much to the forest tradition, just a bunch of people with shaved heads who have nothing, enjoy nothing, and aren't allowed to do anything except meditate all day. It looks monochromatic and monotonous. And I felt that way much of the time I was in robes, just as someone in hospital would probably feel. (Though it still startles me to remember that for all the difficulty I experienced, I rarely felt bored or lonely—making me think that the emotions aren't what they seem to be but appear in different ways according to the influences of the environment we live in.) But when practice is less of a struggle, the richness and color of the lineage become obvious, and inspiring. Having been away so long, fifteen years since my last visit to Ubon, seven years since visiting Abhayagiri in California, things present themselves afresh; I start to think the wonders of the Dharma would be obvious to anyone.

***

Around midday, we get in the van to go to Muang Samsip and Tam Saeng Pet. Ajahn Maha Amorn, abbot of the former, passed away about two weeks ago. That's why Ajahn Sumedho came, to take part in the funeral ceremonies. The casket is in the sala. We go in to pay respects. The sala is not much different from the time of my vassa there, in 1973.

I try not to think irreverent thoughts. My vassa at Muang Samsip was mostly uninspired and forgettable, a dull ache. Ajahn Maha was in frail health and didn't have much interaction with us. I think at that point he wasn't fully accepted by many in the sangha, who considered him first and foremost a scholar, someone who had pursued book knowledge and reputation and found his way into Ajahn Chah's orbit late in his career.

There were two pindapat routes, and I usually went with Ajahn Waeng, a senior monk with a sharp edge who never showed me much friendliness, to a nearby village. But halfway through the vassa we all switched routes, and I was with Ajahn Maha. His route took us up to the small town on the main road, where shopkeepers and their families greeted him as a celebrity.

One morning it started raining hard before we got to the town. The faithful were waiting with umbrellas for us. It was a lovely sight, but Ajahn Maha refused the offer, so the rest of us had to do likewise.

Grumble, grumble, grumble. I was getting soaked and didn't appreciate the heroics. Then as we finished the alms round and were heading back to the monastery, Ajahn Maha stopped, turned around, and said, "Varapanyo! If you don't think about it, there's no dukkha. No thinking, no suffering."

Well, that's cool, I had to admit, and somewhat mollified tried to endure the trek back to the wat without worrying too much about how many hours it would be before my robes would dry. One of the ascetic practices Luang Por urged us to follow was keeping only one set of robes, and most farang did that.

Back in the monastery we emptied our bowls and as usual dispersed for a while as the food was sorted out by the laypeople. When I returned and took my seat, I noticed Ajahn Maha and all the others wearing splendid dry robes. Big talker, I thought darkly.

But before the vassa ended, one day I went to see him about a problem and he offered heartfelt advice that spoke to my faults. "I'm not trying to belittle you," he said, "but these are things I've noticed," and went on to the familiar themes of my attachment to tasty food and my general desire for comfort. It left me with a good feeling and reminded me of the redeeming nature of the way of life, the constant fresh starts and good intentions, the non-sticking quality of stains.

I only saw Ajahn Maha once after I disrobed. A Sinhalese layman was visiting Wat Nanachat and hired a car to take a few of us to Tam Saeng Pet, and we stopped on the way to visit Muang Samsip.

Ajahn Maha was outside the sala. He stopped what he was doing and received us. He asked the man about his life and commitment to Dharma. Ajahn Maha talked about sila and recommended considering a life guided by the eight precepts. But the poor fellow was having a terrible time staying in the wat and not being able to eat dinner. His face fell when he heard Ajahn Maha's suggestion.

"It's like this," Ajahn Maha said consolingly. "You have five baht, and I want you to have eight baht instead." The man who had been known as a scholar with his head in the clouds had come down to earth over the years.

***

It's dark in the sala so I can't make much use of my new camera. But outside, it's Buddhist Disney World. New buildings, grand stupa, huge statues in Thai and Chinese style, as well as colorful sculptures of animals and people. I click away.

Back in the van, I ask if we can stop somewhere so I can buy things to offer Ajahn Vitun at Tam Saeng Pet. The driver pulls into the next 7-Eleven, where I buy tubes of honey from one of the rural development projects sponsored by the Royal Family, and bags of "3-in-1,"individual packets of instant coffee, sugar, and non-dairy creamer mixed together. Yuck! Ajahn Vitun has diabetes now, but the monks assure me this is the popular choice and I can't go wrong by offering it.

The monastery van is big. I sit in the back with the young monk's parents. By now they have learned something of my resume, and the father strikes up a conversation. "Your book saved our son's life," he says. "It saved us too.

"Our son was very confused when he was younger. I was in a bookshop in Monterey one day and I saw *Still Forest Pool*. I took a look at it and I thought he might be interested, so I bought a copy and gave it to him. And now here he is. His becoming a monk has helped us a lot too."

Earlier in the day, Ajahn Kevali told me he decided to come to Thailand and Wat Nanachat after reading *Venerable Father*. It's always gratifying to hear things like that. It provides me with a valid excuse for taking up space in this world. "He wasn't the greatest person, but he left some good books behind," I often imagine people saying *in memoriam*.

Ajahn Kevali was inspired to lead the homeless life through reading *Venerable Father*, Paul Breiter's account of his life with Ajahn Chah. Wat Nanachat, Ubon Province, December 2010.

The town of Amnatjaroen is barely recognizable, like most places. But the road to the monastery is about the same—still not much there. It runs three kilometers from the main road, then a winding climb up the mountain. The road up the hill, hacked out of the forest in the late 1960s by a work gang of monks and novices under Ajahn Chah's direction, is now paved.

One of the best features of Tam Saeng Pet is the open feeling on top of the hill. The familiar black rock is a welcome sight. We park and walk to the huge open-air sala. A monk comes out to greet us and then goes to fetch Ajahn Vitun.

He lights up when he sees us, and further at the sight of me. Seventy years old now and said to be in poor health, he looks pretty good.

Ajahn Vitun asks me the same questions everyone else does. Then he says, "I still remember the words of Varapanyo, even after all these years!" I'd known him at Wat Pah Pong and visited Tam Saeng Pet several times as a layman. I always appreciated his easygoing manner and open-mindedness.

Paul Breiter with Ajahn Vitun, abbot of Wat Tam Saeng Pet, Amnatcharoen Province, December 2010.

Ajahn Pasanno asks about his health. Ajahn Vitun says his doctor got him off medications and told him to adjust his diet. "I control it myself now. I can tell what affects it," he said. "I don't eat much sticky rice." When I used to stay there the food was often meager, and it would have been hard to get by not eating much sticky rice, which has high glucose content. But now Tam Saeng Pet, like so many other monasteries, is well endowed. I wonder what Luang Por Chah would say. He originally refused to allow a fund to be set up for food at Wat Pah Pong, though in later years he relented, after the monastic population had grown along with instances of malnutrition.

I ask after my old cave. "It's still there, waiting for Varapanyo to come back," Ajahn Vitun says. After I offer the honey and coffee, he adds, "Oh! Varapanyo hasn't forgotten me! Now you're really welcome to come back." It was very sweet. Then he adds, "Varapanyo's not old."

I remind him that I am 62—he had just asked my age a few minutes previous.

"I know, but you don't look old."

"It hurts all over," I tell him.

"That's just *tammadah*," Ajahn Vitun responds.

Tammadah, "ordinary" or "natural," is a Thai word of Sanskrit origin that has begun to intrigue me in recent years. It is the Thai corruption of *dharmata*, usually translated as "suchness" or "the true nature of reality." I have started to wonder if it there is, or once was, some implicit or instinctual understanding by Thais that the ordinary and everyday is not separate from ultimate reality.

Like the other places, a lot of building is going on. There is an enormous reclining Buddha and a grand stupa, and other projects in the works. We take a walking tour and see the monks laboring.

The stupa has a glass case inside, filled with rare relics offered by a man from Bangkok who spent a lifetime gathering them. But my camera battery dies. It's disconcerting, making me think my merit is insufficient.

***

Back in my room at Wat Nanachat, I take out a laptop to enter impressions from the day and upload the photos, then plug in the adapter to charge the camera. After that I charge my cell phone. Not your grandfather's forest monastery experience. But still I don't feel that far from my old cave.

***

The next day's trip is to Monastery of the Beautiful Forest in Ampher Detudom, where I spent my first bhikkhu vassa. I tell the monks in the van, "The people were taller than the trees when I lived here." But now it's a mature forest. Like many other wats they've been able to accumulate adjacent land. Ajahn Anek too has become a prolific builder. He's created a unique and pleasant grotto around his kuti and has a lot of amazing Buddhist artwork carved in stone around the monastery—carved by him, I'm told, though no one knows where he learned his craft. He also is a dog lover and has an entourage of canines, and has put in a huge fish pond, teeming with catfish. He too is now called Luang Por, and his presence—happy, humorous, radiant, short and starting to round out—reminds me of Luang Por Chah more than any other Thai monk.

He was at Amaravati when I went there in 1994, and now he recounted our conversations from that time.

"I asked Varapanyo, 'How come you never visit my monastery?' and he said, 'I'm afraid of Luang Por!'" When I was still a bhikkhu, he once told Ajahn Sumedho he worried that I resented him for the arduous training he put me through during my first bhikkhu vassa. It was a surprise to hear that. I long accepted that it was part of the package of submitting myself to Ajahn Chah, and I was truly grateful for the way Ajahn Anek had helped lift me out of the morass of hopelessness.

He shows us the site for the chapel (Uposatha hall, or *bote* in Thai) he wants to build. There is a Buddha statue he's working on, which he says weighs six tons. Once the bote is built he'll figure out how to get the Buddha inside.

We (the no-nonsense farang, who knew better than anyone except maybe Ajahn Chah) used to be skeptical of ajahns with ambitions to build things. It seemed like the abbots of the branch monasteries were in competition to have the biggest and newest sala. And why be so concerned about Buddha statues when we're supposed to be uncovering the real Buddha within? But now I can appreciate such reverence for the physical representations of wisdom and compassion. And in a time where it's hard to get people to practice according to the letter, providing opportunity for generosity and virtuous effort in building monasteries and statues, creating places and objects worthy of worship and respect, all of which can inspire reflection on what is meaningful, may be one of the best things the sangha can do.

But on this trip sitting on the hard floors in "polite posture," with legs folded to one side, is murder. Knees hurt, spine is crooked, neck stiffens up. These courtesy calls take a toll. How long can I last? And while I contemplate that, it's time to get ready for another cold shower.

***

I walk along on pindapat some mornings, to Bung Wai village, where Ajahn Kevali and Ajahn Pasanno go. The first house used to be about a kilometer from the wat (which I seem to recall being stipulated as the minimum distance for a forest monastery to be from the nearest habitations, and which was the case at all the monasteries I stayed in when I was in robes, most of them one and a half to two kilometers from the nearest village), across the highway and up a dirt road. Now there are houses right outside the wall of Wat Nanachat. The road leading to the highway sports a big pink concrete house, next to which workers thresh rice with a big machine. Ajahn Pasanno points out these new features of rural life as I take my camera from its case. I aim at a water buffalo in the field across the road. One of the monks says, "It's good to get a picture of that. It's an endangered species." They used to be as much a part of farming life as the sun and the rain, but mechanization is consigning them to the dustbin.

The road is now paved all the way into and through the village. New houses, no doubt sturdier than the old-style wood structures but mostly either garish or lacking in character, are everywhere. A convenience store, coffee roaster, and travel agency mark the beginning of the village. Previously there might have been one or two pickup trucks in all of Bung Wai village, maybe a few motorcycles, but now shiny new vehicles are everywhere. Satellite dishes and a mobile phone store complete the picture.

But the faithful still come out to offer sticky rice. They look like the same weather-beaten old farmers who lined the village streets in the 1970s, the only missing element being the old man who always used to confide in us as he dropped rice into the bowls, "It's not cold today, but there's a wind" or "There's no wind today, but it's cold." Dogs and chickens everywhere, though designer breeds of dogs are now part of the mix.

We used to get mostly rice, maybe a half-bowlful or so. Now there is such abundance that someone has to follow with a pickup truck so the monks can keep emptying their bowls into basins and buckets. Plenty of fruit and wrapped items now.

We go by the small village monastery. I never paid those places much attention, as they are not known as places of practice, discipline, or even much study, often functioning mainly as social centers for the villages they are located in, but now I notice exquisite little stupas lining the wall of the wat. One lady waits just past that wall to make her food offering. I am a respectful distance from the end of the line, snapping away with my Nikon. The lady stops me.

"Wait. Take this."

I thought she means there's more food to offer that wouldn't fit in the last monk's bowl. But I look at her basin and it's empty.

"Take what?"

"Take my photo!"

She puts on her straightest face to pose and I shoot. But afterwards I think, "She didn't give me her e-mail address" so I could send her a copy.

***

Ajahn Pasanno takes the day off from travel. I wash some clothes. A young layman solicits my advice on ordaining. Usually I tell such questioners to take their time and consider thoroughly, give it a chance as they stay in the monastery and undergo the training. It feels logical to add things like "It certainly can't hurt you" and "What else do you have to do that's so important?"

It's still so hot! Glad I came in "winter." Is it me or are the winters always warmer? It seemed that way when I used to come frequently in the 1980s. I can't begin to imagine what it would be like to spend hot season here.

We visit Wat Pah Pong again, in daytime. I wanted to walk by some of my old kutis but am assured that they're all gone. One of the old models near Luang Por's kuti, which was a new model then, is still standing, looking like it should have a sign designating it a historical heritage site. To my disappointment, we walk by Luang Por's kuti but don't stop to soak up the vibes. It was always the most incredible spot in the monastery, even when Luang Por wasn't there.

New eating hall that can accommodate hundreds of monks. New statues and kutis. The Ajahn Chah Museum at the entrance to the monastery wouldn't look out of place in San Francisco or New York. In front of it is the statue of the Buddha standing with one hand up in the gesture of telling people not to quarrel. Luang Por was keen on that one. He also liked the two-handed version. "People are really stubborn these days, so you've got to be more forceful," he explained.

But I am waiting for Ajahn Pasanno and the other two monks to finish talking with Ajahn Liem, so I don't go inside the museum. Anyhow, I've toured it once before, on my last visit 15 years ago. And still waiting for the Varapanyo Wing.

After passing Luang Por's kuti we walk through the forest to a place where there are steps going over the wall, the shortcut to Ajahn Chah's stupa. There is a wide path parallel to the wall, wide enough for vehicles. We pass the site of a well, now filled in. All the water comes out of taps now, from the many huge storage tanks throughout the monastery.

***

It cools off on my last full day at Wat Nanachat, before I leave to visit an old friend who is working in Laos. "Now I can get out there and sweep some leaves," I think, and then consider that if everyone was like me we'd be knee deep in leaves. Now I remember what cool season used to be like and why it was such a respite from the rest of the year.

One of the layman, an energetic Irish fellow, corrals me and asks about the old days. "You contributed so much just by being here then," he says. I look around and take stock of all that has grown from those humble beginnings and think he might be right. "There are many joys in being here/And just to see it through is something gained," goes a verse written by a Chinese hermit of old.

Walking through the forest, thinking about leaving, I start getting sentimental. Nostalgia wells up and I'm flooded by memories; but when I think how many of the people I remember so fondly are now deceased or infirm, anicca hits me like a blow to the stomach. I get one of those rare inklings that impermanence might apply to my existence as well.

The next morning I say goodbyes. I tell Por Som, "Next year meet again."

"If the breath isn't finished first," he responds, which is what people there will say.

"Don't let it finish," I tell him. He half-rolls his eyes.

***

Though I've done my share of traveling, I've never been much of a tourist. But having bought a new camera, having spent a bunch of money to make the trip, and not having been in the neighborhood for so long, I thought I ought to have something to show for my efforts. I got a few hundred photos of the monasteries and Bung Wai village. After returning to Bangkok, one day I take a taxi to the old part of the city, where Wat Boworn and other grand temples are located. I plan to pay my respects at Wat Boworn, take a tour of the Grand Palace and Temple of the Emerald Buddha and maybe Wat Saket, the Temple of the Golden Mount. I stayed there as monk and layman a few times. The abbot, Chao Khun Prom, was a lovely old monk.

It was 1986 when I last visited Wat Saket. The residential area was divided into square compounds, with courtyards in the center. Chao Khun gave me a room in his compound. It's a Mahanikaya temple but looked neat and clean and showed a firm hand in charge of things. No raucousness from the temple boys, who used to run wild at Wat Boworn.

A friend was in town on a visa run from Japan, and one evening I came back at 10:30. The heavy double door was locked from the inside. I meekly knocked, and who answered but Chao Khun himself.

"Ten p.m. we lock the doors," he gravely informed me in his deep voice.

Shamed and remorseful, I tried to be invisible after that. One night Chao Khun knocked on my door. "Come out and chat," he said.

My reason for being in town, along with helping my friend, was that Ajahn Sumedho was coming from England. We talked about the old days a little. Chao Khun said, "I come out here at night when it's quiet and meditate." He stood up, looked at the sky, and said, "The sky is not good." An interesting statement, I thought.

The next evening when he was sitting outside I offered him a calendar with Tibetan art I had brought from Nepal, where I'd been a couple of months before. He accepted it appreciatively and started studying it.

"And what meaning does this have?" he asked, pointing to a form of Guru Padmasambhava with consort.

I explained the symbolism of method and wisdom. He took it in thoughtfully. "That is the master who established tantra in Tibet, Padmasambhava."

"Oh, right," he remarked, "Patumasompop," which would be the Thai corruption of Guru Rinpoche's name. I was surprised that it was familiar to him.

***

On the way across town, we pass the palace grounds, traveling down fine, tree-lined avenues, a rare sight in Thailand. Then we turn toward the river, and the Marble Temple, Wat Benchamabopit, appears on the left. I'd been there several times in the past, but now it looks especially splendid. The buildings visible from the road have probably undergone major cleaning or renovation lately, and the sight of them makes me think that even in the crazed atmosphere of modernization people still have the same priorities they always did.

Banglampoo district, where Wat Boworn is located, looks mostly unchanged from thirty or forty years ago, the most glaring differences being the presence of 7-Elevens and people using cell phones. Most of the buildings are the same one- and two-story shops and row houses. The sidewalks are still filled with vendors, the streets dense with people and vehicles. Even the Number 56 bus still stops there and doesn't look much different from when I first took it in 1971. The spires of Wat Boworn dominate the skyline.

Entering the temple compound I am greeted by familiar sights: the canals, the main chapel, the same buildings that were there decades ago, seemingly the same Thai people, with a few Western tourists. I head first to the chapel and go inside to pay respects to the gilded Buddhas.

The building is now open to tourists during the daytime, with the front area where senior monks sit roped off. But decorum is maintained. People offer incense and prayers or sit silently, meditating or just taking a breather from the twenty-first century. I sit for a while and memories overtake me. This is the building in which I first heard about the teaching of the Buddha, and this is where I took novice ordination four weeks after that. It doesn't look or feel any different now.

After that I walk around the wat, taking photos, marveling at new and refurbished shrines and buildings, gazing fondly at old ones. After traversing the whole place, I come back to the area where farang monks used to live. There is now a beautiful new building, several stories high, glassed in, air-conditioned, complete with an elevator.

Going inside for a look, I encounter a young Thai monk coming down the stairs and ask if there are farang monks in residence.

In a mixture of Thai and English he explains that one Western bhikkhu lives in the monastery, and he gives teachings, leads meditations weekly, and is available to answer questions at certain hours. The Thai monk leads me to the Westerner's kuti, but it's locked. Then he tells me there is a visiting English bhikkhu. With a little cajoling I get him to take me to see the fellow.

On the way there I ask how long he's been ordained. He says, "This is my second time, actually. I was a monk for three years when I was twenty."

"Oh. Where was that?"

"In Ubon, at Luang Por Chah's monastery. I also lived at Wat Nanachat, the monastery for foreign monks."

Small world.

Pra Robert lives in one of the old wooden kutis. The Thai monk goes upstairs and knocks on the door. An elderly Westerner comes out and invites me up.

After brief introductions, we settle down to a long conversation. The time ticks by and my compulsion to go sightseeing fades away. This is a lot more meaningful, I am thinking—anyone who wants to see pictures of the Grand Palace can look online.

It's an experience I've had countless times, mostly in Thailand but in other Buddhist societies too, and in the West as well. Those who follow the way of liberation and compassion are a true family, and there is instant familiarity and warmth. At the end of our conversation, Pra Robert says, "Well, it's wonderful that you could come back to see your old friends and the places you lived in." I tell him that these are the kind of friendships that are meaningful and stand the test of time, becoming even stronger rather than fading away, based as they are on high purpose rather than confused emotion.

And this being Bangkok, I am mindful of the hour. If I don't get in a taxi by three o'clock I could be stuck in traffic for a long while. Even so, the trip back across town is a crawl much of the way. The driver and I work out a route between us. It often seems these guys are newly arrived, or the regular driver's brother is filling in for him, because they don't know how to find a lot of places. This guy keeps mixing heavily accented English with his Thai so I'm not perfectly sure what we are talking about, but I manage to steer him to the hotel.

***

There were several people I hoped to visit, but Ajahn Pasanno and others have filled me in on the ravages wrought by time and impermanence. Some are dead, some have moved, others are too infirm to receive visitors. But Ajahn did have the address of my old friend Mr. Manun. On my next to last day in Thailand, I take the Skytrain to the end of the line and get a taxi for the remaining miles to Soi 64.

I remember that Manun has long since moved his family out of their cramped quarters, where I was a regular visitor and recipient of his great hospitality in the early and mid-1980s, into new digs. I visited the new place once, in 1988, which was the last time I saw him. The property was about an acre in size, with several buildings, including one for visiting monks to stay in, and even a kidney-shaped pool.

There is a gate with a buzzer and call box. I ring and the gate slides open, no questions asked. I walk inside but don't see anyone. So I peek into the first building, then walk around back. A servant girl comes out, followed by a woman I recognize as one of Manun's daughters. She looks at me quizzically.

"Is your father home?" I ask. She says he is.

Realizing that she isn't sure who I am, I ask, "Do you remember me? I used to visit your father when you lived on Soi Watanawong. But it's been a long time."

She still looks uncertain, but not concerned, and leads me back to a large kitchen. Manun recognizes me instantly, letting out a loud "Ohhoh!"

"Long time, long time," he says, shaking my hand. He reminds his wife who I am, and, ever true to form, asks what he can serve me: lunch, tea, coffee, fruit...

"No problem, I ate before I came," I truthfully reply.

They invite me to have a seat in the stifling kitchen and interrogate me further to make sure I'm not just being polite about not needing food. Then they barrage me with offers until we settle on tea, a good-natured process of negotiation similar to what I used to do with my dear departed Jewish grandmother every time I visited her. Manun gets out his best tea, prepares a pot, and suggests we move to his air-conditioned office, obviously sensitive to the way a non-native will feel in the heat.

He's been retired for several years. "We can't just keep working our whole lives," he says, which is good to hear. Having lived in Taiwan, I am aware that Chinese often view retirement as a death sentence. Manun is now seventy-two but looks well, his hair still black.

The tea comes, along with some sweets and orange slices. "So happy to meet again," he keeps repeating, in the conversational usage that omits pronouns. He asks what brought me. I tell him I've wanted to visit Thailand and the monasteries for many years and finally got around to it after several false starts.

"We are truly fortunate people," he says, "meeting the Dharma, meeting Luang Por Chah. Teachers like that are so rare." He is full of enthusiasm for Dharma. He meditates every day, as much as he can. "I can still sit in the Vajra posture," he says, and gets on the floor to show me. I hadn't heard that term in Thailand—it's what Tibetans use for what Westerners call "full lotus."

"I don't go out much unless it's really necessary. Socializing is a distraction. At night I prefer to do walking meditation outside here."

He still supports monks and monasteries. He and his wife are proud to tell me that their oldest son is a bhikkhu of eighteen vassa, now living at the monastery of the most revered Ajahn Mahaboowa in Udon province. They don't mention anything about the other five children until I ask—the bhikkhu is clearly the one who brings them the most satisfaction.

"Developing the mind with meditation is really necessary," Manun says. "It gives us strength to deal with situations and to face down the defilements. Watch out for defilement! Don't let it trick you. It's dangerous! Keeping good morality is so important.

"I don't forget the words of Ajahn Chah. I still listen to his teachings on tape and read Dharma books. What good fortune we have!"

A small Audi is parked in the driveway. I'd half-expected to see the ancient green Mercedes he used to drive, about as conspicuous as he ever got in his consumption. People used to ask him why he didn't get a newer model. He would tell them, "Luang Por Chah sat in this car! I will drive it as long as I can."

He says he exercises regularly, because it becomes a necessity as we age. I ask what exercise he does, and he gets up and shows me his Chi Gong moves. I can feel power coming out of him as he does them.

The hours pass as we discuss Dharma and mutual acquaintances and I fill him in on my life to date. He keeps reminding me of our good fortune and says, "I do my best to practice. I always make the aspiration, 'At the least, may I reach the first rung on the ladder in this life,'" meaning stream entry. "I will wish that for you too. I don't know if I can make it in this life, but that's my aim."

I tell him that someone such as he, with such a virtuous mind, can be confident, and I mention that there are teachings that point out the moment of death as a special opportunity to achieve liberation. He listens thoughtfully. Chinese Buddhists in Thailand usually are more open to things outside of orthodox Theravada. Unfortunately I am tiring after the hours of conversation, and my ability to explain things in Thai, already pretty shaky after years of disuse, is proving inadequate.

Ajahn Mahaboowa, now ninety-seven years old, is critically ill. Manun is on call for anything that is needed. "Sometimes I fly to Udon and come back the same day. There's a first-class Chinese herbal doctor I know here. I may take him to Udon tonight or tomorrow morning." So as evening approaches I take my leave, with many heartfelt invitations from Manun to come visit again.

***

I walk up Soi 64 to get a taxi on Sukumvit Road back to the train station. Once I get into the air-conditioned cab I think maybe I should just ride it all the way back to my hotel, but soon we hit a wall of traffic and start creeping, which is what usually happens when you take a taxi at any time or any place in the city, so I get out at the On Nut station.

Back in my room, rejoicing in the lives of Manun and so many others wells up spontaneously. It's something that keeps happening. Goodness must be infectious. It is so rare for me to be able to look outside myself and be aware of others, much less care about them, to empathize with their troubles and rejoice in their upside. Hardheartedness, competitiveness, envy—it doesn't take much to fall into those habits. But meeting up with genuine spirituality naturally provokes positive reactions. I visited Abhayagiri in the spring, didn't do anything there but talk with people and walk around the property with Ajahn Pasanno, yet the morning after when I was practicing I was suddenly filled with happiness and rejoicing about the mandala of virtue created and maintained by Ajahn Chah's disciples.

Ajahn Sumedho once remarked on the trappings of ordained life, saying, "Monks are unthreatening. We shave our hair off. We don't have any adornments. We wear sheets of cloth." So how could one not have positive feelings after being around them?

Well, the water buffalo are said to get spooked by the sight of ochre robes, and we were always cautioned to keep a safe distance. Some people likewise feel threatened by the symbols of renunciation and immediately start blurting and babbling: "I don't see why I should have to give up my way of life!" When I mentioned that to Ajahn Sumedho once, he said, "That's the value of the robes!" But it's hard to feel competitive with people who have nothing and want nothing other than peace for themselves and wellbeing for all.

The day I leave, when boarding the China Airlines flight for the first leg of the trip home, I look at the newspapers on offer and select a Thai-language paper just to see if I can still read it. And there on the front page is news of Ajahn Mahaboowa. In critical condition, he has just been brought to a hospital in Bangkok, and the prognosis is not good. After I get home, I will search the Internet in English for news of him, to no avail, and then thoughts of him fade into the background for me. A couple of months later I will find out that after a short time in Bangkok he made the decision to return to his monastery, wishing to pass away there.

***

I used to look back nostalgically on the early 1980s as "Thailand's last gasp," before it became a major tourist destination, before the waves of foreign investment led to the construction boom, the mad race to modernization, and hordes of nouveau riche. Maybe it also felt that way because I was always on a backpacker budget and stayed in temples and cheap guesthouses in the older part of town and rubbed elbows with the hoi polloi on the buses and at sidewalk eateries. Now that I am not thirty-five years old, it's certainly less stressful to stay in decent hotels, take taxis instead of buses, and enjoy the splendor of air conditioning while eating. But maybe I miss something. The closer you get to the major tourist areas, it seems the people are a little harder; but still something shines through. The place has a few gasps left, I think.

I might miss Thailand.

Glossary

P.=Pali; Skt.=Sanskrit; Th.=Thai; Tib.=Tibetan; J.=Japanese

Ajahn (Th.; P. *acarya*)   Teacher. In Thailand it is often used as an honorific for monks of even a little seniority.

anagarika (P.)   "Home-leaver," i.e., one who takes ordination. Commonly refers to white-robed monastics keeping eight precepts.

arahant (P.)   The final level of enlightenment in Theravada Buddhism, literally "one far from afflictions" or "one who has destroyed the enemy."

Ariya (P.)   Noble Ones, those on the levels of enlightenment.

bhikkhu (P.; Skt. *bhikshu;* Tib. *gelong*)   "One who sees danger" in the round of existence; one who begs; a fully ordained Buddhist monk.

bodhicitta (Skt.)   "Mind of awakening." It has relative and ultimate aspects. Relative bodhicitta means love and compassion for all beings, subdivided into aspiration, the wish to benefit all beings, and application, doing something about it, primarily through practice of the six *paramita* (see below). Ultimate bodhicitta is realization of emptiness. As with many Buddhist concepts, it can take on additional meanings in tantric contexts.

Bodhisattva (Skt.)   "Awakening being," one who vows to attain Buddhahood in order to liberate all beings.

brahmacarya (P.)   The pure or holy life, specifically, the way of celibate ordained people.

Ch'an   The Chinese name for Zen, derived from the Sanskrit *dhyana* (see *jhana*).

cetiya (P.)   *Stupa*, a reliquary and symbolic representation of enlightened mind.

dependent origination   The doctrine that everything arises from causes and that nothing exists independently. Traditionally it describes the cycle of existence in twelve "links," beginning with ignorance and ending with suffering and death.

defilements (P. *kilesa*; Skt. *klesha*)   The mental and emotional hindrances that keep the mind in a state of suffering. Also rendered as "afflictions," "conflicting emotions," and "poisons," they are usually categorized as three: greed, hatred, and delusion. Some classifications add pride and jealousy.

deities (P. and Skt. *deva*)   In Theravada Buddhism, this refers to the highest realms of *samsara*; after the good karma that leads to rebirth in realms of pleasure is exhausted, the beings there must take rebirth elsewhere. In Vajrayana, deities can be samsaric or they can be Buddhas.

desana (P.)   Sermon, Dharma talk.

Dhammayuttika Nikaya or *Dhammayut* (Th.; P. *Dhammayuttikanikaya*)   The smaller monastic group in Thailand, founded as a reform movement and generally adhering to the monastic discipline more strictly than the *Mahanikaya*.

Dharma (Skt.; P. *Dhamma*)   The teachings of the Buddha; truth; ultimate truth.

dharma (lowercase d.)   Phenomena.

dharmakaya   See "three *kayas*."

dukkha   Suffering, the pervasive imperfection and unsatisfactoriness of all conditioned existence, i.e., that which appears from causes and is tainted by not knowing the true nature of mind and phenomena; the first Noble Truth taught by the Buddha in his first sermon.

dzokchen (Tib.)   Great Perfection, meaning the natural state of mind and the path of practice for realizing it

empowerment/initiation (Tib. *wang*; Skt. *abhiskekha*) Vajrayana ritual in which an enlightened master transmits the essence of realized mind, usually in the form of a deity, empowering disciples to do the relevant meditation practices. The deities may have a specific function, such as healing, removing obstacles, aiding wisdom or compassion, or attracting wealth, but they are all enlightened Buddhas and their empowerments and meditations are means to attaining enlightenment.

emptiness (Skt. *shunyata*)   The lack of inherent existence of self and all phenomena. According to the view of the Middle Way (*Madhyamika*), which is accepted by all Tibetan schools, emptiness is not nothingness or mere negation: phenomena do appear, as a result of causes and conditions, but lack inherent existence precisely because they appear from causes and conditions.

Geluk (Tib.)   One of the four main lineages of Tibetan Buddhism, in which His Holiness the Dalai Lama is ordained. It was founded by Tsongkhapa (1357-1419) as a monastic reform movement.

Geshe (Tib.; lit. "Virtuous Friend")   A scholar in the Geluk tradition who has completed required courses of study and passed a set of exams.

Guru Yoga   "Union with the [mind of] the Guru," visualizing and praying to the Guru, reciting a mantra, receiving blessings, and uniting with the Guru's mind. It is said to be the most central practice of Vajrayana, which is the path of blessings. The Guru is seen as identical with the Buddha and is usually visualized not in his ordinary form but as a central figure in the lineage; in Nyingma practice the Guru is visualized as Padmasambhava.

Hinayana (Skt.)   "Lesser Vehicle," usually meant to refer to Theravada Buddhism (Southern Buddhism) as compared with the Mahayana ("Great Vehicle") schools of Northern Buddhism, but more accurately describing a spiritual approach focused primarily on one's own liberation.

jhana (P.; Skt. *dhyana*)   States of deep meditative absorption.

Kagyu (Tib.)   One of the four main schools of Tibetan Buddhism, it developed from the teachings brought from India by Marpa the Translator (1012-1097) and transmitted to Milarepa and then Gampopa. There are several sub-schools, including Karma Kagyu, Drukpa Kagyu, and Drikung Kagyu.

karma (Skt.; P. *kamma*)   Action accompanied by intention, the results of which are never lost. Popularly used as meaning cause and result.

Kathina (P.)   Offering ceremony at the conclusion of the three-month rains retreat (P. *vassa;* Th. *pansa*) in Theravada monastic tradition.

koan (J.)   "Public case," a story, phrase, or question-and-answer dialogue that steps outside the boundaries of logic, used as a meditation subject in Zen practice.

Khun (Th.)   Polite form of address, similar to *Tahn* (see below).

kuti (P.)   An individual monastic dwelling. In Thai forest monasteries it is usually a small cabin raised on pillars.

Mahamudra (Skt.)   "Great Seal," the most profound teachings of the New Translation lineages of Tibetan Buddhism (Geluk, Kagyu, and Sakya), similar to *dzokchen*.

Mahanikaya (P.)   "Great Collection," the older and larger monastic sect in Thailand.

Mahayana (Skt.)   "Great Vehicle," the Buddhist path that takes the welfare and liberation of all beings as the focus of practice.

mandala (Skt.)   Literally, "extracting the essence." The Tibetan term, *kyil khor,* means "center and surrounding"; it is usually a symbolic representation of a tantric deity's realm.

mandala offering   Tantric practice for accumulating merit through offering the entire universe and all its desirable objects and qualities to the Three Jewels and Three Roots.

mantra (Skt.)   Literally, "that which protects the mind." Formula recited to invoke and actualize the enlightened mind of a deity.

ngondro (Tib.)   Tantric preliminary practices, involving 100,000 each of prostrations, Vajrasattva mantra, mandala offerings, and Guru Yoga mantra. Refuge and Bodhicitta are also part of ngondro, often recited while doing prostrations. Ngondro is emphasized by all schools of Tibetan Buddhism as the indispensable foundation for tantric practice, as it involves skillful means for purifying karmic obstructions and accumulating merit.

nirmanakaya   See "three *kayas.*"

nirvana (Skt.; P. *nibbana*)   Extinction, the state of liberation from defilements and suffering.

Nyingma (Tib.)   The "ancient tradition," the oldest school of Tibetan Buddhism, founded by Padmasambhava (Guru Rinpoche) in the 8th century.

Pali   The language of the original Theravada scriptures, the vernacular in which the Buddha taught.

pansa (Th.)   See "vassa."

parami (P.)   Spiritual perfections developed as supports on the path to enlightenment. Theravada lists ten: generosity, morality, renunciation, wisdom, effort, forbearance, truthfulness, resolution, loving-kindness, and equanimity.

paramita (Skt.)   The spiritual perfections of Mahayana: generosity, morality, patience, effort, meditative absorption, and wisdom.

Patimokkha (P.; Skt. *Pratimoksha*)   "That which leads to liberation," the 227 main monastic rules in Theravada (253 in Mahayana).

pindapat (Th.)   The daily alms round of Buddhist monks and novices.

Pra (Th.)   Derived from the Pali *vara*, "excellent," it is a widely applied honorific, but also specifically means *bhikkhu*, a fully ordained monk.

Refuge   Recognizing the faults of *samsara* and the difficulty of escaping from suffering, help is sought by making a commitment to the objects of refuge, Buddha, Dharma, and Sangha. In Vajrayana the Three Jewels are the outer refuge; there are also various classifications of inner, secret, and absolute refuges. Upon taking refuge in the Tibetan tradition, one is usually given a card with a refuge name, the date, and the teacher giving refuge.

Rinpoche (Tib.)   "Precious One," an honorific accorded to reincarnated or highly realized masters.

Sakya (Tib.)   One of the four major schools of Tibetan Buddhism, founded by Khon Konchok Gyalpo in 1073.

samana (P.)   A renunciate; "peaceful one."

samanera (P.)   A novice, one who wears yellow robes and keeps ten precepts; "offspring of *samana*."

samatha (P.; Skt. *shamatha*)   Tranquility meditation.

sambhogakaya (Skt.)   See "three *kayas*."

samsara (Skt.; P. *sangsara*)   The round of cyclic existence, which is of the nature of suffering.

Sangha (P., Skt.)   The community of Buddhist practitioners. The

Sangha as one of the Three Jewels and as an object of refuge means the enlightened followers of the Buddha, those with real ability to help others.

sila (P; Skt.*shila*)   Morality, the codes of ethics for Buddhists.

soi (Th.)   A side street off a major road, often designated by the name of the road and the number of the soi.

sotapanna (P.)   Stream enterer, someone on the first level of enlightenment, who will have at most seven more rebirths.

stupa   See "cetiya."

sutta (P.; Skt. *Sutra*)   The discourses of the Buddha.

Tahn (Th.)   Polite form of address (lit. "you"), preceding the given name. (Thais are addressed by their given name.)

tantra (Skt.)   Literally, "continuum" or "weave." The continuum of enlightened mind is the basis of the path of tantric practice; the result, enlightened mind, is taken as the path, as when one meditates on oneself as a deity, which is a manifestation of Buddha mind.

Theravada (P.)   The "Way of the Elders," also known as Southern Buddhism, the form of Buddhism based on the Pali scriptures and practiced in southeast Asia and Sri Lanka.

Three Jewels   The Buddha, the Dharma (the Buddha's teachings), and the Sangha (the community of enlightened practitioners).

three *kayas*   The three bodies of a Buddha: *dharmakaya*, the aspect of emptiness, ultimate reality, the formless Buddha mind which is the source of the forms of Buddhas perceived by beings; *sambhogakaya*, the aspect of clarity, the "perfect enjoyment body," the form of Buddhas perceptible only to highly realized bodhisattvas; *nirmanakaya*, the aspect of compassionate responsiveness, the forms in which Buddhas manifest to ordinary beings.

tonglen (Tib.)   The meditation practice of visualizing oneself taking on the suffering of beings and sending all one's happiness and merit to them.

Tripitika (Skt.; P. *tipitaka*)   The "three baskets" of the Buddha's teachings, the scriptural collections of *Vinaya*, dealing primarily with monastic discipline; *Sutra*, emphasizing the subject of meditation; and *Abhidharma*, teachings of higher wisdom.

tulku (Tib.; Skt. *nirmanakaya*)   A reincarnated enlightened being; the emanation body of a Buddha.

Uposatha   The fortnightly recitation of the *Patimokkha* rules in the assembly of bhikkhus. Can also mean a consecrated building where monastic ceremonies are performed, as well as the four lunar observance days of the month and the eight precepts laypeople may vow to keep on those days.

vajra (Skt.; Tib. **dorje**)   "Diamond scepter"; that which, like a diamond, can cut any other substance but cannot be cut by anything. It symbolizes indestructible wisdom.

Vajrayana (Skt.)   The "diamond vehicle" or "adamantine way"; *tantra,* the way of secret mantra.

vassa (P.; Th. *pansa*)   The three-month "rains retreat," from July to October, during which time ordained men and women remain in one monastery and undertake more rigorous training.

Vinaya (P.; Skt.)   The teachings of the Buddha dealing primarily with the monastic discipline.

Vipassana (P.; Skt. *vipashyana*)   "Special seeing"; insight meditation. In Theravada it usually means experiential insight into the three characteristics of existence: impermanence, suffering, and absence of self-existence.

Wat (Th.)   Monastery.

Wun Pra (Th.)   "Monk's day," the quarterly lunar observance days. Laypeople traditionally go to a monastery to offer food, take precepts, hear teachings, and meditate.

zafu (J.)   Round cushion used for sitting meditation.

zazen (J.)   Sitting meditation.

zendo (J.)   Meditation hall.

Selected Bibliography & Recommended Reading

Breiter, Paul. *Venerable Father: A Life with Ajahn Chah,* Paraview Publishing, 2004.

Brown, Mick. *The Dance of Seventeen Lives: The Incredible True Story of Tibet's 17th Karmapa,* Bloomsbury Publishing, 2004.

Chadwick, David. *Crooked Cucumber: The Life and Zen Teachings of Shunryu Suzuki,* Broadway Books, 1999.

Chah, Ajahn. *Being Dharma: The Essence of the Buddha's Teachings,* Shambhala Publications, 2001.

_____. *Everything Arises, Everything Falls Away: Teachings on Impermanence and the End of Suffering,* Shambhala Publications, 2005.

_____. *Food for the Heart: The Collected Teachings of Ajahn Chah,* Wisdom Publications, 2002.

Chang, Garma CC. *The Hundred Thousand Songs of Milarepa, Vol. I and II,* Shambhala Publications, 1977.

Dalai Lama. *The Way to Freedom: Core Teachings of Tibetan Buddhism,* Harper Collins, 1995.

_____. *Kindness, Clarity, and Insight,* Snow Lion Publications (Updated Edition), 2006.

Gimian, Carolyn Rose (editor). *The Essential Chogyam Trungpa,* Shambhala Publications, 1999.

Gruber, Elmar R. *From the Heart of Tibet: The Biography of Drikung Chetsang Rinpoche,* Shambhala Publications, 2010.

Kalu Rinpoche. *Luminous Mind: The Way of the Buddha,* Wisdom Publications, 1997.

Kornfield, Jack. *Living Dharma: Teachings and Meditation Instructions from Twelve Theravada Masters,* Shambhala Publications (Second Edition), 2010.

_____ & Breiter, Paul (translators). *A Still Forest Pool: The Insight Meditation of Achaan Chah,* Quest Books, 1985.

Lhalungpa, Lobsang D. *The Life of Milarepa,* Prajna Press, 1977.

Martin, Michele. *Music in the Sky: The Life, Art and Teachings of the Seventeenth Karmapa Orgyen Trinley Dorje*, Snow Lion Publications, 2003.

Mukpo, Diana J. *Dragon Thunder: My Life with Chogyam Trungpa*, Shambhala Publications, 2006.

Nalanda Translation Committee. *Rain of Wisdom*, Shambhala Publications, 1980.

Patrul Rinpoche. *Words of My Perfect Teacher*, Harper Collins Publishers, 1994.

Ricard, Mathieu. *The Spirit of Tibet: The Life and World of Khyentse Rinpoche, Spiritual Teacher*, Aperture Foundation, 2000.

Savin, Olga (Translator). *The Way of the Pilgrim and The Pilgrim Continues on His Way*, Shambhala Publications, 1991.

Seung Sahn. *Dropping Ashes on the Buddha: The Teachings of Zen Master Seung Sahn*, Grove Press, 1994.

Sumedho, Ajahn. *The Way It Is*, Amaravati Publications, 1991.

Suzuki, Shunryu. *Zen Mind, Beginner's Mind*, Shambhala Publications, 2006.

Tarrant, John. *Bring Me the Rhinoceros and Other Koans to Bring You Joy*, Harmony Books, 2004.

Thondup, Tulku. *Masters of Meditation and Miracles: The Longchen Nyingthig Lineage of Tibetan Buddhism*, Shambhala Publications, 1996.

Trungpa, Chogyam. *Cutting Through Spiritual Materialism*, Shambhala Publications, 2008.

Tsogyal, Yeshe. *The Lotus-Born: The Life Story of Padmasambhava*, North Atlantic Books, 2004.

Zopa Rinpoche, Lama. *Making Life Meaningful*, Lama Yeshe Wisdom Archive, 2001.

About Paul Breiter

Paul Breiter was born in Brooklyn in 1948. In 1970—after wandering through Europe, Turkey, Iran, Afghanistan, Pakistan, and India—he found himself in Thailand, where he took ordination as a Buddhist monk. He soon met Ajahn Chah, abbot of Wat Pah Pong, and became his student. Breiter learned Thai and the local Lao dialect (Isan) and served as Ajahn Chah's translator for the many Westerners who came to study with him. He kept a journal of his translations of Ajahn Chah's teachings, some of which he published with Jack Kornfield in *A Still Forest Pool* (Quest

Paul Breiter, Ubon Province, Thailand, December 2010.

Books, 1985). He traveled with and translated for Ajahn Chah when he visited the United States in 1979. He later published an account of his time studying with Ajahn Chah, *Venerable Father: A Life with Ajahn Chah*, which has become an underground classic (Buddhadhamma Foundation, 1994; Cosimo Books, 2004). He also published two books of Ajahn Chah's teachings through Shambhala Publications, *Being Dharma* (2001) and *Everything Arises, Everything Falls Away* (2005).

After disrobing in 1977, Breiter returned to the United States and continued Buddhist study and practice with Roshi Kobun Chino Otogawa of the Soto Zen school, and then with Lama Gonpo Tseten and other masters of the Nyingmapa lineage of Tibetan Buddhism. He lives in Florida and tries to keep an open mind.

Colophon

The interior of *One Monk, Many Masters* was designed using Adobe InDesign. The body type is Adobe Minion Pro, 11 points on 14 points leading. Heading typefaces are Adobe Myriad Pro Light and Chalk-duster. The quotations at the beginning of each chapter are also set in Myriad Pro Light.

Publisher: Parami Press, Vancouver, Washington
Developmental Editor: Paul Gerhards
Copy Editor: Jessica Swanson
Interior Design: Paul Gerhards
Cover Design: Anita Jones, Another Jones Graphics
Cover photographs: Paul Breiter
Printer: Color House Graphics, Grand Rapids, Michigan
Paper: 55# natural shade uncoated